THE CONTESTED CITY

THE
CONTESTED
CITY

John H. Mollenkopf

PRINCETON UNIVERSITY PRESS
PRINCETON, NEW JERSEY

Library of Congress Cataloging in Publication Data will be found on
the last printed page of this book

ISBN cloth: 0-691-07659-6
      paper: 0-691-02220-8

This book has been composed in Linotron Times Roman

Clothbound editions of Princeton University Press books are printed on
acid-free paper, and binding materials are chosen for strength and du-
rability. Paperbacks, although satisfactory for personal collections, are
not usually suitable for library rebinding.

Printed in the United States of America by
Princeton University Press, Princeton, New Jersey

CONTENTS

LIST OF TABLES

LIST OF FIGURES

ACKNOWLEDGMENTS

In a project as ambitious and as long in gestation as this, an author accumulates many intellectual debts. On those occasions when I wondered whether it would ever reach a successful conclusion, I consoled myself with the thought that I could save the best part of the chore—writing the acknowledgments—to the last. Thinking about what to say, and all the friendships and intense intellectual exchange which made reaching this point possible, sustained me during those times.

To begin at the beginning, this project grew out of my Ph.D. dissertation and my dissatisfaction with its lack of a structured theoretical perspective different from the received pluralist wisdom of the times in which it was written. The dissertation itself arose from a collaboration with a number of remarkable people to whom I am deeply grateful. My co-workers at Barss, Reitzel and Associates, several of whom were also graduate school colleagues, gave me the challenge of doing a quantitative analysis of the impact of the Community Action Program on neighborhood political mobilization as well as a stimulating and warm environment in which to do the job. This remarkable group included Bruce Jacobs, Stanley Greenberg, Curt Lamb, Dan Linger, Jack Spence, and Emily Starr. Cynthia Hecker, then on the staff of the Cambridge Corporation, helped get me involved in community activism, which, in turn, convinced me to study community organizations in the field as well as at the computer terminal. My association with community activists in Cambridge, Boston, and San Francisco inspired and educated me as well.

In my two dissertation advisers, James Q. Wilson and Barrington Moore, Jr., I found the most challenging, demanding, and admirable tutors that anyone could want. They opened my eyes to the fundamental issues of social history and comparative analysis and set the highest standards for intellectual work. Moore is a master at going to the fundamental questions and in conducting what he once called "participatory autocracy," while Wilson's friendly skepticism and staunch support kept me going. It was a privilege to work with both.

In the late sixties, it was said that graduate students enjoyed the greatest pleasure-to-responsibility ratio that they were ever likely to experience. It was also said that one's peers were one's true faculty. For me, these conditions came together in intense, wide-ranging discussions with friends, the results of which have shaped my subsequent work. Bob Amdur, Gary Orren, Jon Pynoos, Steven Krasner, Margaret Levi, Howard Reiter, and Theda Skocpol, as well as Jacobs, Greenberg, Spence, and Linger, have my thanks for many happy hours, as do my fellow members of the *Upstart!* publishing collective. Another important home during this time was the Joint Center for Urban Studies.

My time at Stanford University, both at the Public Management Program of the Graduate School of Business and in the Urban Studies Program, allowed me to develop a critical perspective on urban politics. The GSB provided me with extensive support and a considerable challenge as the only political scientist among a group of economists. If this work has an impact on policy discourse, it will largely be the result of my contact with Mick Seidl, Bill Moffat, Harry Rowen, John Steinhart, and the fine students who passed through the PMP during my time there. Dauna Moths provided unfailing good cheer as well. My undergraduate teaching in the Urban Studies Program, which later I had the pleasure of directing, was like a second education and a portable seminar rolled into one. My co-teachers in the core seminar, Terry MacDonold, Frederic Stout, and Paul Turner, proved to be extraordinarily valuable friends and colleagues. What a pleasure, and, in retrospect, a luxury, it was to work with an urban historian, an intellectual historian and man of letters, and an architectural historian in developing a synthetic study of American urban development. Our students as well as other faculty and staff members, particularly Len Ortolano, Clay Carson, Jarir Dajani, Madeline Landau, Dick Muth, Sylvia Yanagisako, Lisa Salter, and Nina Farana, enriched this experience. Lisa Salter, Nina Farana, Jeff Fraas, and Ron Jepperson provided valuable research assistance. A grant from the Rabinowitz Foundation also provided support at a critical juncture.

My involvement between 1974 and 1978 with a group attempting to build a Marxist theory of the state had an equally profound impact on my intellectual development. In the midst of a changing membership, Sue Bessmer, Jens Christiansen, Roger Friedland, David Gold, Clarence Lo, Ann Markusen, James O'Connor, Alan Wolfe, and Erik Wright made an indelible impact. Though I finally concluded that an adequate Marxist theory of politics could not be built, much of this work has a lasting value. During these years, my involvement in San Francisco politics, especially with Action for Accountable Government and the stalwart Eric Craven, helped me understand better the inner workings of electoral and bureaucratic politics.

Many people contributed specifically to this book. The community activists interviewed for my dissertation, who heard from me a number of times as I attempted to gauge the impact of a decade of change, once more deserve my thanks. Steven Waldhorn provided important archival material on the Western Addition, as well as an introduction to many of the most innovative planners and planning ideas afoot today. Similarly, Dan Feshbach, Chester Hartman, Roger Montgomery, and Marc Weiss have traded many thoughts about the history and meaning of urban renewal. David Strohm, David Smith, Ann Kerry, and Kietha Fine provided invaluable insights about Boston and South End politics. This book was born in a discussion with David Strohm, as we sat at the foot of the Quincy Market urban renewal project. Lars Lerup helped me work out many ideas during our daily run on the Fire Trail above Berkeley. At the end of the project, Susan Jaster of the Boston Redevelopment Authority and Peter Groat of the San Francisco Department of City Planning were kind enough to supply 1980 census data from the STF 3 file on the two case study neighborhoods and cities.

A group of scholars, many of whom have served as mentors, read and criticized various drafts of this book. They include Robert Alford, Marshall Berman, Manuel Castells, Roger Friedland, Norman Glickman, R. M. Jackson, Ira Katznelson, Michael Lip-

ACKNOWLEDGMENTS

sky, Frances Piven, Martin Shefter, and Arthur Soloman. Their achievements have inspired my work and their friendship and constructive criticism have sustained it. Castells helped me to see the dualism between the liberal and conservative versions of pro-growth politics, while Rick Busacca convinced me that the differences between the two were contained within the Democratic party as well as between the two parties. Richard Ingersoll provided invaluable editing assistance, while Famah Andrew expertly typed and retyped the manuscript. Renetta De Blase and my father gave it a meticulous copy editing.

In the main, this book was written during the summers of 1980 and 1981 between employment opportunities at the New York City Department of City Planning and later at the City University Graduate School. My thanks go to Chairman Herb Sturz of the City Planning Commission for a sojourn in the real world of policy-making, to Howard Lentner of CUNY for inviting me to the Graduate Center, and to Gail Filion of Princeton University Press for her absolutely vital encouragement.

In closing, two special people must be mentioned. The late Tom Brose, then director of labor relations for the Navajo Nation, introduced me to the great Southwest. Without him, the regional aspects of this analysis might never have been developed. I mourn his passing and will cherish always our escapades to Canyon de Chelly, the Goosenecks of the San Juan, and Monte Alban. The most special person in my life, Kathleen Gerson, has made more contributions to this book than I can say. I would like to dedicate it to my family—the family into which I was born, my grandmother Polly Mitchell, my parents Bill and Margaret Mollenkopf, my brother James; and the family which Kathleen and I are making.

THE CONTESTED CITY

What follows is an attempt to reconstruct the logic by which government intervened to shape U.S. urban development since the New Deal and particularly since World War II. It seeks to explain not only the causes and consequences of government intervention, but also how its successes created new conflicts that eventually undermined the political and economic supports upon which that intervention depended. The heart of this work is its effort to explore the dynamic, and ultimately conflicting, interplay between economic and political forces.

The argument relies on two concepts which deserve to be defined because they have not been widely used and could easily be misinterpreted. First, this analysis contends that a "progrowth coalition" was erected in American politics, both local and national, in the postwar period. Varieties of this coalition became prominent in most of the older, larger central cities; local leaders had a large hand in creating these coalitions, but creating them also became a central and defining task for the national Democratic party, and particularly for Democratic presidents and their administrative and legislative allies.[1] Domestic urban development programs, it is argued, became the principal means through which the modern Democratic party was created. Progrowth coalition building thus became a central feature of national as well as local politics. National politicians and the federal government became important actors in local politics, and this involvement, in turn, integrated local politicians, program administrators, and program beneficiaries into a new national political framework. Over time, Republicans and conservatives reacted to the power of this Democratic invention and gradually articulated their own parallel, but opposed, political model for progrowth coalition building.

This varied use of the concept "progrowth coalitions"—local and national, liberal and conservative—raises a question about its analytical specificity. If the term covers so many different situations, how can one tell whether such a coalition really exists and

3

which of its features hold explanatory power? And since it is asserted that these coalitions enabled the transformation of central city and metropolitan development patterns, how can they be distinguished from straightforward power elite or class intervention? On the other hand, are progrowth coalitions really anything more than pluralism dressed up in a new name?

Fundamental to the idea of a progrowth coalition is that political entrepreneurs can bring together widely different, competing, and even conflicting political actors and interests by creating new governmental bases for exercising new powers which none of these actors and interests could otherwise have exercised on its own. This coalition building occurs according to architectural principles that no single interest, no matter how elite, can control. Nor are these principles the mere resultant of a parallelogram of contending interest groups.

To the contrary, political entrepreneurs, to whom we will turn in a moment, construct these coalitions out of disparate elements. Public actors, not private interests (plural or singular), take the initiative in creating a political and programmatic framework which goes considerably beyond its individual components. The resulting programs and policies take on a life of their own. An individual coalition participant may shape or constrain parts or even all of the policies adopted, but it cannot generally exercise direct, instrumental control over them. Indeed, during the periods of economic and political crisis which have fostered the emergence of such coalitions, initiative has typically shifted strongly away from private sector interests toward public sector actors. Progrowth political coalitions thus provide a framework for the creation and exercise of power. They are not a transmission belt by which outside interests manipulate or directly control government. The reverse is rather more true: programmatic initiatives launched by such coalitions have tended to reshape the contours of private sector interests.

This is not to say that progrowth political coalitions have not vigorously and sometimes callously advanced market values. Politics runs on money in many ways. Governments must finance their activities from a strong revenue base. Politicians must recruit

4

supporters from among powerful and propertied institutions. They generally create or win over these supporters by conveying some form of economic reward, be it capital subsidies to particular firms, a favored position in the labor market to construction trade unions, or a broadly dispersed income transfer payment. Political entrepreneurs are always looking for ways to use government authority or government revenues to build up supportive constituencies.

They rarely do so in a strictly economically rational manner, however. (This is a fact against which economists evidently love to beat their heads.) Politicians will frequently impose widely dispersed costs on the many to create friends among a few powerful beneficiaries, especially when they can be cloaked in the public interest, regardless of any resulting economic inefficiencies. Moreover, politicians will even impose costs on the powerful few in order to create a broad class of beneficiaries when the political circumstances demand it. (The subsidization of home-ownership, which arguably deflects capital from more productive investment, might be read in this light.) The construction of progrowth coalitions is thus driven by a political logic even more strongly than an economic one. It is in the interaction between the political and economic logics, and the conflicts between the two, that the guiding force behind the life cycle of progrowth coalitions may be discovered.

Political logic dictates constructing progrowth politics out of disparate and seemingly inconsistent elements. Certainly, this was true of the classic Democratic versions of progrowth coalitions. As Catherine Bauer Wurster once observed of the 1949 Housing Act, seldom had such a diverse group of would-be angels tried tò dance on the same small pin. Private sector actors themselves were diverse, and included large corporations, banks and other investors, developers and builders, merchants, and the construction trades. Along with urban property owners in general, they shared an interest in rising property values, increased investment, and greater returns. But many differences also divided them. Urban renewal, or example, destroyed many small businesses to allow large ones to expand. Developers and the construction trades could agree to back large projects while fighting over whether union workers would be employed.

Public actors were also diverse. In the postwar period, central cities were experiencing economic and political exhaustion. Innovative mayors saw redevelopment as a way to overcome this situation and reap political benefits along the way. Democratic presidents also wanted to reorganize and strengthen their urban bases of electoral support. Democratic legislators, particularly House members, found urban development programs a means to deliver for their constituencies. And the agencies created to deliver these programs generated new careers and a new sense of competence for professionals, planners, administrators, and even academic theorists. Urban reformers, public housing advocates, labor leaders, and civil rights activists also sought to hitch their wagons to progrowth politics. With such support, a new kind of administrative state came into being and developed considerable momentum and leverage.[2]

Local and national political entrepreneurs took the initiative in bringing these disparate interests together and forging the new kinds of power that none of them could enjoy on his or her own. This second key term should not be equated with "politician," for "political entrepreneur" is one who gathers and risks political capital or support in order to reshape politics and create new sources of power by establishing new programs (or "products"). He or she thus does not simply play by the rules of the game, but attempts to win the game by changing them. Using government to create new beneficiary groups, political entrepreneurs create supportive new constituencies. Or as the Republicans say about Democrats, they "spend, spend, spend, elect, elect, elect." Just as there have been many versions of progrowth coalitions, many different kinds of political entrepreneurs have helped to forge them.

Elected chief executives and their immediate circle of policy advisers and program designers have been the most important entrepreneurs in forging progrowth coalitions. Franklin Roosevelt and his New Deal administrators and Lyndon Johnson and the authors of the Great Society programs clearly played key roles in

6

assembling, shaping, and reshaping the Democratic progrowth coalitions. Roosevelt invented federal urban development policy as a way of modernizing the Democratic party. This invention revolutionized American politics and indeed created the modern American state. Johnson carried that modernization an important step further in the 1960s by making the federal government a key force not just in city government, but in neighborhood organization and the growth of a burgeoning network of nonprofit organizations.

Local officials, elected as reformers to bring together new energies and "get things moving," also shaped progrowth politics. In Boston and San Francisco, the two cases analyzed later in this study, Mayors Collins, White, Christopher, and Alioto broke through climates of economic and political stagnation with the help of federal leverage. Strong program administrators, Edward J. Logue and M. Justin Herman, played equally important roles in these two localities. Credit must be given to the political skills and leadership which these entrepreneurs asserted, but it must also be remembered that they had a great deal of help from national political entrepreneurs and powerful local constituencies pushing them forward.

Other political entrepreneurs played important controlling roles, most notably the members of Congress who fashioned compromises among competing interests in the design of federal programs. A recent study by the Advisory Commission on intergovernmental Relations reached a conclusion similar to that offered here: "Public entrepreneurship of one sort or another—congressional, presidential, bureaucratic, special interest— was the dominant factor in policy genesis and maturation."[3] In the programs under study, Congress and the congressional balance of power acted both as a gatekeeper on the flow of program creation and as a shaper of program design. In sum, forces arising within the political system itself, not those imposed from outside, governed public intervention into the urban development process.

The use of these two concepts—the progrowth coalition and the political entrepreneurship which created it—should distinguish the argument presented here from both major traditions of ex-

7

plaining the "dependent variable" of urban development. It rejects economic determinism, whether of the Right or the Left. Mainsteam urban economics has attempted to explain metropolitan diffusion and interregional growth as a simple function of changing production technology, differing land costs, rising personal incomes, and increasing use of cars and trucks.[4] Central-city evolution derives from the demand for office buildings, the distribution of disposable income, and costs relative to suburbs and economies of central location.

The classic Marxist version of the economic determination of urban form holds that it must take whatever shape most effectively creates and realizes surplus value in an increasingly international division of labor. Cities are also shaped by the conflicts (and the need to control them) which arise under capitalism, most particularly within the workplace.[5]

The argument presented here rejects both of these approaches. It does not belittle economic factors. Indeed, the demand and the opportunity for government intervention have been most strong at points of economic collapse, and opportunities for private gain have shaped the manner of intervention. This argument holds, however, that politics and government are independent driving forces which can override economic "functional necessities." It stresses the need to examine how politics and economics interact.

By themselves, economic factors explain relatively little. They are necessarily mediated through, and influenced by, the political system. The classic market approach fails to see that political actors and government intervention help determine the relative costs of different locations, promote some sectors of the economy over others, and guide location decisions for new investments. It is blind to the fact that noneconomic, political factors strongly enter into such decisions.

The classic Marxist approach has similar weaknesses. Cities with the same mode of production have a wide variety of politics and forms, while there are some striking similarities between certain kinds of capitalist and socialist cities. Advanced capitalism has moderated and modified class conflict in the workplace so thoroughly that central social tensions have been displaced into many other arenas—for example, neighborhood-based urban social movements. More fundamentally, this kind of economic determinism fails to see that cities are not just resultants of or arenas for larger forces; they have an active, generative economic and political role all their own. The specificity of urban form, it is claimed here, arises more out of political factors than any purely economic functional requirement.[6]

Similarly, this study rejects the two dominant traditions for explaining the structure of political power: the notion that some controlling "power structure" or capitalist elite intervenes to determine what decisions are made, or, alternatively, that they result from the contention among private interest groups. The political entrepreneurs who put together progrowth coalitions were not operating according to some class-conscious scheme. Few of the actors involved were aware of the systemic consequences of their actions, and when they were, it was the political consequences they most often had in mind. They were searching for concrete solutions to pressing problems. They developed a progrowth programmatic framework with a jumbled character because they had to accommodate and logroll among many different interests, none of whom—even the most powerful corporate chieftains—could control the entire process or even assume that its interests would be taken fully into account. Public actors, not private actors, generally possessed the critical initiative, and the results of their actions shaped private interests just as much as private interests shaped public action. A power structure, power bloc, or capitalist class model must be rejected because each draws the causal arrow in the wrong direction, or, at any rate, in only one direction, and because even capitalists must achieve popular support for measures government takes to benefit them. Politics runs on votes as well as money.

That government intervention follows its own logic rather than that of private interests also differentiates this argument from traditional pluralist analysis. Pluralist analysis fails to see the structural logic which governs the assembly of political power and governmental capacity and which tends to give it an inherently regressive quality despite its often populist origins. It is obvious that since political and economic resources are unequally distributed, political entrepreneurs have a strong incentive to give greater weight to powerful interests whether or not they participate directly in politics. It is less obvious, but equally true, that powerful interests cannot count on having their way, can be frustrated by the inertia of government practices, and that government can (at least at times) operate independent of them, and can even reorganize the constellation of private interests. Neither the classic pluralist position nor one which weighs pluralist actors by their economic power takes sufficient note of these facts.

In contrast, this study seeks to explain the structural principles which led political entrepreneurs to assemble support for the government intervention which transformed both metropolitan spatial structure and the organization of national as well as urban politics. It asserts that the initiative for government intervention welled up within the political system itself instead of being imposed by private sector actors, whether singular or plural. Though private interests clearly shaped the nature of government intervention, the reverse is even more strongly true. Finally, it argues that the demise of progrowth coalitions stems more from the political conflicts it created than from its economic performance, which has been extraordinary. It develops a political economy in which, in contrast to much of Marxist analysis, the political receives its due.

Two caveats must be offered in closing. Despite the fact that this study covers a great deal of ground, some may feel that it tries to make a partial analysis too general. The reader may object to the central role given to urban development programs in the construction of the modern party system. He or she may point to other factors—the traumas of war and inflation, for example— that have shaped domestic policy, politics, and Washington decision-making. The reader may also emphasize that other policy systems, be they income transfer payments or social service spending, have also had a major impact on national political development. To a degree, one can only plead guilty and recommend that the reader undertake similar analyses of these other policy areas which have so obviously contributed to the making of the

10

modern American state. But while it must be conceded that such areas held sway at crucial points, it can be argued that as an urban nation, urban development issues have been a primary, if not exclusive, factor in our national political development.

Second, some will object that this treatment is flawed by a failure to put the evolution of domestic policy and politics in the framework of a rapidly changing international order. To this charge, too, only a guilty plea can be entered. It is hoped that this omission is mitigated by the fact that for much of the period under examination, the United States could behave as if it lived in a world by itself, or, at any rate, in a world to which it could export its problems. Today, this situation has changed, with the result that new analytic problems have emerged.

Overview of the Argument

1. INTRODUCTION

A century ago, the industrial revolution transformed the thinly settled agrarian and small-town landscape of the United States into a series of large, dense, smoky, and brawling cities. The factories of these new cities brought together great concentrations of labor and capital. The falling cost of goods, their increasing supply, improving means of transportation and communications, emigration from the U.S. and European countryside, and the rise of an urban mass market all fed on each other. These forces, in turn, propelled the market system outward from the swelling urban centers, penetrating and reorganizing rural as well as urban life.

The United States became an urban nation in a matter of decades. Between 1850 and 1920, the proportion of Americans who lived in urban places rose from under one-fifth to over one-half. By 1920, one in four persons lived in a central city with more than one hundred thousand residents. The national population rose four times to 106 million, and industrial production jumped a thousandfold.[1] In this way, the historical linking of the factory and the city transformed the United States into urban society. Even today, big cities retain the imprint of the urban-industrial revolution.

Since 1920, however, a second and equally profound transformation has seriously eroded the nineteenth-century industrial city. For lack of a better term, it might be called "the postindustrial revolution." This second urban revolution grew out of and in many ways constituted a reaction against the first. If labor and capital concentrated into factories defined the industrial city, the postindustrial city is characterized by the geographic diffusion of production and population. The office building, not the factory, now provides the organizing institution for the central city. The postindustrial transformation of the U.S. city system has been destructive. Speaking of the displacement of industrial investment away from old industrial cities like Cleveland, Detroit, and St. Louis, George Sternlieb has foreseen "the decline of the historic industrial metropolis—the endpoint of industrial urbanization" and "a virtual dismantling of the traditional urban complex."[2] Change has also dismantled the mosaic of blue collar ethnic segmentation which developed within the occupational and residential order of the older industrial cities. This mosaic has largely given way to a new central-city mosaic dominated by more recent, lower-status minority groups, particularly blacks and Hispanics.[3] In all the older cities, the hallmarks of the nineteenth-century industrial revolution, whether physical or social, are in decay.

For each measure of disinvestment in the old order, however, the postindustrial transformation has produced an equal measure of investment in new institutions. Like its predecessor, the second urban revolution has stimulated tremendous urban—or, more precisely, metropolitan—growth. Since 1930, when the census first collected data on metropolitan areas, the proportion of the population living within them has increased from 51 to 74 percent, the national population has doubled, and real economic output has risen fivefold. While the larger, older central cities lost some of their population, their surrounding suburbs for the most part grew rapidly in the postwar period and a whole new group of cities, typified by such southwestern cities as Phoenix, grew from small-town beginnings.

The second urban revolution created new defining institutions within central cities. High-rise office buildings, government centers, cultural complexes, hospitals, and universities displaced aging factory districts, wholesale markets, and rail yards. These new institutions, in turn, produced a new ethnic-occupational order, rooted in administrative and service institutions and a new segmentation in metropolitan residential patterns.

The postindustrial transformation also altered the relations among

13

cities. The interstate highway system, air travel, and mass communications put cities in much closer touch with each other. Moreover, the growth of multilocational organizations internalized many of the exchanges between cities which had formerly taken place in open markets; large cities actually penetrated one another through the institutional networks embodied by large corporations, government agencies, and non-profit organizations.[4]

The two urban revolutions thus provide a study in contrasts. While the first concentrated urban growth, the second diffused it. While the first created an ethnically segmented occupational and residential order based in industrial production, the second dissolved that order and created a new one based in administrative institutions and further balkanized by suburbanization. Most crucially, however, while the weakness of government and the absence of political influence hastened the first transformation, government intervention and the interplay of political forces have accelerated and directed the second transformation of American cities. This has been true in at least three senses.

First, and most obviously, the postindustrial transformation did not "just happen," but grew out of the nearly universal rejection of the kind of city which the rapid, haphazard, and rapacious growth of industrial capitalism produced between 1850 and 1930. As Lewis Mumford once observed of this earlier period, "That a city had any other purpose than to attract trade, to increase land values, and to grow is something that, if it uneasily entered the mind of an occasional Whitman, never exercised any hold on the minds of our countrymen."[5] But though this triumph of the entrepreneurial spirit produced tremendous wealth, it also created new miseries and intense new forms of political and social conflict.

By the turn of the century, the intellectual critics who castigated these cities found a wide variety of receptive audiences. Radical socialists hoped and Yankee businessmen feared that the newly formed urban, ethnic working class would become a politically dangerous and destabilizing force. Though big-city machine politicians may have served the business elite by effectively compromising whatever radical potential the urban working class had, the two nonetheless resented each other and blamed the other for the ills of urban life. The emerging middle class sought physical distance and social isolation, while the working class engaged in bitter ethnic competition over who would be lucky enough to turn their dreams of upward mobility into reality. Very few raised their voices to defend the quality of city life.

This widespread, varied criticism of urban industrial life contributed heavily to the postindustrial transformation. Though each grouping had its own theory about what needed reforming in urban life and none ever fully dominated the government policies growing out of reformist sentiment, government intervention was nevertheless central to the postindustrial revolution which transformed U.S. cities. Deliberate local attempts at social engineering to improve cities began during the Progressive era. Not until the Depression and the advent of federal intervention during the New Deal, however, did government truly develop the muscle to shape urban development patterns.

During and after World War II, the federal intergovernmental program delivery system had an increasing impact. It meshed with and reinforced key parts of the expanding national economy, promoted the outward expansion from the older central cities, as well as the reorganization of these centers, and spurred the rise of entirely new metropolitan areas.

Political factors also influenced this transformation in a second and even more profound sense. While the fact of government intervention was important, the balance of political alignments at both the national and local levels also determined the rate and extent to which these programs had an impact. From the New Deal onward, national and local political entrepreneurs, for the most part Democrats, constructed new political alignments and new coalitions around the framework of federal urban development programs. These programs provided a means by which diverse local constituencies, all of which had some stake in stepping up the rate of urban development, could be brought together in new "progrowth" coalitions. These local coalitions, in turn, pushed for the expansion of federal programs and provided organizational and political support for the national Democratic political entrepreneurs who had established them. They also had a direct impact

15

on how fully these programs were implemented, and thus on the rate and depth of the postindustrial transformation of the major cities.

This process has been political in a second sense, then, not only because government intervention had an impact on urban form, but because local and national political entrepreneurs used federal programs to introduce and solidify a new system of alignments in American politics. In a sense, the New Deal Democrats had little choice about using federal urban programs to build their political base, for a newly mobilized urban electorate forced them to do so. In the following years, their successors used these programs to shape that electorate and continually modernize and adapt the organizational base on which their national majority status rested.

For this reason, however, the postindustrial transformation has also been a profoundly political phenomenon in a third sense. At the outset, Democrats succeeded in making the political and the economic impact of their programs reinforce each other. But their success at this task gradually generated new forms of conflict, distinct to the twentieth-century postindustrial city, which ultimately broke their strategy apart and left traditional Democratic progrowth coalitions in disarray. As the accumulation of these conflicts shattered the political integument which protected federal urban development programs, the fact of continued urban growth itself has become problematic for many of the nation's oldest and largest cities.

Three conflicts have contributed to the disintegration of traditional progrowth politics. As Democratic entrepreneurs succeeded in using federal programs to consolidate their political position, they triggered countermovements from conservatives, led by Republican national political entrepreneurs, with support from the conservative coalition in Congress and local conservative elites. These countermovements, which enjoyed political ascendancy during World War II, the Eisenhower years, and the Nixon-Ford administrations, undermined those aspects of the intergovernmental program delivery system which favored Democratic constituencies and replaced them with programs favoring conservative ones. Over time, this partisan competition severely eroded the political and substantive coherence of the program delivery system.

The progrowth coalitions formed by Democratic political entrepreneurs also triggered opposition within their own constituencies. The Democrats' urban liberalism promised to improve life for the poor as well as the rich, the central-city neighborhood resident as well as the suburbanite. In practice, however, Democratic programs have exacerbated differences between these groups and worsened conditions for poor central-city neighborhood residents, particularly those living in minority areas. From the late 1950s, for example, freeway construction and urban renewal directly threatened central-city neighborhoods, particularly black communities. The result was an explosion of protest and community activism during the mid-1960s, which necessitated politically difficult efforts to absorb dissent and further modernize central-city politics.

In the final analysis, the Great Society failed to bridge the gap between the actual operation of federal programs and the needs and aspirations of central-city neighborhood residents. Democrats were caught in a bind. Measures responding to newly mobilized groups heightened conservative opposition and threatened to rupture local progrowth coalitions. Retreat from such measures and a renewed emphasis on traditional coalition partners, however, did not appease them, but succeeded only in demobilizing the central-city minority voters upon whom Democrats rely to get national electoral majorities. Even today, neither national nor local Democratic entrepreneurs have been able to overcome the objective conflicts within urban areas that federal programs enacted largely by Democrats have exacerbated.

The increase in urban conflict during the 1960s, and the Democratic reactions to it, also provoked a third reaction. Though the heads of large corporations headquartered in central cities had often played key roles in forming local progrowth coalitions, private sector decision-makers as a group reacted strongly against both the political challenge of the 1960s and attempts by Democratic entrepreneurs to absorb it through community action, cit-

17

izen participation, social service programs, and the growth in spending and the taxes required to support them.

Private sector decision-makers exercised an implicit veto power against these trends by shifting investment away from politically contested jurisdictions and toward those where a more conservative brand of progrowth politics reigned intact. This displacement of investment away from the older central cities of the Northeast toward their suburbs and the newer cities of the Southwest exerted market discipline on the core of the Democrats' political strength.

During Republican administrations conservative national political entrepreneurs sought to foster this movement (and benefit from it politically) by shifting the emphasis of federal urban development programs. In this climate, even local political leaders in liberal big cities had little choice but to trim their sails.

In addition to provoking these three kinds of essentially political conflict, federal urban development programs also had a fourth unexpected consequence. By their very success in hastening the postindustrial transformation, they dissolved the social base upon which the New Deal majority and Democratic urban programs had originally been built. Development trends created new constituencies in suburbs and new metropolitan areas as well as in central cities. Programs and political coalitions defined in an earlier era could not always respond effectively to the needs and perspectives of these new constituencies. In a sense, progrowth politics generated demographic and social trends which led to its own obsolescence.

Taken together, these four conditions have brought the political alignments and programs first established by the New Deal Democrats to the end of their life cycle. These programs began with great vigor, causing tremendous innovation both in politics and in the urban development process. With success came maturity. But success also stimulated counteractions from conservative political competitors, from within the Democratic coalition, from private sector decision-makers, and from altogether new constituencies. The net result has been what some observers have called "political dealignment."[6] Plagued by economic uncertainty, fiscal distress, and a lack of consensus about their proper role, the nation's cities face a problematic future.

However painful, this impasse has also created new political opportunities. The weakening of the New Deal political order has created the political space in which a new generation of political entrepreneurs can try to build new coalitions aroung a new national political consensus. At present, the outcome of these attempts remains uncertain. Can traditional, urban Democratic liberals overcome their accumulated internal differences? Will their conservative opponents succeed in lodging themselves in a commanding position? Or will some third alternative emerge? The answers are unclear, but the future of urban development will certainly hinge on the outcome.

This study, then, asks three questions. First, what forces have shaped the postindustrial transformation of the largest central cities of the United States? The study argues that while its origins may be found in economic forces, federal urban development programs and the local progrowth coalitions which implemented them have magnified and channeled these economic forces.

Second, since progrowth politics played such an important role, what factors have accounted for its rise and subsequent decline? Like-minded private elites did not join together to manipulate public policy toward their own ends. To the contrary, this study argues that political entrepreneurs ardously built progrowth coalitions out of conflictiing interests, mass as well as elite, and that each element had its own reasons for joining forces. It also argues that the successes of these coalitions increased rather than decreased disagreement over the content of progrowth politics.

Finally, what can be learned from this experience which would be relevant to the design of new programs and a new political consensus concerning the course of urban development, given the collapse of the old ones? This study concludes by examining current efforts by a variety of political entrepreneurs with this question in mind.

Before turning to these issues, however, we need to take a closer look at the nature of the postindustrial transformation of U.S. cities which set the stage for political intervention and influenced the course which it followed. A complete analysis of how the structure of the national economy has changed and how such changes encouraged suburbanization and the reorganization of central-city economies would go beyond the scope of this study. Some appreciation of these things is necessary, however, in understanding the context in which progrowth politics emerged.

2. DIMENSIONS OF THE POSTINDUSTRIAL TRANSFORMATION

Scholars have written a great deal about the coming of postindustrial society without reaching a consensus on its causes or essential characteristics.[7] The term is employed here to denote two basic and interrelated trends. The first involves the organizational revolution which has overtaken nineteenth-century capitalism, dominated as it was by relatively free markets and small enterprises. The rise of the modern corporation has been a major aspect of this organizational revolution, but the rise of the modern state and the development of what some have called "the service economy" and others "the third sector" have also been basic ingredients. As a result of this organizational revolution, large, multilocational organizations, using educated labor and applied social science, have come to dominate the economy. In many instances, they have displaced markets as the institution for allocating scarce resources. Whether private firms, government agencies, or nonprofit institutions, these organizations have become economically predominant.[8] Central cities continue to house disproportionate numbers of such organizations and their support systems.

The growth of mass consumption created the conditions under which multiunit business enterprises could emerge triumphant, and provides the second defining aspect of the postindustrial transformation. As A. D. Chandler, the leading historian of the modern corporation, has noted, "Without the rapidly growing urban market, there would have been little need and little opportunity for the coming of the corporation in American industry."[9] The organizational revolution thus went hand in hand with the emergence of new consumers who made it profitable for multiunit enterprises to organize mass markets and integrate them on a national and increasingly on an international scale. The construction of a new metropolitan form played a key role in expanding consumer demand.

These two aspects of the postindustrial transformation of the national economy have had an enormous, if contradictory, impact on urban development patterns in the United States over the last five decades. The shift of population and employment away from the central cities and toward the suburbs and newer metropolitan areas has been widely noted. Simultaneously, however, the organizational revolution has thrust a new set of institutions into dominance of the central-city economy, displacing the goods production and distribution activities which organized it a century earlier. While postindustrial institutions have followed the factories to locations in the suburbs and newer metropolitan areas, they have done so far more slowly than goods production. Indeed, many continue to show a distinct preference for central-city locations.

Table 1 shows the impact of the organizational revolution on the sectoral composition of national employment. Although total national employment doubled, "old industries" such as steel and automobiles remained steady, despite their migration to suburban locations. "New industries" encouraged by government intervention, such as electronics and aircraft production, chose suburban and new metropolitan locations from the outset. In contrast to the older industries which had grown up before 1930, their employment tripled between 1929 and 1974.

Perhaps the most noteworthy feature of Table 1, however, is that it shows that the organizational revolution has produced the great bulk of new employment over the last half century. All of manufacturing together accounted for only one-fifth of the expansion of employment during this period. Despite the growth of new industries, manufacturing employment declined in relative importance from one-third of the total labor force to less than one-quarter. In contrast, more than half of the increase in national employment came in business and professional services and the growth of such private "third sector" institutions as hospitals,

21

TABLE 1 The Changing Structure of the National Economy, 1929–1974

	1929	1974	Increase	Industry Proportion of Total Employment Gains
Total FTE employment	35,338	76,342	41,004	100.0%
Agriculture and mining	3,945	2,005	−1,940	−4.7%
Total manufacturing	10,428	19,499	9,071	22.1%
Old industries:				
Textiles	1,262	954	−308	−0.8%
Iron and steel	1,217	1,237	20	0.1%
Automobiles	540	899	359	0.9%
New industries:				
Electrical machinery	519	2,015	1,496	3.6%
Fabricated metal products	325	1,472	1,147	2.8%
Aircraft	150	1,087	937	2.3%
Chemicals	397	1,045	648	1.6%
Wholesale and retail trade	5,846	14,543	8,697	21.2%
Total services	9,731	32,022	22,291	54.4%
Finance, insurance, and RE	1,415	4,037	2,622	6.4%
Business services	157	1,780	1,623	4.0%
Professional services	125	1,073	948	2.3%
Medical and health services	429	3,457	3,028	7.4%
Education (private)	224	1,011	787	1.9%
Federal government (civilian)	267	1,956	1,689	4.1%
State and local government (includes public education)	2,357	9,911	7,554	18.3%

SOURCE: U.S. Bureau of Economic Analysis, "National Income and Product Accounts of the United States, 1929–1974, Statistical Tables," 1975, Table 8.6.

Right column does not add to 100.0% because construction, transportation, and communication have been excluded from the table.

schools, and universities. Further, the growth of government, particularly local government, added as many jobs as all of manufacturing.

These broad trends worked two kinds of changes on the industrial central cities. As we shall see in a moment, newly dominant postindustrial institutions transformed the central-city economy. Along with this positive economic impact, however, came a tremendous disinvestment in and decentralization of traditional central-city economic activities.

The Displacement of Manufacturing and Population from the Older Cities

The central-city concentration of population and employment reached a peak around 1919 in New York and a number of other older cities. Since that time, population and employment have been decentralizing, first to these cities' suburbs and then to new metropolitan areas. The rate of suburbanization has not been constant. After a beginning in the teens and twenties, the Depression and World War II slowed the process, but it surged again after the war.

In the northeastern cities, the rate of suburbanization has slowed with each passing decade. Central cities have continued to decline, but their suburbs have also aged and grown less slowly. Between 1970 and 1980, slow suburban growth contributed to net population declines in a number of the older SMSAs. In the wake of the urban turmoil of the 1960s and the 1969–1970 and 1973–1975 recessions, the focus of metropolitan growth shifted from the older northeastern cities to new metropolitan areas, particularly those in the Southwest.

Between 1947 and 1967, the suburban rings captured 111 percent of the manufacturing employment gain and 100 percent of the population gain in the sixty-nine largest SMSAs with populations over five hundred thousand. During these two decades, the sixteen largest and oldest central cities, located primarily in the belt stretching from New York and Boston to St. Louis and Chicago, lost an average of 34,751 manufacturing jobs, while

23

their suburbs gained an average of 86,358. By contrast, the seventeen largest southern and western central cities gained an average of 19,756 manufacturing jobs, while their suburbs also gained 64,937 on average during these two decades.[10]

Between 1960 and 1976, regional differences grew more substantial. The Northeast-North Central region lost 10 percent of its industrial job base. Industrial employment rose 59.3 percent in the South, putting it ahead of the North in total industrial jobs, while the West also gained 44.4 percent in manufacturing employment.[11] It is not surprising that over six decades these trends would lead observers to characterize the older central cities as suffering from "urban blight" or worse.

"OLD" INDUSTRIES

In analyzing these trends, it is useful to note that manufacturing suburbanized more rapidly than population and that "old" industries such as apparel, steel, and automobiles and "new" industries like electronics and aerospace followed distinct locational patterns. The old industries had been established in central-city locations long before the Depression. They were the stuff of the nineteenth-century city, having fashioned its blue collar ethnic makeup and having contributed the industrial strife which plagued big cities from the turn of the century to the union recognition battles of the 1930s. The departure of these industries after 1930 has been a primary source of central-city decline.

As plants in old industries increasingly became units of multilocational enterprises, and as these enterprises sought to build their plant capacity according to a rational market strategy, enterprise decision-makers increasingly questioned the continued use of pre–World War II central-city plants. As Roger Schmenner, an astute analyst of the plant location decision-making process, has observed, "The location decision is best viewed as an integral part of the corporation's planning of capacity."[12] As demand grows, a corporation must choose between expanding existing plants, creating new branch plants, or relocating existing plants.

In most cases, a corporation's already large plant commitment in an existing area deters it from making large-scale movements in the location of its production facilities. But certain conditions can weaken this constraint. When old and crowded plants which have grown up in a haphazard manner cannot be rebuilt or expanded to meet demand, management is forced to take a new look at the location issue. This is particularly true where the corporation can substantially upgrade its production technology. Schmenner cites "an urgent need for increased space" and "an opportunity to alter the production technology significantly" as the major factors causing plants to move.

In choosing new sites, Schmenner finds "most companies do not view site choice as a means to save money for the company, except in the long term." Indeed, site-specific costs have tended to become fairly homogeneous. "It is here," Schmenner notes, "that a wealth of qualitative concerns get produced," such as evaluating attitudes "of local people to work or of government to business or of potential company managers to live in the area."[13] The run-down condition of an old plant, the inability to start from scratch on an old site, and the availability of a more supportive (but not necessarily cheaper) site elsewhere can thus combine to make an otherwise difficult move possible and even necessary.

These exact conditions faced the industries concentrated in the older central cities during and immediately after World War II. Their production facilities were multistory loft buildings and old plants which the Depression and later World War II (in the case of nondefense plants) had prevented from being reorganized and recapitalized. Their locations were often congested. With the advent of postwar prosperity, with the negative political legacy of the central cities, and with the political and physical *tabula rasa* provided by the suburbs, relocation became the logical choice. Even during World War II, plants funded by the War Production Board were located disproportionately in suburban sites. After 1946, manufacturing employment suburbanized even faster than residential population. The pent-up demand for new housing, new job opportunities, and considerations similar to those facing industry stimulated rapid residential suburbanization as well.

Because they were toward the end of their product development life cycles, the "old" industries could increase production without

25

commensurate increases in employment. Since the ratio of production workers to total employment also declined in these industries—down 10 percentage points in the steel industry and 15 in the auto industry between 1947 and 1976—the new suburban, blue collar labor force in the old industries was smaller than it previously had been in the central cities. Owing to unionization, they were also better paid. As these industries abandoned central-city locations for new suburban plants, they spurred considerable suburban population growth.

The auto and steel industries illustrate this pattern. Only 37 out of the 297 bargaining units represented by the United Auto Workers in 1979 are located outside the old industrial belt. Of the remaining 260 units, half are located around Detroit, but only 29 remain within the central city itself.[14] Similarly, only twelve out of the fifty-eight raw steel plants are located outside the Pittsburgh-Detroit belt, mostly in the steel centers of Alabama and the Texas Gulf Coast. The forty-six plants in the old industrial belt are not usually located in central cities, but rather in industrial suburbs like Bethlehem, Aliquippa, Lackawanna, East Chicago, and Dearborn.[15] The wave of wartime and postwar suburban-plant construction, such as the Willow Run plant 25 miles outside of Detroit, U.S. Steel's Fairless plant between Philadelphia and New York, or the auto factories in Hayward and Milpitas, California, hastened suburban population growth and central-city manufacturing employment decline.

"NEW" INDUSTRIES

Federal defense spending during and after World War II fostered "new" industries which chose an even more pronounced pattern of suburban location. Between 1950 and 1980, military spending accounted for one-quarter of the growth in federal spending, a larger share than any other function except income security payments to individuals. Between 1932 and 1952, military spending accounted for over half the growth in federal spending. This spending created the electronics and aircraft industries as we know them today. For both industries, federal defense procurement has provided half the market demand. Table 1 shows that since 1929, their employment has tripled and that they account for most of the employment growth for manufacturing in the economy as a whole.

Unlike the old industries these industries were not tied down to existing plant concentrations. Because of their heavy reliance on inputs of knowledge and educated labor, universities and research laboratories were far more likely than the presence of previous industrial capacity to influence their initial locations. The relationships which grew up between the federal defense establishment, universities like MIT and Stanford, and nascent high-technology firms during and after World War II had a tremendous impact on the growth of such areas as Route 128 around Boston or the Silicon Valley complex south of San Francisco.

Electronics clearly shows this pattern of suburbanization. Of the 430,000 jobs presently located in electronics plants in California, only 100 are located in San Francisco and 992 in San José. In contrast, suburban Palo Alto has 119,453 jobs, Santa Clara 60,730 jobs, and Sunnyvale 39,809 jobs. Other smaller nearby suburbs contain plants with employment totaling 40,400. Similarly, although Los Angeles houses electronics plants employing 26,683, the Southern California suburbs contain far more: Culver City employs 36,591, Century City 24,000 and Anaheim 20,774. Other Los Angeles suburbs account for 138,687 jobs. Although Boston has only 1,340 jobs in electronics plants, towns along the Routes 128 and 495 radial highways have far more. Waltham contains 23,961 jobs, Maynard 19,058, Wellesley 13,700, and Lexington 8,355.[16] The pattern in the aerospace industry, which is concentrated in the West and South, has been similar.

The new industries not only have located in the suburbs from the start, they also have preferred the newer metropolitan areas over old ones. Studies of the geographic pattern in military prime-contract awards show that this locational preference has strengthened over time. As a recent congressional research service literature review noted, "A definite shift . . . from the Northeast and North Central regions to the South and West" has occurred in the awarding of prime contracts between 1950 and 1976, especially in the years after 1968.[17]

27

With the suburbanization of old central-city industries and the emergence of new suburban industries leading the way, suburban populations increased dramatically after 1946. In the old industries, the recognition of labor unions in the latter 1930s helped to create the foundation for a new and more prosperous ethnic, blue collar working class. With the production of new housing, the growth of new suburban plants, and the contraction of old central-city plants, ethnic blue collar workers deserted old, crowded, and often decaying central-city housing stock for better conditions in the suburbs. Similarly, the growth of new industries heavily staffed by engineers and other kinds of educated labor and the increase in central-city administrative activities created a new middle class which also chose to live in the suburbs.

The Depression and World War II had constrained both the household-formation decisions and the housing choices available to the age cohorts which benefited from economic expansion in both the old and new industries. The postwar economic boom, the postwar suburban housing boom, and the postwar baby boom thus went hand in hand.

The suburbanization of blue collar ethnics, the new professional and managerial middle class, industrial employment, and the retail and service activities which followed them created a stark contrast between healthy suburbs and declining central cities in the years after 1946. The vacuum left by their departure was not negative for everyone, however, because it fostered a substantial migration of blacks and other minorities into the central cities. Though some seven million whites left central cities between 1950 and 1970, five million blacks, largely from the South, moved in. Minority groups were not, however, the only growing presence within the older central cities.

The Rise of New Institutions in the Central-City Economy

The growth of new institutions within central-city economies also contrasts with the displacement of manufacturing investment and residential population away from them. Although these new institutions also developed in suburban locations, the most important of them continue to be clustered in central-city locations. Unlike manufacturing, they also substantially increased their employment.

In the business world, these newly dominant central-city institutions include corporate headquarters, banks, and advanced corporate service firms in management consulting, law, accounting, advertising, and other professional fields. In the public sector, they include local government agencies, public benefit corporations, and federal agencies.

A "third sector" of private, nonprofit, but often publicly supported, organizations has also expanded tremendously. Hospitals and universities offer the two most obvious examples of third sector growth in central cities, but a wide range of activities comes under this heading. As Table 1 shows, administrative and service institutions account for three-quarters of the total growth in national employment since 1929. The largest and most specialized institutions remain located, more often than not, inside the central cities.

CORPORATE HEADQUARTERS

Ever since 1913, when President Wilson pressed a button in Washington to turn on the lights in New York's new fifty-five-story Woolworth Tower, the increasing dominance of the modern corporation has profoundly influenced the economic, social, physical, and political structure of big cities. The modern corporation was based on the fact that corporate managers could make allocation decisions more profitably than markets had previously. In A. D. Chandler's words,

> The modern multiunit business enterprise replaced the small traditional enterprise when administrative coordination permitted greater productivity, lower costs, and higher profits than coordination by market mechanisms.[18]

By using sophisticated analytic techniques, corporate managers could allocate capital, labor, and raw materials strategically across production units to control costs and match output to demand; they could also market and deliver production through a stable

29

organization. In this way, corporations increasingly dominated most sectors of the economy on an increasingly international scale (although some sectors, like apparel, naturally resist this trend).

"As the large enterprises grew and dominated major sectors of the economy," Chandler notes, "they altered the basic structure of these sectors and the economy as a whole."[19] As the postwar experience indicates, part of this changed structure involved decentralizing plant production capacity to suburbs and new metropolitan areas. Simultaneously, however, the corporate form concentrated decision-making and administrative capacity into units typically located in central cities. The multiunit corporation thus became the basic organizing institution of the metropolis as well as the economy.

In 1919, some 5,838 central offices controlled 21,998 plants, accounting for only 7.8 percent of all plants but one-third of all industrial employment. By 1929, roughly the same number of central offices accounted for 12 percent of the plants and 48 percent of employment. These figures held through the Depression. In the immediate postwar period, however, the rate of concentration took another surge. By 1974, the five hundred biggest corporate offices controlled 71 percent of all manufacturing assets and 76 percent of the employment.[20]

Many corporate headquarters followed their branch plants to the suburbs, especially after the turmoil of the late 1960s. Smaller SMSAs have also been gaining headquarters relative to the largest SMSAs. Nevertheless, corporate headquarters in the aggregate remain heavily concentrated in the central cities of the largest metropolitan areas. Two-thirds of the *Fortune* 500 largest manufacturing company headquarters are located in the twenty-five largest metropolitan areas. Despite a decline from 128 such firms in 1965 to 72 today, New York City still contains 1 out of every 7 headquarters, three times more than Chicago, the next largest corporate center. Most of New York's decline represented movement to nearby suburbs, which now contain 60 corporate headquarters. These corporations still rely heavily on New York's banks and corporate service firms. Large new cities like Dallas and Houston have also increased their role as headquarters centers. Even Los Angeles, a city once known for its lack of a downtown, has developed a new corporate center in and around the Bunker Hill redevelopment project.[21]

The increasing importance of corporate headquarters in the economy has created new kinds of interdependence among cities. Though these new links do not strictly correspond to hierarchy in which one "pinnacle city" influences all the others, the few cities with corporate headquarters complexes nevertheless exert influence over and benefit from growth in many other cities populated by branch plants.[22] New York—or at least its corporate headquarters complex—can benefit from growth lower down in the hierarchy even though it happens thousands of miles away.[23] The economic prospects of cities with large corporate headquarters thus increasingly depend on the economy as a whole rather than what may be happening in the nearby region. Further, for a city to keep a prominent role in this intercity network, it must have first-rate communications and transportation facilities.

ADVANCED CORPORATE SERVICES

The rise of what Robert Cohen has called "advanced corporate services" (ACS) has had perhaps an even greater postwar impact on central-city economies. Cohen sums it up this way:

> As corporations have evolved since World War II, they have faced an increasingly complex business environment, in which major changes have occurred with increasing frequency. To adapt to this climate, corporate managers have found themselves in need of certain skills, information, and strategies which could not be developed within the corporation itself. They have demanded these inputs from a number of specialized corporate service firms . . . which have become full-fledged partners in corporate decision-making and strategy formulation. . . . As specialization within corporate service firms has increased, concentration and economies of scale have been attained. The cities have been the natural magnet for this growth of the corporate services sector.[24]

The growth of corporate headquarters created a demand for specialized corporate and investment banking activities, corporate and international law, accounting, management consulting, ad-

31

vertising, and even architectural and urban design services. The highly specialized firms providing these services have tended to cluster even more strongly in central cities than corporate headquarters activities themselves. In those cities with substantial headquarters representation, employment in advanced corporate services has risen more rapidly than in any other sector.[25]

Cohen examined three advanced corporate services in detail: investment banking, corporate law, and accounting. He found an extraordinarily high concentration of these firms in such cities as New York, Chicago, Boston, San Francisco, Los Angeles, and Philadelphia. New York City alone, for example, contains 31.2 percent of all bank deposits, 53.9 percent of all foreign deposits, and almost one lawyer out of every ten in the nation. He concludes his investigation in these terms:

> Thus, in the '60s and '70s, a few cities have emerged as centers of corporate headquarters and strong ACS firms. In these places, the city has become more than just a center for companies which manage and coordinate a widely dispersed network of productive operations. It has become, as Hymer suggested, the center of corporate planning and strategy formulation for the large business corporation. But its strength and status are founded not only upon the existence of major multinational firms, *but also upon* the existence of large ACS firms, whose activities are usually also multinational.[26]

Despite the post-1970 suburbanization of corporate headquarters, these highly sophisticated corporate service activities have remained clustered in the central cities. One study has shown that the more sophisticated, the more likely firms providing these services are to have remained in or near the city center.[27] These firms have scored substantial employment gains, which were reflected, in turn, in the high-rise office construction booms of the late 1960s and the late 1970s.

THE GROWTH OF GOVERNMENT

Private, profit-making, multilocational organizations have not been the only force behind the organizational revolution in the major central-city economies. As Table 1 shows, the single largest source of employment gain between 1929 and 1974 has been government. By 1974, government employed one out of almost every six workers. This government employment gain has been concentrated in the central cities, which have more public workers in relationship to the population, more kinds of services, and receive proportionately more support from federal intergovernmental assistance.

In the years between 1955 and 1975, the growth in federal spending was three times the growth in local government spending, but the increase in federal employment was only one-fifth the growth in local government employment. This apparent disparity arises from the fact that the federal government has increasingly become a "banker government" for local governments and a wide variety of private, nonprofit service agencies, rather than a direct service provider. According to the Advisory Commission on Intergovernmental Relations, by 1978 direct federal aid constituted 50.7 percent of locally raised revenues in forty-eight large central cities.[28]

The increase in state and local employment between 1953 and 1975 came mostly in education, and thus mirrored the life cycle of the suburban baby-boom generation born just after World War II. Half of the 5.9 million new state and local employees during this period worked on some aspect of education. Reflecting the source of demand, more than half of these workers were located in the suburbs.

The other half of the growth in state and local employment has, by contrast, been concentrated in the central cities. In the years since World War II, local governments took on new functions ranging from housing and physical development to social services and manpower training. The largest cities have the highest ratio of municipal labor force to population and the broadest spectrum of services, including municipal hospitals and even, in some cases, municipal universities. The federal aid which supports these activities has gone disproportionately to larger central cities. Markusen and her colleagues, for example, conclude that "central cities receive higher per capita allocations of federal aid than either

33

their suburbs or nonmetropolitan counties'' and that ''the record on state aid to cities by size is fairly straightforward: the bigger the city, the larger the per capita allocation.''[29] Robert Yin has shown how federal aid programs stimulated the growth of local ''counterpart bureaucracies.''[30]

As a result of the growth in public employment, the upward and outward expansion of ''government centers,'' city agencies, City Halls, courts, state office buildings, and federal office buildings has typically accompanied the similar expansion of central business districts. As with the growth of corporate headquarters complexes, expanding government centers often provided the catalyst for major redevelopment projects. Boston provides a particularly striking example of a trend which has influenced many major cities, particularly those which are federal regional administrative centers.

THE ''THIRD'' SECTOR

Federal spending increases have also fueled the growth of private, nonprofit service providers engaged in government by contract. As the case of defense spending shows, this phenomenon has not always favored the central cities. Increased federal spending on education, research, social services, and health, however, substantially favored central cities. The 1950 federal budget allocated less than half a billion dollars to either education or health. By the 1979 budget, these figures had risen to $12 billion and $49.7 billion, respectively.

The local nonprofit institutions which benefited from this increase in grants and contracts, such as universities and medical complexes, did not suburbanize nearly so rapidly as manufacturing employment or residential population. Research universities offer a case in point. Commenting on the fact that the Defense Department put more than two-thirds of its research funds into ten research universities during the 1950s, Don Price observed that

Here was a system in which the federal agencies could do business not only with state government agencies, but with private universities and corporations as well. . . . This new system almost wipes out the distinction between public and private affairs and gives great segments of industry and education a stake in federal programs.[31]

Some of these segments, of course, grew up in suburban settings, particularly those which, like Lincoln Laboratory or the Lawrence-Livermore Radiation Laboratory, were closely identified with the Defense Department. And many state universities are located in small cities.

Despite the fact that some suburbs also benefited, a striking amount of university growth occurred in central-city locations. Such major institutions as Harvard, MIT, Yale, Columbia, the University of Rochester, the University of Pennsylvania, Johns Hopkins, the University of Pittsburgh, Carnegie-Mellon, Case-Western Reserve, the Universities of Ohio, Minnesota, and Washington, and UCLA are all located in or near central cities. All expanded greatly in the years after World War II, and most served as a focal point for redevelopment activities in adjacent areas. None moved to new suburban locations. Indeed, in cities with large concentrations of colleges and universities like Boston and New York, higher education has become a significant export activity.

Table 1 shows that another example of the "third sector," the health industry, has also grown rapidly since the New Deal. It accounts for 7.4 percent of the total increase of employment in the economy. The health industry has also been a major recipient of federal assistance and accounts for almost 11 percent of the increase in the federal budget since 1950. Even more than institutions of higher learning, major medical centers are concentrated in the largest metropolitan areas and most often are located in the central cities.[32] In New York City, the twenty-two major medical centers and their allied activities increased their employment from less than 90,000 in 1958 to more than 190,000 in 1980.[33] In Boston, Massachusetts General and its associated activities helped to spur the redevelopment of the West End; Boston City Hospital and the Tufts-New England Medical Center did the same for the South End. These institutions, together with Harvard Medical

35

School and numerous other health centers, make Boston one of the major health services exporters in the United States. Similarly, in San Francisco, while the University of California Medical Center is the city's largest employer, the city has more than twenty additional hospitals, including two adjacent to the Western Addition urban renewal area.

In contrast, therefore, to the decreasing importance of industry in central-city economies, the organizational revolution has thrust new institutions into dominant positions within central-city economies as well as within the national economy. Despite the suburbanization of service activities and despite the rise of new headquarters centers in suburbs like Westchester and cities like Houston, cities such as New York, Chicago, Los Angeles, Philadelphia, Boston, and San Francisco remain leading centers of corporate headquarters, advanced corporate services, government agencies, and nonprofit service providers. Their impact on these central cities has been as large and as profound as the more frequently noted flight of industrial employment.

The Cities of 1930 and the Cities of 1980

Over the last five decades, the two primary forces of the post-industrial revolution have substantially altered the physical form of big cities, their economic and social structure, and the system of cities as a whole. One primary force, the displacement of industrial capacity and residential population, contributed both to the rise of the modern metropolitan form and to the rise of new cities which now rival the old ones in economic and political importance. The metropolitan areas produced by this force are much more spread out, socially segmented, and politically fragmented than the cities of 1930.

In its study *Our Cities*, released in 1937, the National Resources Committee noted the "dominance of the machine over the ways of life in cities" and characterized them as "the dusty and sometimes smoldering and reddened arena of industrial conflict."[34] As of 1930, the ninety-six metropolitan areas with populations over one hundred thousand contained 45 percent of the national population, three-quarters of which lived in the central cities. The 155 counties containing the larger industrial cities accounted for 74 percent of all industrial employment and 79 percent of the output.[35]

By 1980, the nation had become much more urbanized, but the urban population is now much less concentrated in central cities. New metropolitan areas located largely in the South and West increased the overall number of SMSAs from 96 to 279. The proportion of national population contained by SMSAs rose from 45 to 75 percent. The central-city proportion of the metropolitan population fell substantially, however, from three-quarters to less than half.[36] In many cases, the population of the older central cities which formed the nucleus of the city system in 1930 fell in absolute as well as relative terms between 1930 and 1980. The older central cities were no longer the "workshops of industrial society," having declined in manufacturing employment even more precipitously than in population. In contrast to 1930, central cities accounted for only 25 percent of industrial employment in 1980.

In 1930, the central cities housed great extremes of wealth and social background within single political jurisdictions. As annexations halted during the 1920s and suburbanization progressed swiftly after World War II, metropolitan areas became steadily more segmented in social and political terms. In a study of the Los Angeles metropolitan area, Gary Miller has shown how industries seeking to escape central-city burdens, public officials seeking to keep tax rates low, and suburban residents seeking to avoid paying for services to the less affluent combined to produce exclusionary and discriminatory incorporation practices. He concluded that "during the period 1950 to 1970, municipal boundaries increasingly served to separate races and income classes in the Los Angeles area." Reviewing a larger sample of metropolitan areas, Urban Institute scholars also concluded that "when computed for entire metropolitan areas, segregation generally increased over the decade" of the 1970s.[37] Metropolitan income inequality also increased.

The suburbanization of population and industry also industrial-

37

ized the occupational structure of the suburbs. By 1980, the suburban rings of the SMSAs contained 41.6 percent of all manufacturing employment, while nonmetropolitan areas accounted for another 33.2 percent. While the largest and oldest central cities lost blue collar employment most heavily, "the largest growth in suburban blue collar employment has also been in the outer rings of the largest and oldest SMSAs."[38] During the 1960s alone, the proportion of the blue collar labor force which worked and lived in central cities in 101 SMSAs declined from 47.6 to 35.6 percent of the total. By contrast, the percentage who lived and worked in the suburbs rose from 30.2 to 36.1 percent, while the total proportion of blue collar workers residing in the suburbs increased from 45.7 to 54.6 percent.

If suburbanization and decentralization shifted the traditional, ethnic, blue collar labor force out of the older central cities and built up suburbs and new metropolitan areas, the second primary force of the postindustrial transformation, the organizational revolution, played an equally important role in shaping the current system. As *Our Cities* observed, even in 1930 large cities were "the nerve center of our vast and delicate commercial mechanism" whose growth "of late . . . has reflected their increasing importance as commercial and service centers rather than as industrial centers."[39] What had only begun in 1930 had reached full force by 1980.

The most obvious physical impact has been the postwar boom in central business district office-building construction, especially during the latter 1960s and the latter 1970s. Despite the growth of suburban service employment and the movement of some corporate headquarters to the suburbs, central-city office construction has been substantial. The New York and Chicago central business districts alone account for 45 percent of all office space within the twenty largest SMSAs and 10 percent of the total national office space inventory. Together, they accounted for 148 million square feet, or 40 percent of the new office space constructed in these twenty SMSAs between 1960 and 1975. In 1982 and 1983 alone, New York City is scheduled to complete 20 million square feet of space in development. Other major gainers between 1960

38

and 1975 included Washington (36 million square feet), Los Angeles (26 million), Houston (22 million), and Boston and San Francisco (21 million each).[40]

These physical changes had occupational consequences. As central-city employment related to the production and distribution of goods fell and blue collar occupations declined, service sector employment and white-collar occupations, such as professional, managerial, and clerical work, have increased. The growth of service occupations has brought a second group of immigrants into the central cities alongside the well-known migration of blacks and other minority groups.

As the baby-boom generation born in the suburbs has moved through its life cycle, it has been educated more thoroughly than any of its predecessors. As a result, it has moved into the new professional jobs created by the expansion of new institutions. In so doing, a significant proportion of this cohort has made different household formation and location decisions than their parents made. Deferring or choosing not to bear children, most women of this cohort have moved into the labor force. This cohort has formed a greater variety of households, many with several workers, most without children, which are quite unlike the child-centered, single-income households of their parents. For such households, central cities provide a far more appealing location relative to the suburbs than was true for their parents. Though the in-migration of young white professional residents to central cities has not numerically offset continued minority immigration or the continued overall white exodus, their numbers have nonetheless increased greatly. Moreover, their market power is so great that their impact reaches far beyond their numbers.[41]

In new and different forms, the urban social and income inequalities of the 1930s are thus perpetrated in the central cities of 1980. In 1930, such differences were largely among whites and revolved around the industrial occupational order. The five subsequent decades largely dismantled this occupational order and replaced it with a new one based on administrative and service institutions. The better jobs in these now-dominant organizations are held by suburban commuters and the new stratum of young

39

professionals. Central-city minority-group members, in turn, are clustered in lower status clerical jobs and especially in services which are outside the newly dominant institutions but which support them, such as the restaurant industry.[42]

The forces which have transformed individual cities have operated across the system of cities as well. As cities have become more interdependent, those which play a nodal role have fared much better than those which, like Youngstown and Gary, were mainly centers of industrial production.

Indeed, three broad kinds of cities can be distinguished. Old cities which were major industrial centers but which never became administrative and service nodes have fared worst. Suburbanization hurt these cities and the organizational revolution did not help them. These cities also carried legacies of industrial conflict from the period before the New Deal and from the urban unrest of the 1960s, and scored high on what Nathan and Adams have called the "hardship" index.[43] By contrast, a second group typified by the new cities of the Southwest had no industrial legacy at all. Instead, they grew up during and after World War II on new, high-technology industries as well as on administrative and services activities. Typically, these cities have had no legacy of urban conflict and have grown far more rapidly than any of the other cities.

A third group mixes the two elements which define the postindustrial transformation. They may have been significant production centers between 1880 and 1930, but they also developed strong corporate, banking, and "third sector" activities, often because they were cultural and commercial centers before they industrialized. New York, Chicago, Philadelphia, Boston, and San Francisco exemplify this pattern. Because these cities contain all the conflicting elements of the postindustrial transformation within them, they provide the most interesting and revealing cases for analyzing how it happened. In subsequent chapters, two such cases, Boston and San Francisco, will be used to show the political forces which hastened the postindustrial transformation.

Finally, one similarity between the cities of 1930 and those of today is also worth noting. In 1930, the postindustrial transformation was just beginning to be felt. In the following decades, especially right after World War II, it picked up tremendous momentum. Today, however, both suburbanization and central-city transformation appear increasingly problematic. The rate of suburbanization has slowed, opposition to further suburban development has increased, and social diversity and political conflict within the suburbs have grown. The children who grew up in suburbs often cannot afford them now, nor do they want to. Though the urban conflicts of the 1930s have been dissolved, the postindustrial transformation has created new conflicts and problems in the central cities and suburbs alike. Many older central cities have experienced fiscal and economic distress, heightened urban conflict, and new kinds of racial and ethnic tension. In some, infrastructure built by the New Deal is literally collapsing. In all, housing is tight. Thus just as the New Deal attempted to grapple with the urban problems of one era, the political leaders of today face a similar challenge.

3. Government Intervention into the Postindustrial Transformation

As the previous discussion suggests, government intervention fostered both the displacement of industry away from the central cities and the organizational revolution within them. A whole series of government actions encouraged the suburbanization of employment and residential population. The new industries which arose in the suburbs and the new metropolitan areas were either capitalized by the War Production Board during World War II or stimulated by federal defense spending in subsequent years. Federal investment in the interstate highway system after 1956 also strongly favored suburbanization as did federal tax treatment of industrial depreciation. Federal housing policies, such as the standardization and insurance of home mortgages through the VA and FHA programs, channeled capital into suburban housing construction through the federal secondary mortgage market. Favorable tax treatment of homeowner interest payments strongly promoted suburban housing construction, while the treatment of

41

commercial investment stimulated office construction. Finally, the growth-oriented political climate in suburban jurisdictions contrasted with big-city politics, which often favored rent control and public housing.

On the whole, government intervention transformed the central cities in ways suited to the needs of newly dominant postindustrial institutions. Federal funds fueled the expansion of many of these organizations, such as hospitals and universities. Local government took increasing initiative in shaping the central-city environment. It cleared industrial areas and low-income residential districts, built freeways, expanded airports, developed new commercial and government centers, built luxury and subsidized housing, and became an increasingly important employer and service provider on its own account.

Although many of these efforts depended on entrepreneurial political leadership at the local level, few could have been undertaken without the leverage of federal assistance. Between 1954 and 1969, federal assistance allowed local redevelopment agencies to acquire and clear 57,300 acres of central-city land in 1,600 projects. After deducting space for streets, 60 percent of the disposable land went to nonresidential uses, particularly office buildings, other commercial buildings, government buildings, schools, and hospitals.[44]

The National Resources Committee observed in 1937 that although "the city has come to play such a preponderant role in our national existence," the relations between cities and the federal government "remain in an amorphous and anachronistic state."[45] The 1930 federal budget contained virtually nothing specifically targeted to urban development. Between 1950 and 1980, however, programs influencing some aspect of urban development accounted for almost 10 percent of the entire growth in the federal budget. This amount does not include the tax expenditures derived from favorable treatment of depreciation and homeowner interest payments. If still amorphous, federal-city relations are certainly not anachronistic.

When all aspects are considered, metropolitan physical development accounts for perhaps one-fifth of the GNP and perhaps one-fourth of its growth since World War II. (Physical capital investment alone accounts for 16 percent of the GNP.) In relationship to these amounts, government tax expenditures on physical development amount to about 20 percent of the private capital invested. Direct government capital expenditures are also considerable. Currently, government at all levels accounts for nearly 27 percent of all construction as measured by value. Many of these government construction projects, such as roads, schools and other public facilities, and sewer and water systems, have a determining effect on where private physical investment goes.[46]

In addition to the dozens of federal programs encouraging and shaping urban physical capital investment, federal assistance has also influenced urban social services, the structure of urban government, the city planning process, the urban labor market, and the forms of citizen participation. Together, more than two hundred fifty federal program titles influence urban development. In 1978, a single department, Housing and Urban Development, published a book outlining seventy-four major and minor program categories ranging from the solar heating and cooling demonstration project to the GNMA secondary mortgage market.[47]

If the local implementation of federal urban development programs has had such a substantial impact on the postindustrial transformation of U.S. cities, how did these programs come about? As the next chapter will show, the answer lies largely in two discoveries which Democratic national political entrepreneurs made during and after the New Deal. They discovered first that they could bring together formerly feuding urban constituencies around a program of federal intervention into the urban development process. By making economically vital physical changes possible, federal urban development programs could create local coalitions of producer interests. The disparate urban constituencies of the national Democratic party—machines as well as reform groups, big business as well as labor, blue collar ethnics as well as minorities—could each find reasons to be united behind a program of growth and development. As Catherine Bauer later observed of the urban renewal program, "Seldom had such a diverse crew

43

of would-be angels tried to dance on the head of the same small pin.''

National Democratic political entrepreneurs' second discovery stemmed from the first. During and after the New Deal, national political leaders used federal programs not only to bring local constituencies together, but also to unite them organizationally. In other words, they could augment and ultimately replace the particularism and uncertainty of the old-fashioned machine with a new kind characterized by bureaucratic certainty and funded by the U.S. Treasury. Government programs could thus solidify national political power. No less an observer of American politics than V. O. Key first described the process by which this end was accomplished.

Most federal grant programs, Key observed, ''were preceded by long periods of agitation and pressure by interested groups, and of study by congressional committees and commissions,'' in order to ''meet certain problems where state action had been inadequate.'' He added that ''the spearhead of the movement for Federal aid for a particular governmental function is usually a nationally organized pressure group whose cause would benefit by the proposed legislation.'' Such pressure groups could and did provide political support in both national and city elections. When successful, Key concludes, such groups possessed ''a powerful weapon in dealing with hesitant state legislatures.''[48] He might have added that they also possessed a powerful weapon for dealing with the local physical and political obstacles to new patterns of urban development.

Roosevelt, Truman, Kennedy, and Johnson may have been influenced by such advocacy groups, but they were also past masters at using new federal programs to turn such constituencies to their own political advantage. During their years of political success, they built up ''iron triangles'' between federal program managers, congressional political supporters, and local beneficiaries.

Given the political as well as the economic efficacy of federal intervention into the urban development process, it might seem that federal policy would strongly favor the central cities under

Democrats, since they provide Democrats with most of their electoral support. Republicans, by contrast, would shift the emphasis away from central cities and toward more conservative constituencies in the suburban and new metropolitan areas. To some extent, as the next two chapters will show, this kind of pendulum swing did in fact occur.

There are several important reasons, however, why no simple correlation can hold between the party in power and the *pro* versus *anti* central-city emphasis in federal urban development policy. Most obviously, the diversity of constituencies which national Democrats sought to favor was sufficiently great and the congressional balance of power sufficiently narrow that Democrats promoted *both* kinds of programs at the same time. To please its diverse constituencies, and to reduce its exposure to political opposition, Democratic urban development policies have ridden off in several directions at once. This is particularly true because the Democrats have repeatedly abandoned programs of domestic reform in order to fight World War II, the Korean War, and Vietnam. Whereas Republicans can and have fairly consistently opposed central-city measures and favored aid to suburban constituencies, the Democrats have, in a sense, been for and against the city at the same time.

The second reason that federal urban policy has not completely responded to political shifts lies in the certainty that those shifts will take place. In order to preserve politically favorable programs, their proponents have sought to remove them from immediate accountability. In the Ramspeck Act of 1940, for example, Democrats ensured that political appointees administering the New Deal agencies would, through noncompetitive examinations, be granted civil-service tenure. Civil service, as well as such devices as independent boards and agencies, increased such political insulation. As administrations changed and more programs were passed, this created an increasingly less coherent and more politically responsive sedimentary layering of programs.

Finally, the fact that program managers themselves became political entrepreneurs guaranteed that the programs of one political era would, for the most part, survive into the next. Political and nonpolitical appointees alike came to identify with their program, sought out and mobilized local support, and effectively lobbied Congress for expansion of their programs. The real political clout of an "iron triangle," once fabricated, mostly blunted severe partisan shifts in the overall content of the intergovernmental program delivery system from one era to the next.

Nonetheless, despite these difficulties, generations of national political entrepreneurs on both sides of the aisle have used the expansion of federal urban development programs as a tool for assembling and solidifying national (and local) political power. The Democrats, who invented this technique, in particular have used it to maintain their normal majority status. As succeeding chapters will show, however, it has proven to be a double-edged sword.

The New Deal and After:
The Political Determination of
Federal Urban Policy

1. INTRODUCTION

Before the New Deal, "the great majority of federal-city relations were casual and incidental, if not extralegal."[1] Federal and state government displayed a fundamentally antiurban disposition. At both levels, legislative representation was heavily biased toward rural areas, and the programs these legislatures enacted followed suit. The few pre–New Deal federal grant programs dealt with such matters as land grant colleges, rural road projects, and agricultural subsidies.

Beginning in 1932, however, the New Deal and subsequent Democratic administrations dramatically overturned this *status quo*. By 1980, they had made the federal government a major source of funds for urban infrastructure, a major force in the urban housing industry, and a major revenue source for big-city operating budgets.

What factors explain this federal intervention into urban development patterns? Some have argued that federal urban programs evolved in response to needs of the national economy. According to this view, urban programs were initially developed to promote economic recovery from the Depression and were continued after World War II to keep up aggregate demand and provide work in the construction sector. This view of policy development is also reflected in the recent discussion about how best to target countercyclical federal assistance to "distressed cities." However, if one examines the timing of the major federal urban programs or their distributive impact, it becomes clear that abstract economic factors do not explain the growth of federal urban programs.

Instead, the evolution of federal urban programs may best be understood as resulting from the competition among national political entrepreneurs to strengthen their political position by enacting new national programs which bolster their local constituencies. Economic crises have increased the scope of action available to these entrepreneurs and have underscored the kinds of problems needing government attention. But factors rooted within the political system itself, not the economy, have accounted for the actual design of the resulting federal programs.

Beginning with Roosevelt's invention of national urban policy during the New Deal, federal urban programs have provided a principal method—perhaps the *key* method—by which national Democratic political entrepreneurs have attempted to widen and organize their political support. Urban programs enabled Democrats to build national political power on a base of urban electoral majorities, and to sustain that influence over time through new nonparty organizational forms. In achieving these ends, their efforts have been shaped by political imperatives and by political constraints.

Perhaps the most obvious constraint has been the national electoral balance, which has repeatedly shifted against urban Democrats since the New Deal. Republicans have repeatedly won the White House. In Congress, the influence of the conservative coalition between Republicans and southern Democrats has also repeatedly blocked national Democratic entrepreneurial attempts to expand urban programs.[2] Congress's representational bias toward rural, conservative districts, though now attenuated, reinforced this constraint. Similarly, conflicts among the local political interests which Democratic program entrepreneurs sought to unite in a coalition have also shaped program development. In contrast to these constraints, the chief imperative for Democrats has been the determining role the urban electorate has played in giving them national political majorities.

At many points, the constraints have blocked or delayed the

development of federal urban programs. At a few key points, however, the mobilization of the urban electorate has enabled Democratic political entrepreneurs to overcome these constraints, although they still shaped legislative design. During these periods, Democrats enacted urban programs in great surges. Particularly during the New Deal and the Great Society, but also during the Fair Deal and the Carter years, a mobilized urban electorate, a favorable congressional balance of power, local support, and, as time passed, advocacy from government agencies themselves led Democratic presidents to advocate and Congress to enact dramatic expansions of federal urban development programs.

Between these points of expansion, as the next chapter will show, Republican political entrepreneurs attempted to curtail or modify Democratic programs and to change their overall emphasis to favor conservative constituencies. World War II, the Eisenhower administration, the Nixon-Ford years, and the Reagan administration all represented unfavorable swings of the national political pendulum which undermined Democratic achievements.

Despite these adverse periods, Chart 1 shows that the New Deal erected the basic framework for federal urban policy, much of which survives today. Conservative swings weakened some parts, added new programs with different emphases, but could not dismantle the overall program structure. In contrast to the 1920s, the federal government today strongly influences the patterns of urban physical development and urban political participation. Chart 1 sums up the major legislative titles through which this impact has been achieved. While conservatives have also influenced policy over the years, urban liberal Democrats can rightly take credit for creating this program structure and its consequences.

Chart 1 also shows that the major spurts of growth in federal urban programs came during the New Deal and the Great Society. The factors which at other times constrained policy development encouraged and even demanded its expansion during these periods. Congress was a gatekeeper on change.[3] As Figure 1 shows, the strength of northern, urban liberal Democrats relative to their Republican and southern Democratic conservative coalition adversaries in Congress reached all-time peaks during the New Deal

49

CHART 1 Evolution of the Federal Urban Development Program Structure, 1933–1980

	New Deal '33-'38	WWII-Fair Deal '39-'52	Eisenhower '53-'60	Great Society '61-'68	Nixon-Ford '69-'76	Carter '77-'80
Physical Development						
FHA Insurance	NHA '34					
BMIR Loans	NHA '34		HA '54	HUDA '68	Freeze '73	Thaw '77
Urban Renewal	USHA '37	'39	HA '54		HCDA '74	HCDA '77
EDA-Type Grants	RFC '32		'54	ARA '61 PWEDA '65		HCDA '77
Freeways		FAHA '44	IHA '56		FAHA '73	
Mass Transit				UMTA '64		
Public Works	{ CWA '33 / PWA '33	'43	HA '55	APWA '61 PWEDA '65 { PWEDA '65 / HUDA '65	PWEA '76	IAA '77
Airports	WPA in '39/Defense	FAA '46				
Social Welfare						
Public Housing	USHA '37	'39 HA '49		HUDA '65	HCDA '74	
Labor Market						
Wagner Act	WA '35	T-H '47				
Davis-Bacon Act	D-B '32					
EEO				CRA '64-EO11246 '65		
Public Employment	FERA '33 WPA '35	'39		MDTA '62	CETA '73	CETA '77
Government Structure						

	USHA '37	HHFA '47 / HA '49	s701 '54	HUDA '65	HCDA '74	Urban Initiative / HCDA '77(UDAG)
HHFA/HUD	USHA '37	HHFA '47		HUDA '65		Urban Initiative
UR Agencies		HA '49			HCDA '74	HCDA '77(UDAG)
701 Grants			s701 '54		HCDA '74	
Model Cities				DCMDA '66	HCDA '74	
Community Organization and Citizen Participation						
OEO/CSA				EOA '64	CSA '70	
Model Cities				DCMDA '66	HCDA '74	
PAC's				RHA 7217.1 '68	HCDA '74	
Delegate Agencies				sXX '67		

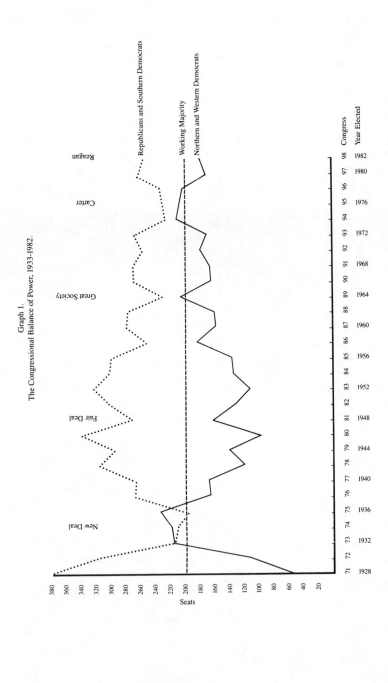

Graph 1.
The Congressional Balance of Power, 1933-1982.

and the Great Society. More importantly, during these two periods local pressures for a national political response to urban political constituencies also became intense. By passing new urban development programs, national Democratic political entrepreneurs sought not only to respond to this pressure, but to capitalize upon it.

The New Deal and the Great Society illustrate two fundamental features of this process. First and foremost, national Democratic political entrepreneurs sought to ensure that a mobilized urban electorate would identify with the Democrats and thus offset the traditional sources of Republican support. In 1932, as in 1896, the party capable of dominating the urban electorate could also dominate national elections. Before the realignment of 1932–1936, in which the Democratic party became an urban party, Republicans had taken advantage of this fact. After 1932, because it was willing to become the urban party and enact federal urban programs, the Democrats benefited from it.[4] The Democratic party was not only a party of the city (given the importance of agriculture to the southern wing), but it became more so over time.

The New Deal and the Great Society also illustrate, however, that the use of federal programs to secure urban loyalties must evolve. Great differences divide urban constituencies. As past federal programs have had an impact, they have generated new constituencies and new conflicts. These, in turn, have required subsequent cohorts of national Democratic political entrepreneurs to enact new programs which modernize old political alliances in order to incorporate the newly created urban constituencies. The New Deal and the Great Society illustrate the difficulties inherent in this process of adaptation, for political innovation is a painful, conflict-laden, risky process. It was not one which Democratic presidents could avoid, however. Only by building sufficiently large urban majorities could they hope to win national elections. Despite resentment and resistance from established local program beneficiaries and political supporters, and indeed from among the conservative southern Democrats who made it possible for Democrats to organize Congress, New Deal and Great Society entre-

53

preneurs found it mandatory to develop new programs which would enable them to reach out to new urban constituencies.

The national Democratic administrations since the New Deal generated power for Democrats by expanding federal urban development programs, but program growth also generated conflicts among Democrats. These conflicts, rooted in the differences of interest among urban (now metropolitan) constituencies, have challenged Democratic political entrepreneurs from the New Deal to the present. The New Deal established the Democratic urban political strategy and worked out its initial forms. After the conservative war years, the Fair Deal preserved and institutionalized those forms, creating the basis around which powerful local institutions could join to use federal programs to shape urban development. It also thus created the basis for major urban conflicts over the impact of these programs. After the conservative Eisenhower years, the Great Society attempted to revitalize federal urban programs and to close the breaches which those programs had opened.

2. THE NEW DEAL AND THE INVENTION OF FEDERAL URBAN POLICY

Franklin Delano Roosevelt's New Deal administration amounted to a "geological fault line" in partisan alignments, the federal government's role in national affairs, and intergovernmental relations.[5] The partisan realignment crystallized by the 1932, 1934, and 1936 elections has shaped the patterns of American political competition to this day.

The breakdown of the old political order made this realignment possible. The Depression severely undermined both traditional Republican rule and the traditional bases of support for the Democratic party. As two astute observers of the American polity have noted, "Instead of being custodians of prosperity, the business elite suddenly found itself custodians of an extraordinary collapse."[6] With the decay of the old order, and with economic distress spurring forward new voices within the political system, political actors seeking to forge a new Democratic party found an unusually wide scope of action open to them. FDR and his New Deal allies were not slow to exploit this opportunity.

The New Deal accomplished three interrelated and mutually reinforcing tasks. It brought previously unrepresented constituencies to bear on national government. It reconciled them with more traditional participants to form a new coalition of forces on behalf of national (and local) Democratic elected officials. Finally, it cemented this coalition by shifting "the thrust of American nation building from the business community to the public sector."[7]

Although the term "national urban policy" was not in use at the time, the New Deal accomplished these three tasks largely by inventing one. President Roosevelt and the New Deal created a variety of devices with which to reach down from the national center of power to shape the local bases of politics. FDR's fireside chats made him the first "media president"; legislative accomplishments like the Wagner Labor Act created politically supportive, extraparty, organizational vehicles which linked his administration to the political grass roots. Most important, the many urban-oriented New Deal programs simultaneously made the federal government a key actor in local politics and provided FDR with a framework for pyramiding local political organizations into national political power.

Discussions of the New Deal political coalition—liberal reformers, labor, working class ethnics, and minorities—often miss the point that these groups were brought together in particular places (cities) around particular programs (the New Deal "urban policy"). To appreciate the magnitude of this political achievement, let us consider the shifting electoral climate from which the New Deal sprang.

The Political Determinants of New Deal Program Expansion

Historian Carl Degler has pointed out that since the turn of the century, the political party which dominated big-city election returns has also dominated national presidential politics. "Taken together," Degler has written, "the elections of 1894 and 1896

55

mark the emergence of the Republican party as the party of the rising cities."[8] Perturbed by the mass influx of immigrants into the major cities and shocked by the urban labor violence of the 1890s, the urban business elite united behind the Republican party. With its social roots in the urban middle class, its commitment to industrial expansion and the rising corporate elite, the Republican party successfully mobilized the dynamics of urban growth on its own political behalf. The Democrats could offer no alternative because they were "the party of the provincial idea, of Protestant fundamentalism, . . . of small towns and farms, . . . of localized interest, a party lacking vision of the national idea."[9]

After 1896, powerful demographic, social, and economic forces built up underneath the partisan alignments which Republicans had established in 1896. Prefigured by Al Smith's 1928 Democratic presidential candidacy, and then powerfully expressed through FDR's victory, these forces broke through the old alignments, created new ones, and made the Democrats the party of the new urban majority. In Ladd and Hadley's view, "The dynamic of the era of industrial nation-building [between 1870 and 1929] carried with it processes leading necessarily to yet another social setting, with a new political agenda, with a new fabric of conflict, with new claimants for power, economic benefits, and recognition."[10] The Depression broke down the impediments which had restrained the entry of the urban industrial working class into national politics.

Observing the Democrats' rise to power in 1932, Samuel Lubell put it this way: "No segment of the population was more ready for a 'new deal' than the submerged, inarticulate urban masses. . . . The really revolutionary surge behind the New Deal lay in this coupling of the Depression with the rise of a new generation, which had been malnourished on the congestion of our cities and the abuses of industrialism." Roosevelt "awakened the climbing urban masses to a consciousness of the power of their numbers."[11]

In many ways, the Republican party had built its national strength by opposing the urban, immigrant working class and blunting its electoral force. The numerous children of the late nineteenth-century immigrants came of political age in the 1932 election and were not to be excluded any longer. They had more education and a stronger political standing than their parents, and they shared a grievance against the unbridled urban industrial city. The Depression galvanized them into political action. For the established political parties, particularly the Democrats, this mobilization constituted both a threat and an opportunity. If the Democrats failed to enlist this generation, it might be outflanked. But if the New Deal could win the allegiance of this politically unincorporated yet potentially powerful population, it would "stand like a wall between the Republicans and their past dominance."[12]

In a brilliant monograph, Kristi Anderson has shown how the New Deal did indeed mobilize the second generation, ethnic urban electorate in order to create a Democratic majority.[13] She shows that the upsurge in Democratic votes came heavily from those who had previously been nonvoters and those coming of voting age between 1928 and 1936. These voters joined previous Democratic partisans and a very limited number of converted Republicans. After a careful review of polling data and electoral data from Chicago wards, Anderson concludes that "the Democratic majority was built partially with the support of millions of those voters who came of age in the late twenties and early thirties (many of whom were the children of immigrants) as well as on the mobilization of their heretofore nonparticipating elders."[14]

So it is hardly surprising that the New Deal gave its highest political priority to legislation which spoke directly to urban blue collar constituencies. This legislation responded to profoundly felt needs, but even more to the imperative of the ballot box. It also provided the organizational means by which the New Deal could channel and absorb these constituencies. While the electoral context dictated the general direction in which New Deal programs ought to flow, however, it did not determine the exact content of these programs nor the method by which they would be administered. The balance of power in Congress and among the local organized interests through which the New Deal sought to operate shaped the details of program design.

The same forces operating in the 1932 presidential election also shaped the 1932 and 1934 congressional elections and thereby

57

influenced the balance of power within Congress. Since the House failed to reapportion itself after the 1920 census, congressional representation was based on the outmoded 1911 census until 1932. Only then did congressional districting come to reflect the fact that the United States had become a decidedly urban nation.[15] This change, together with the electoral mobilization of urban voters behind the Democratic party, thrust an extraordinary number of northern, urban liberal Democrats into Congress and the Senate. Indeed, as Figure 1 shows, the 1932 and 1934 elections constituted the high-water mark for nonsouthern Democratic representation for the entire post-Depression period. Though this index does not exactly track urban liberalism, it is an excellent proxy.

The 1932 elections turned 150 members, or more than one-third of the House, out of office. Almost one hundred of the newly elected congressmen were Democrats, many elected for the first time from northern urban districts, and they gave the Democratic party a 312 to 117 advantage over the Republicans (five members were Farmer-Laborites). In the Senate, fifty-nine Democrats faced thirty-six Republicans. With initiative coming from the heavily urban Ohio and New York House delegations, the House elected the first northern Democratic Speaker in over fifty years, by a vote of 166 to 112. Many of the members were new to national politics, unaccustomed to congressional byways, and possessed unusually strong political convictions. As E. Pendleton Herring, who chronicled congressional affairs for the *American Political Science Review*, reported, these new congressmen made quite an impact, "bringing novel proposals for national salvation and knowing little of legislative problems."[16]

With perhaps one-third of the nation's labor force out of work, many banks closed, and the electorate up in arms, Congress pressed for action. Rexford Tugwell, FDR's chief brain truster, was later to recall that "on March 4, we were confronted with a choice between an orderly revolution—a peaceful and rapid departure from the past concepts—and a violent and disorderly overthrow of the whole capitalist structure."[17]

These conditions clearly required FDR to present a strong legislative program. The administration responded with the National Industrial Recovery Act, which included a $3.3 billion public works appropriation, a Home Ownership Loan Corporation to refinance strapped homeowners, a Federal Emergency Relief Act, and, in a later session, the 1934 National Housing Act. Contrary to previous patterns, the 1934 off-year elections produced thirteen more Democratic seats in the House and nine more in the Senate, giving the Democrats the largest majorities a party had ever enjoyed in Congress.

Many aspects of New Deal legislation were designed to ease its way through Congress. Even at the height of the New Deal's push toward expanded federal intervention, its legislation stressed partnership with the private sector, decentralized local government administration, nonpartisan distribution criteria, and something for every major interest and every congressional district. The New Deal's emphasis on various forms of physical capital investment was a key to its political appeal. As Herring commented about the close of the 1933 session, it "indicated that the consummation of a national program of legislation is greatly aided by transmuting through patronage of the localism of our politics into support of the Chief Executive."

Urban development programs provided the chief source of such patronage for FDR's key political constituents, the cities. Herring elaborated:

The President accepted the principle of vast federal expenditures on public works as a means of seeding recovery. Journalist Hearst and Economist Keynes endorsed the move, as did the majority in Congress. The cost was necessarily high. Although its justification was placed on economic grounds, the move was certainly politically expedient. It is unlikely that the Chief Executive could have acted otherwise and still retained a semblance of control over Congress. The great majority that voted to override his veto of the Independent Offices Appropriations bill showed the readiness with which representatives and senators deserted the President when they thought his measures were bad politics for home consumption. The individual con-

59

gressman could not risk his chances for reelection; nor could the Administration afford to endanger the position of its supporters. The President's policy, therefore, was one of compromise and concession directed toward curbing the more extreme demands of regions and classes.[18]

The balance of power in Congress thus pushed the New Deal forward and shaped the design of its proposals, which FDR had, in turn, framed with an eye toward majority-building in Congress.

Local interests also shaped program design. The New Deal did not initially have a clearly defined strategy about what kinds of local political coalitions it was trying to build or what policies would promote them. As the biographer of the Senate's leading New Deal legislative craftsman has written, "The President, who brought no overall plan of his own to Washington, picked and chose in his pragmatic way from among the proposals presented by competing brain trusters, congressmen, and pressure groups, and fashioned from them a program—a New Deal—that was 'highly experimental, improvised and inconsistent.' "[19] But if the New Deal lacked conceptual consistency, it provided a political framework within which "a number of persuasions and interest groups competed for supremacy"[20] and around which new coalitions could be constructed.

The New Deal sought to bring previously conflicting elements—machine politicians and reformers, business and labor, established ethnic groups and more recent southern European and southern black arrivals—into a consolidated electoral alignment. In sectional terms, the New Deal was a combination of the cities and the South. It responded to these two core constituencies with urban development programs for one and agricultural policies designed to raise farm incomes for the other. The New Deal also bid for western constituencies with such measures as the Taylor Grazing Act and water project construction.

Since the big-city vote was central to the achievement of the New Deal electoral majority, however, the New Deal's core programs aimed at urban public works investment, urban public employment, direct relief for the urban unemployed, and strengthening the labor market position of the urban working class. Though these tasks had to be achieved in the abstract, the issue of who would administer these programs and reap their political benefits remained open.

The New Deal national political entrepreneurs in the Roosevelt administration—men like Farley, Hopkins, Ickes, and congressional allies like Senator Wagner—were ambivalent about the New Deal's most obvious source of urban political support, the big-city Democratic political machines. On the one hand, the New Deal needed urban votes, which were the machines' stock-in-trade. On the other, many New Deal political entrepreneurs wanted to reach beyond the narrow social base of the machines to groups they had excluded, such as the growing reform-minded professional middle class, labor unions, and minority groups. To bring these divergent groups together, the New Deal sought to restructure and modernize the local organizational base of its national power. To achieve this end, the New Dealers encouraged the development of new organizational vehicles for urban political mobilization.

Martin Shefter has brilliantly described the motives for adopting a program-based strategy for building political power:

The New Deal realignment brought new elements—most notably, labor and the liberals—into the Democratic Party. After entering the party, these groups sought to overthrow the incumbent leadership of the party, which, in their view, was not sufficiently committed to the principles of the New Deal, but was interested merely in reaping the spoils of the victory. By attacking the patronage system—by building a wall between the bureaucracy and the political parties—the New Dealers sought to deprive the incumbent Democratic leaders of the resources they employed to sustain their organizations. The reformers could use the institutions which *they* commanded to seize control of the party.[21]

These institutions included professional societies, labor unions, reform organizations, and the program delivery agencies themselves.

61

The New Deal worked closely with some urban machines, which provided crucial backing for it, including the Pendergast organization in Kansas City, the Cook County organization, boss Crump in Memphis, and Bronx County regulars.[22] (Since most Tammany sachems had supported Al Smith against FDR, FDR favored New York reform mayor La Guardia.) In Pittsburgh, the New Deal was instrumental in helping the Lawrence organization dominate that city's politics.

But in just as many cases, the New Deal opposed local Democratic machines, especially those which did not embrace the New Deal, such as Tammany and the Curley organization in Massachusetts. And in all cases, the New Deal entrepreneurs set up parallel administrative organizations which limited regular party control over patronage. James Farley, FDR's patronage chief, wrote that "the administration of WPA and PWA has been remarkably free from the blight of partisanship and politics," and that highly politicized administration of these programs would have jeopardized them.[23] Contemporary academic evaluations of the WPA confirm Farley's views.[24]

Though New Deal programs did not condition the distribution of benefits on political service, they were, nonetheless, "political." They strengthened constituencies important to Democrats, responded to congressional pressure in the appointment of top administrators, and generated new interest groups which influenced subsequent policy development. The New Deal caused big-city mayors to organize the U.S. Conference of Mayors as a key supportive lobbying group for federal urban programs. "In effect," notes one observer, "USCM rose out of crisis conditions, with members strongly bound in the common goal of assisting the President and federal agencies in their urban relief efforts. . . . Direct federal-local ties multiplied under the New Deal recovery programs and were further promoted by the Conference of Mayors, which organized to sustain, protect, and nurture these newly established bonds."[25]

New Deal programs were thus an independent, extraparty method for rewarding FDR's key constituencies and for advancing his political agenda. The New Deal administration probably had more continuity with the Progressive era tradition of middle-class, professional reform activities than it did with urban political machines.

The New Deal program also played both to business and labor. At the national level, the New Deal attempted to bring these two parties behind the administration through the NIRA. Business leaders helped to draft the legislation, which legalized cartelization and business administration of the price system. Though the NIRA's codes failed to induce recovery, and though most businessmen bitterly opposed the New Deal's intrusion on private sector prerogatives, the New Deal was continually at pains to point out that it had the capitalist economy's best interests at heart.[26]

The New Deal also launched national labor legislation both to countervail "economic royalism" and to create a new, organized constituency supportive of the New Deal. "For the most part, [New Deal labor legislation] was the result of the initiatives of New Dealers themselves" and, in turn, laid "the foundation-stone of the labor-Democratic party coalition that has functioned almost intact for three decades."[27] Through the Wagner Act, union membership rose from less than three million in 1935 to over sixteen million in 1945.

The New Deal search for business and labor support also took place at the local level. The massive public works investments undertaken by the PWA, CWA, and WPA generated business and labor support by boosting the severely depressed construction industry, thereby winning support from building contractors and suppliers as well as from the building trades and unemployed, unskilled WPA workers. More importantly, these investments provided the means by which big-city business elites began to realize their plans for reforming and modernizing the urban built environment. New Deal funds produced the first limited-access, high-speed highways, new airports, subway lines, bridges, and slum clearance projects. These programs thus laid the foundation for the postwar progrowth coalitions which transformed the major metropolitan areas.

The New Deal also extended benefits to urban ethnic groups, including blacks, which previously had been excluded from local politics. Blacks occupied one-third of the public housing units constructed by the U.S. Housing Authority.[28] The Russell Sage Foundation found that 15 percent of all WPA workers were black, and that while the WPA employed 4.2 percent of all white workers, it employed 5.5 percent of black workers.[29] As a result of the New Deal's programs, blacks swung away from the Republican party after 1932, and by 1936 were among the most pro-Democratic of all urban ethnic groups.[30]

From the outset, however, the New Deal Democratic commitment to urban blacks was limited. As one observer noted, "The fear that any challenge to white racism would alienate the South and thus endanger the administration's entire program for economic recovery also dissuaded President Roosevelt from endorsing the major civil rights proposal of his time, the NAACP-sponsored anti-lynching bill."[31] While blacks were incorporated into the New Deal coalition, it clearly subordinated their interests to other political considerations.

The New Deal Delivery Systems

The programs developed by the New Deal strongly reflected the need to mobilize the urban electorate, the need to command congressional majorities, and the need to align competing interests in urban politics. These political requirements led the New Deal to benefit big-city working-class and minority-group constituencies as parts of larger packages which also benefited more powerful and established constituencies. Success in Congress and at the local level called for logrolling, horse trading, and something for everyone, even potential opponents. As a result, the New Deal built conflicts into its program structure from the outset.

The four principal elements which constituted the New Deal urban policy included the Public Works Administration (PWA), established through one of the sections of the National Industrial Recovery Act of 1933; the Works Progress Administration (WPA), established by the Emergency Relief Appropriations Act of 1935; the PWA Emergency Housing Division, which became the U.S. Housing Authority (USHA) through the U.S. Housing Act of

1937; and the Federal Housing Administration (FHA), established by the National Housing Act of 1934. Through these legislative titles, the federal government began all the basic activities which have come to be called "national urban policy."

The Public Works Administration

Between 1933 and 1939, the PWA spent $4.8 billion building highways, bridges, dams, airports, public buildings, sewer and water projects, and other public works. More than half this money went to urban areas. Passed as Title II of the National Industrial Recovery Act, it was envisioned by its main champion, Senator Robert Wagner, as "ideally suited as a means of priming the pump of business," and received support from business and labor lobby groups as well as Brookings Institution economists.[32]

The PWA made grants and loans to local jurisdictions for large, durable public works built at "prevailing rate" union wages. These included 17,800 federal projects costing $1.8 billion and 16,700 state and local projects costing $2.4 billion, representing an unprecedented federal contribution to local infrastructure.[33] While WPA administrator Harold Ickes gave Roosevelt every project he wanted "without demur," he not only wanted to keep agency appointments and project designations "outside of partisan politics, but . . . want[ed] to avoid the appearance of politics."[34] He did this by creating a professionally strong central staff which carefully reviewed applications on their merits and by building up "complicated and extensive ties with thousands of municipalities, counties, and special districts."[35]

The PWA often established these ties by working with a local "authority" which could condemn property, borrow money, and build its own staff while operating beyond the control of local party machines. After 1935, the PWA legal division crafted more than five hundred proposals to state legislatures for creating such authorities. In New York alone, such PWA beneficiaries included the Triborough Bridge Authority, the New York Bridge Authority, the Jones Beach State Parkway Authority, the Henry Hudson Parkway Authority, and some twenty others. "Much of the impetus'' for state enactment of these authorities ''came from . . . local businessmen or attorneys, local contractors groups, or industries . . . that would profit by PWA allotments.''[36] The building trades also strongly supported the PWA and shaped its labor policies.

The PWA thus laid the institutional groundwork for postwar progrowth coalitions in urban politics. It created ''new machines'' which worked with party regulars to advance urban development, but were neither staffed by them nor accountable to regulars for their development agenda. Instead, these ''new machines'' fostered cooperation between business, labor, and local elected officials, and funded highly visible results for which all could take credit.

The Works Progress Administration

Because the PWA was slow to spend its money and generate employment, the New Deal also undertook a series of direct employment measures. These began with the Civil Works Administration which, under the direction of Harry Hopkins, spent $400 million in PWA money during the winter of 1933–1934 to put four million people to work. (At this point, fifteen million were out of work, and the PWA had only managed to absorb one million.) In 1935, Congress created the WPA, a $4.8 billion work-relief agency, to replace both the CWA and the Federal Emergency Relief Administration, which had supported more than four million families in 1935.

The WPA directly employed workers through a network of local offices at a minimum wage beginning at $50 per month to work on labor-intensive local public works projects. Its funds were distributed by an allotments committee which included Hopkins, Ickes, the budget director, several other New Deal officials, the Business Advisory Council, the American Bankers Association, labor groups, and Mayor La Guardia, the U.S. Conference of Mayors representative.

Between 1936 and 1940, the WPA employed an average of 2.35 million workers each year, or about one-sixth of the unemployed. Its efforts went primarily into highways (39.5 percent of the labor effort), water and sewer systems (9.3 percent), public buildings (8.3 percent), and recreational facilities. WPA employment was heavily concentrated in urban centers; it constructed more than 67,000 miles of urban streets and more than 25,000 parks, athletic fields, and playgrounds. Its projects included the Central Park Zoo, waterfront parks in Chicago and San Francisco, and La Guardia Airport. WPA efforts significantly helped to renew the infrastructure of the major cities.[37]

Given the WPA's importance in employing the big-city, blue collar labor force, it is surprising that it was not more intimately enmeshed in patronage politics. But as one contemporary scholar put it, the WPA "did not have to resort to favoritism in the selection of its beneficiaries in order to win their support," and indeed "favoritism was a deadly boomerang. For those few whose goodwill might thus be cultivated, many more were antagonized. Efficient and impartial administration was the safer political course."[38]

Hopkins and his associates allocated WPA funds through "executive understandings with individual legislators" using the standard of "loyalty . . . to the broad purposes of the Roosevelt Administration."[39] Thus while the WPA did not build up local political machines or a national Roosevelt machine, it did build New Deal influence in Congress and win support from new constituencies. These included recipients, of course, but also the large cadre of middle-class professionals who administered the agency, whose ranks numbered some fifty-three thousand. Like the PWA authorities, these federally funded, locally situated social service professionals helped to modernize urban government.

The PWA Housing Division—U.S. Housing Authority

Through the lobbying efforts of the National Public Housing Conference, formed in 1931, slum clearance and public housing construction had been designated as an objective for the PWA. Soon after the NIRA's enactment, Ickes established a housing division to undertake such projects. It began by supporting local

67

limited-dividend developers, such as the American Federation of Hosiery Workers' Carl Mackey Houses in Philadelphia, but soon went on to direct federal construction when this method proved to be slow.

Direct efforts by the PWA Housing Division immediately ran into local opposition to its exercise of eminent domain, however, and a landmark 1935 case (*U.S.* v. *Certain Lands in City of Louisville*) forced it to cease this practice. By the termination of its activities in 1937, the housing division had built 21,769 units in fifty-one projects in thirty-seven central cities at a cost of $136 million.[40] After the Louisville case, the New Deal urged states to adopt enabling legislation creating local housing authorities to carry this program forward. By 1937, thirty states had passed enabling legislation, and forty-nine local housing authorities had been established.[41] In 1937, the administration proposed, and, after substantial negotiation, Congress enacted the Wagner Housing Act, which created the U.S. Housing Authority and provided a funding mechanism for continued federal support of local slum clearance and public housing construction.

The campaign to enact the 1937 Housing Act illustrates the cross-pressures which continued to whipsaw urban redevelopment legislation for the entire postwar period. One set of forces, led by Wagner and backed by social workers, housing officials, local affiliates of the Labor Housing Conference, and the AFL, sought to emphasize public or subsidized housing for the broadest possible range of urban residents with only so much emphasis on slum clearance as was necessary to secure sites for this housing. The importance of the urban vote to Roosevelt's 1936 reelection, as well as his 1937 inaugural promise to provide housing legislation for "one-third of a nation ill-housed, ill-clad, and ill-nourished" gave weight to their position.

Opposing them, however, were key congressmen, such as House Banking and Currency chairman Steagall, Treasury Secretary Morgenthau, and an in-house administration review committee, whose members were against any large spending program on public housing. Interior Secretary Ickes wanted control over any program successfully enacted, but housing advocates opposed this because of the PWA's slow and small production record. Finally, though they liked slum clearance and subsidies for private construction, housing industry lobby groups strongly opposed any kind of public housing program. The politically powerful National Association of Real Estate Boards (NAREB), the U.S. Building and Loan League (USBLL), the Chamber of Commerce, and the National Retail Lumber Dealers Association all railed against the idea.

In 1936, a Wagner housing bill had died in Congress for lack of support from Roosevelt and Steagall. After the 1936 election, Wagner decided to press the issue and Roosevelt went along with him.[42] Although he gained victory in the end, Wagner had to give away key elements of the bill to gain votes or forestall opposition. The Senate imposed strict income limits, thus restricting the beneficiary group, and also limited the quality standards and cost of the housing to be built. To placate industry lobbyists, the Senate also required that for every new public housing unit built, at least one "unsafe or unsanitary" housing unit be demolished. This amendment tilted the bill's emphasis from housing production to slum clearance, "precisely the type of amendment that the USBLL and NAREB wanted put into the bill if there was to be a public housing bill."[43] It subsequently passed by large margins.

Even this crippling restriction did not prevent further restrictions on USHA activities, however. In 1939, as the New Deal's influence waned, 55 mainly southern Democrats joined 136 Republicans in the House to vote down further authorizations. Nonetheless, the USHA managed to commit $800 million in project loans to local authorities to build 169,451 units located mainly in the major central cities, which accounted for one-sixth of all housing production during the New Deal.

The Federal Housing Administration

If the New Deal was divided about public housing and enacted the program only when urban liberal legislative power reached its zenith, it wholeheartedly favored public assistance for private, single-family housing. This support led to the creation of the FHA

69

in 1934. Its immediate predecessor was the Home Owner's Loan Corporation (HOLC), set up in 1933. HOLC saved from default one million homeowners, or one in five mortgaged urban homes, at a loan cost of $3.1 billion dollars. HOLC revolutionized home loan practices by providing for twenty-year repayments and loans of up to 90 percent of value. As Arthur Schlesinger has noted, "Probably no single measure consolidated so much middle class support for the administration."[44]

Unlike most of Wagner's major bills, the HOLC and the 1934 Housing Act, which created the FHA, were written by industry experts along with the treasury secretary and budget director. NAREB executive vice-president and chief lobbyist Herbert U. Nelson drafted the initial legislation, commenting that "we believe that public credit can properly be used to help sustain home ownership and private enterprise."[45] The bill passed overwhelmingly, with rural and southern as well as northern urban support. By standardizing mortgage lending and channeling capital to the building industry, FHA contributed heavily to the rise in home-ownership from 39 percent in 1937 to 57 percent in 1950. Later termed by Nelson "the greatest piece of legislation for home ownership ever adopted by any government," the 1934 Housing Act certainly did aid the immediate postwar suburbanization of upwardly mobile, urban blue collar workers, perhaps the New Deal's most pivotal constituency.[46] It did so, however, by working strictly through local private institutions.

The New Deal and the Birth of Federal Urban Programs

By inventing national urban policy as a method for capturing the allegiance of a newly powerful urban electorate, the New Deal unquestionably revolutionized both national partisan alignments and American federalism. It broke all precedents, spending nearly $20 billion in new federal funds to put nearly one-fifth of the unemployed to work at transforming the urban infrastructure. Although this $3 billion a year effort did not succeed in lifting the country out of the Depression, it did consolidate urban blue collar support together with a wide variety of other constituencies to provide Democratic electoral victories. Historian Gavin Wright has used quantitative techniques to show convincingly that the New Deal spent program dollars to maximize its electoral support, and further "used discretionary spending power to build congressional support for these programs." FDR was the first president, in other words, to use federal urban program dollars to build national political power and leverage over Congress. Friedland and Wong have shown that urban renewal spending patterns continued to be shaped by Democratic congressional representation.[47]

New Deal spending did not completely transform the urban infrastructure any more than it raised the national economy out of the Depression. But just as federal urban programs radically changed the character of national political alignments and the role of the federal government, they also modernized local, urban political patterns and created the initial organizational models through which the postindustrial transformation of urban land use would later be accomplished. The New Deal established a national template that shaped subsequent local program implementation.

This template established the link between federal program dollars and the local development agenda as well as the administrative structure and practices, with their emphasis on professionalism, which would put them to work. Although it did not consolidate them, the New Deal template also patterned new coalitions in urban politics between party regulars, reform-minded professionals, labor, business, and minorities. Finally, the great physical accomplishments of the New Deal programs pointed the way to future directions in urban land use. The slum clearance projects, the parkways, the new public buildings, and publicly subsidized private housing construction all showed how government could accelerate and direct market forces.

No case better illustrates these conclusions than New York City. FDR himself was the product of reform Democratic politics in New York, while the regular party provided him with Senator Robert Wagner, his most stalwart legislative ally and prod. Because Tammany regulars had supported Al Smith, FDR chose to work through reform mayor Fiorello La Guardia, founding head of the U.S. Conference of Mayors. FDR and La Guardia, in turn,

71

provided the money and political support that Robert Moses needed to set in motion projects which ultimately transformed the New York metropolitan area. Moses created effective links with local Democratic bosses, but he also responded to middle-class reformers by building organizations with large, highly qualified staffs which produced results. Notwithstanding occasional fights between Moses and the Regional Plan Association, these results closely followed lines first articulated by the city's business elite in the RPA's 1927 *Regional Plan*.[48]

New Deal urban programs also contained the seeds of future conflicts. The New Deal encompassed many competing and conflicting interests. Its assistance set them moving off in different and ultimately conflicting directions. Also, conservative interests within the New Deal tended to drive out the liberal commitment to direct government intervention, to urban workers, and especially to urban blacks. When faced with a choice between principled but sure-to-be-defeated allegiance to liberal values and compromising them in order to gain power, New Deal Democratic political entrepreneurs and their Fair Deal successors never hesitated to choose the latter. The demobilization and decline of the urban electorate and periodic national swings toward conservatism may have made this a rational choice, but it was not without long-run costs. In particular, the related issues of race and urban poverty would ultimately test urban liberalism.

3. The Fair Deal and the Evolution of Urban Liberalism

The conservatism and economic growth brought on by World War II and its aftermath presented the heirs of the New Deal with two challenges. They had to battle in Congress to preserve the New Deal urban programs, which the conservative coalition had begun whittling away after 1938. And they had to reshape the New Deal agenda to reflect the ways in which wartime economic mobilization and the postwar expression of pent-up demand had changed the interests and outlook of both their core urban, blue collar constituency and the local alliances through which the New Deal operated.

With the advent of war and growing resistance to the New Deal, the conservative coalition had become increasingly effective in Congress. It terminated the WPA, refused to fund further public housing construction, and ensured that war mobilization would not be used to foster social change. In their postwar attempts to preserve the administrative structures and funding streams which the New Deal had put in place, Democrats faced difficult political circumstances. Republicans controlled both houses of Congress in 1947 and 1948. Considering these odds, the fact that Harry Truman and his Fair Deal colleagues won any victories at all was a tribute to the continued power of New Deal ideas and the continued national importance of the urban electorate.

The young, second generation, urban working-class voters who had made the New Deal possible had been swept off to war or into new, often suburban, production facilities. Having deferred family formation during the Depression and war years, and having gone without improved housing as the war claimed the increase in national productive capacity, this pivotal element of the electorate was more than ready to enjoy a better standard of living. The Fair Deal was in considerable part an exercise in adapting the New Deal to the needs of this emergent middle class in competition with Republican efforts to capture the same group.

As white unionized workers and middle-class professionals increasingly moved to the suburbs to work and form new households, they emptied out the old central-city blue collar neighborhoods. Manufacturing investment also shifted rapidly away from dense, cramped central-city locations to new suburban plants. Black immigrants from the South partially offset the white exodus from the central cities, but racial prejudice led many to see this change as only one more sign of central-city decline. These trends tested the local coalitions upon which the administration of New Deal programs had rested. "Attacking blight" and stimulating downtown investment became increasingly focal interests for the mayors, business associations, planners, and trade unions which

73

the New Deal had brought together around slum clearance projects.

Fair Deal political entrepreneurs responded to these changing conditions by modifying the New Deal urban programs, largely giving up any emphasis on aiding the urban poor, and institutionalizing them on a long-term basis. Many of their proposals were defeated—public employment was not revived, broad public intervention into housing production was never achieved—but their two major successes were considerable. They consolidated housing and urban development programs into the Housing and Home Finance Agency (HHFA), forerunner of the cabinet department, and enacted the Taft-Ellender-Wagner Housing Act of 1949, which put the urban renewal and public housing program on a permanent basis. Through these successes, however, they set the stage for the great urban conflicts of the 1960s.

The Political Context of the Fair Deal

Between 1939 and 1959, the real median family income in the United States doubled. Wartime mobilization, increased federal spending, and the creation of a new metropolitan physical form contributed heavily to this remarkable increase. These forces also dissolved and transformed the urban, ethnic, blue collar social base which had given rise to the New Deal Democratic party. The obvious contrast between the unemployed, young, blue collar worker in a central-city neighborhood in 1936 and that same person ten years later, as a returning veteran or a unionized worker in a new suburban plant or as a newly minted manager or professional, had clear implications for the Democrats.

Change segmented the homogeneity of the Democratic urban electoral base of the 1930s in at least three ways. Those who remained manual workers but worked in industries where strong unions increased their real incomes generally moved to the suburbs, where their work was also increasingly located. The manual workers who remained in more competitive, less unionized sectors of the economy tended to remain in the central cities, having less financial ability to leave. Their ranks increasingly came to be made up of blacks and other minorities. Finally, through the expansion of education and the professional and administrative occupational order, many people from blue collar backgrounds entered a rapidly growing middle class. These, too, suburbanized during the 1950s.

Deferred household formation, the stagnation of housing production, and the opening up of suburban development posed Democratic political entrepreneurs with perhaps their greatest challenge and opportunity. Homeownership was a nearly universal goal and twelve million new units were needed during the decade of the fifties, but a 1945 National Housing Agency study showed that 75 percent of the five million families seeking new housing in 1946 could afford no more than $50 a month in rent or $6,000 for a purchased home.[49] How could housing be provided?

This pent-up demand within the electorate bore heavily on the 1948 presidential elections. As one historian has observed,

> With the politically powerful veterans' organizations in the lead, the housing issue was forced onto the front pages of the newspapers and into the halls of Congress. The aroused public bombarded Congress and the White House with cries for immediate action. Thus, inadequate housing, affecting several million families directly, created a sense of urgency for housing reform, something most other Fair Deal programs lacked.[50]

Truman used this pressure effectively against Dewey in the 1948 presidential campaign, and it might have been the decisive factor. Accusing Dewey of having revised the 1928 Republican campaign slogan from "two cars in every garage" to "two families in every garage," Truman won a 2.1 million vote plurality over Dewey. Approximately 1.4 million of this plurality was provided by the twelve largest cities. Though this was down substantially from the 3.6 million plurality that these cities had given Roosevelt in 1936, it was still sufficiently strong to show that the route to national electoral victories for the Democrats still ran through the central-city electorate. It also put housing programs at the top of the Fair Deal agenda.

The urban vote gave Truman a narrow victory in 1948, but left

Congress dominated by conservatives. Between 1946 and 1948, the Democrats lacked even nominal control. Afterward, their margin of control was slight compared to the heyday of the New Deal. As Figure 1 shows, the balance between northern Democrats and their conservative coalition opponents was not favorable. According to political scientist John Manley, the conservative coalition lined up twice as frequently between 1943 and 1953 as it had during the New Deal, and it won 90 percent of the votes on which it appeared, regularly including "many of the most consequential issues decided by Congress."[51]

Even after Truman's 1948 victory, Democrats still held only 185 House seats and 54 Senate seats against 150 House seats and 42 Senate seats for the Republicans. In 1949, northern Democrats numbered only 160. Clearly, to get the 218 House votes needed to carry urban legislation, Truman would have to bring along many Republicans and conservative Democrats. Further, legislation would have to be tailored to suit the conservative southern Democrats who dominated the Banking and Currency and Appropriations Committees of the two chambers. Even if electoral factors and local pressures had not already pointed in this direction, this barrier would have proved sufficient to shear away such redistributive substance as remained in the New Deal urban programs.

Truman also faced a significantly altered local political situation. Industrial decline, the suburbanization of population, and the influx of southern blacks thrust "blight" in place of unemployment as the issue of most concern to local Democratic organizations and their allies among dominant local institutions.

In physical terms, "blight" described the urban areas which had been built up between 1860 and 1930 around factory production and blue collar housing, which investment and population had subsequently forsaken in favor of suburban locations. As Miles Colean put it in an important 1953 study for the Twentieth Century Fund, "No matter in what city we may be, we see broad areas of deterioration. . . . Old buildings are rarely replaced and old districts rarely renewed to their former vitality."[52] While this concern for "blight" dated back to President Hoover's 1932 Conference on Home Building and to the real property inventory conducted by the PWA Housing Division in 1934, it became the predominant concern of local elites in the 1950s.[53]

The spread of what Colean called "an accumulation of decadence" threatened central-city property values and prevented the reuse of central business district land for "higher and better" uses. To mayors, developers, downtown businessmen, the construction trades, and urban planners, urban renewal became an increasingly popular rallying cry. Only if the government stepped in to buy out "blighting" but nonetheless profitable slum communities—typically black communities—could new investment and the expansion of dominant but threatened institutions be undertaken. These pressures for a new program welled up from below, in the form of state enabling legislation enacted during the 1940s for local redevelopment agencies in New York, Illinois, and California.

The Fair Deal Programs Delivery System

The Fair Deal was marked by Congress's failure to pass the twenty-one major items which Truman presented in his 1949 inaugural address. The 1949 Taft-Ellender-Wagner Act (T-E-W) was his only major success. Congress defeated proposals for aid to education, fair employment practices, national health insurance, and middle income cooperative housing.

Before his election in 1948, Truman succeeded only in reorganizing existing housing programs into the Housing and Home Finance Agency (HHFA) on a permanent basis. Either House could prevent this reorganization by a majority vote. Real estate lobbyists opposed the HHFA for fear that "their" agencies, the FHA and Federal Home Loan Bank Board, would have to support public housing. House conservatives failed to get the Senate to reject the reorganization, and when Truman promised to appoint Raymond Foley, an FHA administrator with little sympathy for public housing, to head HHFA, he was able to prevail. For the

77

first time, the federal government got a single permanent agency charged with conducting a comprehensive housing policy.[54]

After 1949, Congress defeated most of Truman's housing program. It ended federal rent controls despite the advent of the Korean War. The Senate also defeated Truman's ambitious $3.6 billion proposal to subsidize construction of a quarter of a million cooperative housing units for the middle "forgotten third" of the urban population. NAREB and the private lending industry attacked the measure as "pure socialism," and a majority of southern Democrats joined Republicans in the Senate to defeat the measure 43 to 38.[55]

This inauspicious climate made it clear that the T-E-W Act needed support from southern Democrats and Republicans such as Ellender and Taft if it were to pass. To get such support, the bill was clearly designed to benefit private development. Much of the bill had first been drafted in 1943 by economists Guy Greer and Alvin Hansen and had been adopted by the Urban Land Institute, NAREB's research arm. In introducing the measure in 1943, Wagner had stressed that it was "primarily a private enterprise bill."[56] This aspect of the bill, Title I, provided for the creation of local redevelopment agencies and a $1.5 billion federal write-down of the land acquisition and clearance costs.

Title II of the bill put the public housing program on a permanent footing, authorizing 810,000 units over six years. Both Truman and Republican Senator Robert Taft insisted on its inclusion. The AFL, the CIO, the U.S. Conference of Mayors, various veterans organizations, and the NAACP strongly supported Title II and the omnibus bill as a whole. The HHFA staff, which had drafted the most recent version of the bill, lobbied for it in their off-hours. Public housing advocates were skeptical of the urban renewal title, but felt that an omnibus bill was the only way that public housing was likely to be sustained. As a result, they became a focal point for lobbying on behalf of the bill. Because of Title II, the public housing title, NAREB and the Savings and Loan League opposed the bill.

Despite their opposition, the Senate endorsed the bill 57 to 13.

After being pried loose from the Rules Committee, the T-E-W bill faced a close House vote on an amendment to remove the public housing title. After initially prevailing 168 to 165 on a teller vote, a final roll call vote defeated it by a mere 5 votes. The final measure passed by a margin of 23 votes, with support from forty-seven southern Democrats.[57]

Even during its first years, the 1949 Housing Act clearly disappointed its public housing supporters. By 1952, only 85,000 units were under construction, and HHFA Administrator Foley had little interest in bettering that record and no incentive to do so. Congress reduced public housing authorizations to 50,000 for fiscal year 1951 and 35,000 for 1952. As one observer put it, the conservative coalition, the Korean War, and three years of record private housing production "applied the *coup de grâce* to the high hopes of urban liberals for a breakthrough in housing reform."[58] NAREB and the real estate lobby also conducted a massive campaign to hold local referenda against public housing, and won twenty-five out of the thirty-eight which were held.[59]

The Fair Deal and the Institutionalization of Urban Liberalism

Although conservative opposition negated what many urban liberal Democrats hoped the federal government could do for the major cities, the Fair Deal did succeed in making federal intervention a permanent part of government policy. And it did so under difficult political circumstances. The 1949 Housing Act committed the nation to providing "a decent home and suitable living environment" for every American family, set public housing production targets, and created a new and powerful mechanism for transforming land use in the central cities. It embodied the best that Democratic urban liberals could achieve at the time.

Although a dozen states had passed redevelopment enabling acts by 1949, none had much practical experience in doing it. Metropolitan Life's Stuyvesant Town in Manhattan and R. K. Mellon's Golden Triangle in Pittsburgh provided the only working models for urban renewal. One participant commented that "the

79

urban redevelopment mechanism was a product of theorists, consultants, and bureaucrats at least once removed from operating programs and electoral politics."[60] The 1949 Act did provide, however, the tools with which, after some fine tuning, local political actors could create powerful operating programs.

The new administrator of the HHFA's Division of Slum Clearance and Urban Renewal (DSCUR) left little doubt about where the program would head. He observed that

> It was important to avoid the crystallization of conservative, doctrinaire business opposition which was hemming in the public housing program, and to seek a broad base of support. To this end, I initiated a series of conferences with the local power structure in communities with an identified interest in redevelopment, including business leaders as well as city hall, labor, and local public interest groups.[61]

DSCUR resisted not only public housing, but any residential reuse for land cleared by urban renewal. "After 1950," one observer noted, "a new administrative heartland for the program was created. This was the central commercial district and its adjacent industrial and institutional areas."[62]

As in other cases, Robert Moses' activities in New York led the way for local patterns of implementation of the new legislation. In 1951, he proposed to build a coliseum and luxury housing project at Broadway and 57th Street. By including a few rundown tenements sheltering less than three hundred people, Moses used urban redevelopment to gain control of more than two square blocks of thriving commercial land. With $26 million in federal assistance, and despite a precedent-setting legal challenge which validated the legality of urban renewal, Moses built an exhibition center, a parking structure, and luxury housing on the site.[63]

Moses clearly demonstrated that the 1949 Act would not be used to meet the housing needs of the urban poor, but would be used instead to advance the development agenda of the dominant institutions emerging in the central-city economy. These institutions, along with local Democratic officials, urban planners, labor unions, and middle-class sentiment, supported Moses, and together they defined the meaning of Democratic urban liberalism for the postwar period.

4. THE GREAT SOCIETY'S MODERNIZATION OF THE NEW DEAL COALITION

During the 1950s, a Republican national administration implemented the federal urban program apparatus which the New Deal and the Fair Deal had constructed and begun. In Eisenhower's hands, urban renewal focused even further on downtown commercial development, while the public housing program was reduced to a nominal level. The Eisenhower administration made its own contribution to the program delivery system, particularly in creating the interstate highway program in 1956.

Because they lacked control of the White House, and for a time of Congress as well, Democrats were severely limited in the degree to which they could further shape and use the federal urban program delivery system for their own ends. They insisted on larger appropriations for their favored programs and also modified Eisenhower administration initiatives. For example, Democrats made Eisenhower design the interstate system so that it built urban freeways as well as intercity links. For the most part, however, Democratic legislative initiatives were restricted to the tentative formulation of policies which, though vetoed by the Republican president, would serve their party well when it returned to power.

The changes which had begun to be felt during the Truman administration continued during the rest of the 1950s with such force that they gave national Democratic entrepreneurs a considerable challenge during their years out of power.[64] Freeway construction, FHA assistance to private housing development, and federal stimulation of the growth of new suburban industries all benefited both the suburbanizing, unionized labor force and the emerging professional stratum.

Changes in the central city proved more problematic, however. As the central-city industrial base suburbanized, the growth of new institutions produced a new central-city service-sector labor force, the lower occupational rungs of which were increasingly

81

composed of blacks and other minorities. Between 1940 and 1960, 3.1 million blacks migrated from the South to northern cities. World War II alone brought 1.6 million blacks North to work in war industries. Despite their New Deal attachment to the Democratic party, these groups found themselves excluded from political power by the regular Democratic organizations and from the better blue collar jobs in industries where unions controlled access to the labor market. Nevertheless, this migration increased the national black electorate from less than one million in 1940 to over five million by 1960 and concentrated it in the large northern cities.

Through the New Frontier and the Great Society, a new generation of political entrepreneurs sought to adapt old approaches and old political alignments to these new and changed circumstances. To do so, they had to confront and attempt to resolve the serious conflicts which had grown up within the New Deal coalition. In particular, New Frontier and Great Society political entrepreneurs could not modernize the New Deal unless they could respond to the increasingly restive central-city black population.

This was a risky proposition. Moves toward the central-city black and minority population could and did cost support from southern Democrats, where increases in the electorate were coming among white, middle-class voters who were "militantly anti-trade union, opposed to large-scale governmental intervention in social and economic life, and generally conservative."[65] They promised also to arouse opposition from the blue collar ethnic and middle-class beneficiaries of existing policies and from regular central-city political organizations.

Democratic political entrepreneurs had to bridge the gaps among its constituencies in order to sustain a national majority status. The conflicts among them operated on many dimensions—in politics, in the job market, and in the competition for urban space— and past Democratic policies as often as not had exacerbated them. That the Great Society failed, in the final analysis, to reconcile the two should not obscure the reality either of its aspirations or of its actual programmatic achievements, both of which rivaled those of the New Deal.

The Political Context of the New Frontier/Great Society

John F. Kennedy won the 1960 presidential contest by the narrowest of margins. The change of a few thousand votes in Illinois would have given the election to Nixon. As in Truman's case, the larger northern cities gave Kennedy a large enough margin to barely offset Republican sentiment in rural and suburban areas. Twenty-seven of the thirty-nine largest cities were in his favor, and he got 75 percent of the black vote. After this victory, New Haven Mayor Richard Lee exclaimed that "Kennedy, more than anything else, is the president of the cities."[66] To the new urban minority voters, Kennedy added support from such straying New Deal constituencies as northern white Catholics and blue collar suburban families.

The 1959–1960 recession, the fourth since the end of World War II, provided the backdrop for the campaign. The Eisenhower administration had maintained strict monetary and fiscal policies, and Richard Nixon campaigned on this record. During the campaign, he attacked "the concept of artificial growth forced by massive new federal spending and loose money policies."[67] The prevailing beneficiaries of the federal urban program delivery system did not share this belief, and backed Kennedy. As one former federal official noted,

> The outpouring of mayors, builders, developers, labor officials, and representatives of liberal organizations indicated that a broad consensus in the field was looking to a Kennedy victory to break through the political stalemate which had frustrated them during the Eisenhower years.[68]

These elements of the electorate looked for national economic stimulation through new housing and urban development programs.

An unfavorable balance of power in Congress and then Kennedy's assassination prevented any great progress from being made on this agenda between 1961 and 1963. They did, however, set the stage for the 1964 Johnson landslide. LBJ swept to victory over Barry Goldwater with support from all parts of the electorate, including some traditionally Republican elements like northern white Protestants. In the Democratic heartland of the central-city working class, Johnson did extraordinarily well, however. He got over 90 percent of the black vote and 75 percent of the ballots cast by northeastern white Catholics. He also did particularly well among blue collar and union families.[69]

Johnson faced even more pressure from central-city blacks than these election returns might have implied. Civil rights leaders had organized a March on Washington for Jobs and Freedom on August 23, 1963, which attracted more than a quarter of a million people. Civil rights activists were mounting protests in northern cities at an increasing pace. By the fall of 1964, SNCC, CORE, and other civil rights organizations were organizing sit-in and demonstration campaigns against employment discrimination, urban renewal displacement, and other issues in northern cities.[70]

Simultaneously, a series of riots broke out in northern urban ghettos, beginning in the summer of 1964 in Harlem and Bedford-Stuyvesant. "As the summer wore on," Piven and Cloward note, "the rioting spread to Rochester, Jersey City, Paterson, Elizabeth, a suburb of Chicago, and Philadelphia. It was the beginning of a series of riot-torn summers unlike any period in the nation's history."[71] Many of these riots occurred in or near urban renewal areas, and they constituted a kind of revolt against the heritage of New Deal urban programs. They certainly showed that Johnson's most critically located and supportive political constituency could be extremely volatile. Such events led Johnson to make choices that his predecessors, Truman and Roosevelt, would not or could not make.

He was able to do so by a tidal shift in the congressional balance of power. For most of the 1950s, Republicans enjoyed a strong *de facto* position in Congress, though Republicans lost control in 1954. In 1958, the off-year referendum on the Eisenhower administration and its recessionary policies gave Democrats fifteen Senate seats and forty-nine House seats, mostly in northern and urban jurisdictions. This power poised urban Democrats to change the direction of federal urban programs and increase their funding. While they could not enact new programs, "working in alliance with organizations outside the government they *did*," according to Sundquist, "develop a program aimed at the solution of the country's major identified domestic problems."[72]

Unfortunately for Kennedy and his backers, the Democrats lost twenty House seats in 1960, mostly in northern, urban liberal districts. Nor did the 1962 election change the legislative stalemate: the 174 Republicans elected that year could join with 104 southern Democrats to take working control of the House from the 159 nonsouthern Democrats on the urban measures JFK sought. Congress did pass the Housing Act of 1961, substantially increasing funds for subsidized housing and urban renewal programs, but it voted against establishing a cabinet level Department of Urban Affairs and Housing.

Just as Johnson's landslide gave Democrats the White House, Figure 1 shows that it also put more northern, urban liberal Democrats in Congress than at any time since the New Deal. The ranks of the southern Democrats shrank to ninety-two, while the Republicans lost twenty-nine seats. This gave urban liberal Democrats almost enough votes to command majorities on their own. They needed only 15 votes from among northern, urban liberal Republicans or "TVA district" southern Democrats to pass legislation.

To Speaker McCormack, the result was "the Congress of fulfillment, of accomplished hopes, . . . of realized dreams." To conservative *New York Times* columnist Arthur Krock, it was a Congress which "moved the country nearer to state collectivism at the federal level than in any previous time."[73] Congress was certainly willing not only to extend federal urban grant programs, but also to use those programs to reach all the way down to the neighborhood level to pattern political activism.

Great Society entrepreneurs did not want to dismantle the program structure and coalition and coalition pattern which the New Deal and Fair Deal had erected and which Democratic Congresses had nourished between 1954 and 1965. To the contrary, they wanted to reform it by adding on new programs which would widen and deepen Democratic support within the growing central-city constituencies. They sought, however, to follow FDR's lead

85

by using these new programs to modernize local political alliances, the exclusive character of which they had rightly diagnosed as a cause of the deepening division among Democratic constituencies.

Such beneficiaries of the prevailing programs as big-city mayors, developers, downtown business leaders, and agency professionals were not, for the most part, keen on admitting new partners, however junior. But years of tight Republican budgets, national recession, and urban decline had made them strongly support increased federal funding for urban development programs. If the cost of getting this funding came in the form of Great Society community action programs, most would grudgingly accept. A number of local political entrepreneurs even came to see these programs as a way of expanding their own political bases.

The excluded groups—black and minority groups and liberal, young activist professionals—naturally had quite a different view of what should happen in local and national politics. They sought to make radical reforms in the federal urban programs which had damaged central-city neighborhoods and advocated community control as a new basis for urban politics. These groups and the Great Society political entrepreneurs sought to use each other without ever seeing eye to eye about the outcome of their plans.

In the short run, the Great Society entrepreneurs succeeded to a remarkable degree. With a rhetorical emphasis on concepts like community action, citizen participation, and equal opportunity, they created new bureaucracies alongside the traditional ones, thus modernizing the structure of urban government. In an increasing number of cities, after initial rounds of conflict, Democratic mayors used these bureaucracies (and created new ones of their own) to expand their neighborhood political bases.

They also incorporated two new constituencies. Great Society social programs provided employment and status for the "substantial corps of professionals, committed to reform, inside government or shuttling between government and the academy."[74] It is only a slight exaggeration to say that they provided a kind of outdoor relief for the growing stratum of educated young professionals in the central cities. Also, "community action . . . became an attack on political poverty, oriented toward increasing the po-

86

litical participation of previously excluded citizens, particularly black Americans."[75] Consciously or not, the result was, as Piven and Cloward have argued, to "shape and direct the political future" of "a new and unstable electoral constituency," and to "prod the local Democratic party machinery to cultivate the allegiance of urban black voters."[76]

The New Frontier/Great Society Program Delivery System

New Frontier/Great Society entrepreneurs enacted substantial changes in federal urban development programs through the Housing Acts of 1961 and 1964 and the Housing and Urban Development Acts of 1965 and 1968. These bills increased federal financing for public, subsidized nonprofit, and private housing, enlarged and modified the urban renewal program, and raised the HHFA to cabinet status. Together, they powerfully expanded the 1949 Housing Act, largely within the parameters it set.

The Great Society also established the Community Action Program, the Model Cities Program, and a raft of new social service programs ranging from manpower training to social welfare to education. While these programs vaguely resembled the old WPA, they broke new ground by funding local nonprofit groups to deliver community services. They often bypassed local as well as state government, thus dramatically extending the tactic FDR had invented when he used federal programs to reach directly into and organize local jurisdictions. Nor did the Great Society restrict itself to creating new peak organizations like urban renewal agencies. It reached directly into the complex web of neighborhood social networks in order to pattern political participation.

Urban Development Programs

In their years out of power during the Eisenhower administration, congressional Democrats sought to increase funding for federal subsidized housing and urban development programs and to expand the array of such programs. The Eisenhower-era budgets had, they felt, slowed national economic growth and central-city

87

development. The liberals within the Democratic party also felt strongly that the Eisenhower-era urban program emphasis on central business district projects should be augmented with new and larger subsidized housing programs. Despite the narrow political majorities upon which the Kennedy presidency rested, the New Frontier moved ahead on this agenda.

The Housing Act of 1961 essentially updated and reinvigorated the 1949 Housing Act. It tripled previous public housing authorizations to 100,000 new units, authorized $2.5 billion for urban renewal (more for four years than had actually been spent in the previous fourteen), and established a new below-market interest rate (BMIR) subsidy program for private, limited-dividend, multifamily housing production. Under this new program, known as Section 221(d)(3), FNMA provided mortgage money at the federal funds rate (3⅛ percent at the time) to subsidize housing for families with incomes below the median but above public housing eligibility limits. It was the first real advance in urban housing policy in more than a decade. Though Republicans strongly attacked the bill, on the key vote it passed the House by 18 votes. Seven urban Republicans and forty-four southern Democrats sided with the administration. In the Senate, the measure passed by only 5 votes.

Other New Frontier initiatives did not fare so well. Kennedy's proposal to raise HHFA to cabinet status lost soundly in the House, at least partly because he proposed to appoint a black as the new secretary.[77] Kennedy's assassination, Johnson's 1964 landslide victory, the importance of the city vote to it, and the stirrings within the black community combined, however, to remove many of the political obstacles which had impeded the New Frontier. At the same time, they made new urban program measures even more imperative for the Great Society.

The omnibus 1965 Housing and Urban Development Act increased urban renewal authorizations an additional $2.9 billion, authorized 240,000 more units of public housing construction over four years, and created a local public works construction grant program, a new communities program, a matching grant program for constructing neighborhood multipurpose centers, a rent supplement program to put public housing families into subsidized private housing units, and Section 23, which allowed local public housing authorities to lease privately developed new housing.

Though Johnson commanded large majorities in both houses, the vote on key parts of this omnibus bill was extremely close; the new housing programs, for example, cleared the House by only 6 votes, while a move in the Senate to strike the rent supplements was defeated by 47 to 40. As usual, Republicans and southern Democrats combined to provide the opposition. In a companion measure, LBJ also succeeded in creating the U.S. Department of Housing and Urban Development, though to moderate the opposition from NAREB and other consumer groups he had to grant the FHA and FHLBB continued operating autonomy.[78] Together, these two measures constituted a dramatic reinvigoration both of the 1949 Housing Act and the Democrats' traditional commitment to the program framework around which local progrowth coalitions had been built.

The 1965 Act pumped $4.5 billion in additional money into the existing urban program delivery system, added new components to it, and gave it a much stronger bureaucratic position. If these achievements did not quite equal those of the New Deal, they decisively broke away from the patterns of the Eisenhower administration. On the basis of the Kaiser Housing Commission's final report, the 1968 Housing and Urban Development Act went even further. It set a ten-year housing production goal of 26 million units, 60 percent more than the private market was constructing, and introduced two new interest subsidy programs, Sections 235 and 236, to replace, consolidate, and speed the earlier BMIR programs.

A Nixon-era HUD policy review commented that this "extremely significant expansion of the subsidy concept" resulted in "a rapid increase in all appropriations for housing subsidies."[79] Sections 235 and 236 provided for the federal government to pay the difference between market rates and a 1 percent mortgage for privately constructed single-family and multifamily projects. By the time the Nixon administration suspended the programs in 1973, these titles and the rent supplement program had committed

89

the federal government to financing $24.5 billion in mortgages at an annual cost of $1.37 billion for 1.2 million units of housing. The Acts increased subsidized housing production from less than 40,000 units annually under Eisenhower and 60,000 under Kennedy to 430,000 units annually by 1970 and 1971. In keeping with the importance of the South to the Democrats, that region received more than a proportionate share of these units.[80]

These Acts also shifted the emphasis of urban renewal. Before 1966, urban renewal projects had demolished more than a quarter of a million low-rent central-city units, displacing almost a million people. Only 114,829 new units had been built in cleared areas, and only 45,861 of these were subsidized. After the passage of the 1965 and 1968 Acts, the rate of urban renewal demolition and displacement declined, the emphasis shifted to housing rehabilitation rather than clearance, and the number of subsidized units constructed in renewal areas between 1966 and 1972 tripled to about one hundred twenty thousand. Though downtown development remained the focus of many of the more than three thousand urban renewal projects, the national Democratic legislative response to community protest at least slowed the extent to which urban renewal constituted "Negro removal."[81]

Patterning Community Action

The most ambitious of the Great Society's programs sought to go far beyond these triumphs in revitalizing federal urban development programs, substantial as they were. Through the War on Poverty, the Johnson administration extended the reach of federal programs into central-city neighborhoods to absorb the political mobilization taking place within them. More than any other Great Society program, the Office of Economic Opportunity's Community Action Program (CAP) embodied the Great Society's uneasy marriage between professionalized reform, federal sponsorship of new forms of political participation, and the disruptive political thrust emanating from big-city neighborhoods, particularly black neighborhoods. To some, an attack on poverty, and to others, a device for administrative coordination, CAP ultimately became a method for advancing "the political concerns of racial minorities, whose status as citizens remained so problematic."[82]

OEO gave Johnson what he wanted, "a bold and attention-getting proposal on which he could put his personal stamp" from the outset of his administration in 1964.[83] Despite its initial ambiguity, the measure, which Johnson convinced a Georgia Democrat to sponsor, won a 226 to 185 majority in the House (with support from sixty southern Democrats and twenty-two urban Republicans) and 61 to 34 in the Senate. The sixty-five freshman Democrats that the 1964 elections brought into the House helped pass the 1965 CAP reauthorization by even larger margins.

The Community Action Program (Title II of the 1964 OEO Act) pumped funding which rose from $350 million in 1965 to $1.1 billion in 1969 into central-city "target-area" neighborhoods, 55 percent of which were black. Over one thousand Community Action Agencies (CAAs) were ultimately established. By 1969, the average CAA had a budget of $5.2 million and 230 staffers.[84] CAP's dedication to "maximum feasible participation" created a great deal of controversy. An early CAP manual issued by OEO stressed the need to "assist the poor in developing autonomous and self-managed organizations which are competent to exert political influence." Richard Boone, who had helped to write the legislation, stressed the need for "new, private, nonprofit local structures for policy and administration [because] many local governments were themselves unresponsive to the poor."[85] Though the poor rarely dominated CAA boards, 60 percent of all CAA directors stated that effective participation by the poor was their most important goal. Contrary to the perception among some mayors and legislators, CAAs tended not to participate in direct protest, but they did engage in neighborhood organizing and undoubtedly added to the ferment of community mobilization that was taking place in the mid-1960s.[86]

While CAP "had the effect of absorbing and directing many of the agitational elements of the black population," as Piven and Cloward argue, it also provided training and legitimacy for a new stratum of political leadership within black, Hispanic, and white ethnic working-class big-city neighborhoods.[87] CAP's ability to

91

mobilize these neighborhoods and to lend federal recognition to their leaders' status was resented and resisted by many local officials. Their reactions, in turn, led to the Green Amendment in 1967, which gave mayors control over OEO grants to CAAs. This kind of opposition from political regulars ultimately caused CAAs to shift their activities away from political action and toward service provision.

Just as CAP brought formerly excluded urban constituencies within the ambit of federal aid, a second Great Society program, the Model Cities, sought to reform urban government decision-making with respect to neighborhood development issues. It was also designed, to some extent, to supplant the controversial CAP with something local elected officials would accept and support. Where CAP sought to co-opt the mobilized urban poor, Model Cities, in effect, sought to co-opt local government (and HUD as well) on their behalf. Model Cities would balance "bricks and mortar" advocates with "important 'human' dimensions in a Department that would otherwise be excessively preoccupied with the physical environment alone," according to one participant in crafting the legislation.[88] Model Cities would concentrate and coordinate federal resources from all relevant departments behind locally devised neighborhood plans, thus further shifting the emphasis of the federal urban development program structure.

To win passage, LBJ had to reduce the overall budget of the Demonstration Cities and Metropolitan Development Act of 1966 and increase the number of cities in which the Model Cities coordination experiment would be tried. After the budget had been revised downward from $2.3 billion to $900 for two years, the number of eligible cities increased from sixty to twice that number, and the interdepartmental coordination powers substantially weakened, the measure passed, though with the relatively close vote of 142 to 126 in the House. Mayors joined administration officials in lobbying heavily for the measure, while beneficiaries of existing program priorities had voiced the most skepticism.

In all, the Model Cities Program disbursed nearly $2.3 billion in operating grants to 150 "first-round" and "second-round" cities between 1967 and 1973. On the positive side, Model Cities provided a new constituency within HUD and within city governments which advocated neighborhood development and rehabilitation as a counterbalance to what the major grant programs had been funding. It is not surprising, however, that Model Cities failed to change the thrust of other federal urban programs. It neither coordinated the complex and segmented federal urban program delivery system nor did it stimulate innovations in local government neighborhood development practices. It became simply another fragment of the larger picture, with its own narrow but not inconsequential constituency among mayors and Model City neighborhoods.

The Great Society and the Revitalization of the New Deal Coalition

The New Frontier/Great Society years worked a revolution in federalism which was almost as profound as that of the New Deal. In 1960, the federal government had forty-four grant programs sending about $3.9 billion annually to the big cities. By the end of the Great Society, over five hundred grant programs delivered $14 billion to urban areas, and momentum carried that figure to $26.8 billion in 1974 despite the advent of a Republican administration. In 1960, big cities received one federal dollar for every ten they spent; by 1974, this figure had risen to one in five. As in the New Deal, federal intervention into urban politics and the urban development process took a leap forward during the Great Society.[89] While the Great Society spent only half in real terms what the New Deal had pumped into a Depression-era economy, its spending sharply contrasted with the previous Republican period and dramatically expanded federal urban programs in order to reach new constituencies.

Moreover, like the New Deal, the Great Society sought to modernize local political alignments. Where FDR had limited his efforts to direct federal dealings with local governments, LBJ took this strategy a step further, directly shaping the networks of neighborhood political leadership. By creating new parallel bureaucracies to incorporate these new constituencies, the Great Society

93

had a lasting impact on the structure of urban politics, urban government, and intergovernmental relations.

Sundquist has described how these new programs and their constituencies modernized the New Deal Democratic party:

> Activist politicians looking for public support and interest groups looking for political support were natural allies. . . . While maintaining their official nonpartisan stance . . . such groups were admitted to full participating status in the Democratic party's inner councils on matters within their field of interest . . . and the participants in a very real sense formed a single institution, unorganized and amorphous but self-conscious and cohesive.[90]

The Great Society did not rationalize and coordinate federal urban programs. If anything, it fragmented them further. It did, however, develop a new generation of nonparty methods for bringing central-city minority neighborhoods and reform-minded professionals into the fold alongside the dominant organizational interests which had long prospered from Democratic urban programs. This marriage proved difficult at the time and has been troubled by conflict since. The fact that it could have been consummated at all, however, testifies to the skill with which the Great Society, with its New Frontier provenance, faced its political challenges.

5. Conclusion: Democratic Political Entrepreneurship and the Growth of Federal Urban Programs

Traditional pluralist analysis holds that the interplay among organized private interests acts upon an essentially passive executive and legislative machinery to produce policy outcomes. Economic analyses, whether of the traditional or radical variety, tend to argue that broad economic or demographic trends produce policy outcomes regardless of the interplay of political factors. Contrary to these views, the review of federal urban programs presented here suggests that the initiative for policy expansion comes from within the political system itself. From the New Deal to the Great Society, national Democratic political entrepreneurs have enacted federal urban programs in order to expand, shape, and institutionalize their support from urban constituencies and, in turn, sustain their national political power.

"Objective" economic conditions gave these entrepreneurs a chance to act, but did not govern their response. FDR seized his opportunity by using the "output" side of government to consolidate his urban support. Though he designed programs for the rural South and West, the heart of the New Deal was in the big cities. Roosevelt's strategy contrasted with that of the traditional urban political machines which had built their support on the "input" side of government through direct exchanges between party leader and voter. FDR's political descendants in the Fair Deal, New Frontier, and Great Society developed increasingly sophisticated methods for using federal programs as a substitute for party organization in building national political power.

This use of urban programs began as a peculiarly Democratic strategy. The New Deal invented it and in the process established national government as an ongoing powerful entity for the first time in U.S. history. As institutionalized during the Fair Deal, federal programs provided a framework around which Democrats could organize a supportive political coalition from among quite disparate urban interests. In a second great expansion of federal urban programs, the Great Society sought to modernize this framework by enlarging federal intervention and reaching far more deeply into the urban social and political fabric.

Shifts in national political sentiment as embodied in the competition for the White House and in the balance between non-southern Democrats and their Republican and southern Democratic conservative coalition opponents controlled the degree to which Democrats could pursue their urban strategy. When these factors were unfavorable, urban programs at best grew slowly and at worst were terminated. However, when there was a Democrat in the White House and a nonsouthern Democratic majority in Congress, urban programs grew with almost explosive force.

In the final analysis, the emergence and evolution of the urban electorate as a pivotal force in national politics has governed the growth of urban programs under Democratic administrations.

95

Franklin Roosevelt and the New Deal rode to national power on the emergence of the urban blue collar vote in 1932 and 1936. Lyndon Johnson was no less a beneficiary of mobilized urban sentiment in 1964, though by that time the nature of the metropolitan electorate had changed substantially.

If Johnson was a creature of the New Deal urban strategy, however, he was also its victim. The success of the programs enacted by the New Deal and the Fair Deal faced the Great Society with two kinds of problems. As these programs reshaped the metropolitan electoral terrain, they increased the need to reform the program structure. But because the programs were enacted to aid specific constituencies and were designed to survive adverse political shifts, they resisted adaptation to the needs of emergent constituencies.

What is even worse, federal urban programs created and exacerbated new kinds of conflicts among urban Democratic constituencies. None was more acute than the disparity of treatment between upwardly mobile whites and dominant central-city institutions on the one hand, and central-city black neighborhoods on the other. Not only did federal urban programs advance the interests of the first without "trickling down" to the latter, they often systematically attacked the latter. Perhaps because of the need for southern Democratic votes or because of implacable Republican and conservative opposition, the Democratic party never made good its commitment to the central-city poor. Growing conflict within metropolitan areas thus became growing political conflict within the Democratic party. This condition challenged the Great Society political entrepreneurs, and it continues to haunt contemporary Democratic efforts to build a new consensus on urban development policy.

The Conservative Response to Democratic Urban Program Expansion and the Construction of an Alternative Policy Emphasis

1. INTRODUCTION

As national Democratic political entrepreneurs succeeded in expanding federal urban programs, they produced two kinds of conservative countermovements. Democratic programs helped private sector decision-makers decentralize new plant investments away from the central cities and to reshape central-city land-use patterns. Chapter six will show that the urban protest and political challenge of the 1960s and their penetration of Democratic federal programs and local politics hastened the exodus of private investment from the older central cities to their suburbs and, above all, to newer metropolitan areas like those of the Southwest. In contrast to the 1950s and early 1960s, even corporate headquarters joined this movement during the latter 1960s and 1970s.

The Democrats also generated a conservative countermovement in national politics which paralleled and reinforced this private sector response. During World War II, the Eisenhower administration, and the Nixon-Ford years, conservatives in Congress and the White House attempted to build an alternative emphasis within the federal urban development program structure. Their aim was to undermine those parts which flowed to the Democrats' central city-electoral base, demobilize the central-city electorate, make the program structure more responsive to the private sector, and add new programs aimed at conservative constituencies.

Ironically, Democrats themselves opened the way for this con-

97

servative challenge. FDR, Truman, and Johnson all turned from domestic reform to armed conflict. To rally support for the conduct of war, these Democratic presidents had to sacrifice their commitment to urban reform and play heavily toward conservative constituencies and increasingly conservative public opinion. The Republicans who succeeded them resolutely extended these beginnings.

Republican national political entrepreneurs and their conservative southern Democratic allies had two basic motives. The first was essentially reactive: conservatives sought to terminate the most "political" Democratic programs by capitalizing on the conflicts and controversies which they had created. Because Republicans faced the same political constraints as the urban liberal Democrats, they often failed to terminate these programs outright. More often than not, however, conservatives so altered the environment within which these programs operated that they were forced to behave far more circumspectly. Conservatives thus crippled the programs which Democrats had developed to mobilize urban mass constituencies, even when they could not terminate them.[1] This pattern began during the latter 1930s and continued in more recent Republican administrations.[2]

Republicans sought to adapt the federal urban program delivery system to their own ends. In place of the Democratic orientation toward public sector providers and central-city recipients, Republicans emphasized private sector providers and suburban and nonnortheastern beneficiaries. The 1954 reform of urban renewal illustrates how they made Democratic programs respond better to private sector needs while the 1956 Interstate Highway program and the 1974 Community Development Block Grant program exemplify how conservatives used the Democratic strategy of inventing federal programs to build up favorable local constituencies.

2. World War II and the Militarization of the New Deal

The years between 1938 and 1945 saw the federal government intervene in private sector development to an unequaled degree on the condition that this intervention would not become a tool for further social reform. The militarization of the New Deal demonstrated both that Keynesian intervention worked and that it could be harnessed to essentially conservative ends. During World War II, the federal government almost doubled the economy's productive capacity, eliminated unemployment through war mobilization, set loose migration patterns which continued after the war, and established patterns of infrastructural investment which private investment subsequently followed throughout the postwar years. Yet public control of the economy during World War II was organized so that it could be terminated without having changed the previous balance of power between the public and private sectors.

The Political Context of Wartime Domestic Policy

After 1936, Roosevelt's appeal to city voters declined heavily. In the Midwest, cities with heavy concentrations of German-Americans resisted Roosevelt's turn toward war in 1938 and 1939.[3] Many of the New Deal's later proposals, such as "packing" the Supreme Court, also turned public opinion against Roosevelt and the 1937–1938 recession did not help his cause. According to historian Richard Polenberg, "Every opinion poll in 1938 and 1939 indicated much the same thing: between two-thirds and three-fourths of the American people preferred that the Roosevelt administration follow a more conservative course."[4] The labor movement, which engaged in a growing number of strikes after 1937, including the Flint sit-down strike against General Motors, also caused problems. According to his detractors, FDR's refusal to call out federal troops to evict the Flint strikers showed that he was playing into the hands of Communist agitators.

Simultaneously, war in Europe caused a shift in Roosevelt's political priorities. The legacy of isolationism in American politics was great and Congress had mandated American neutrality. To overcome this neutrality policy and build up the nation's defense posture, Roosevelt began to "virtually abandon" his social programs and court the southern conservatives, midwesterners, and business leaders, whose support he would need in time of war.[5]

In August 1939, he named a War Resources Board which included the heads of U.S. Steel, American Telephone and Telegraph, Sears Roebuck, and a General Motors director.

After December 7, 1941, the electoral context shifted further. War mobilization ended unemployment and brought the problems of rapid growth, rather than decline, to many parts of the country. Urban workers no longer faced desperate circumstances, and the labor movement and other reformist interest groups found new roles in the war effort. To perform well as "Dr. Win-the-War," Roosevelt sought support from the largest business organizations, whose leaders wholeheartedly opposed further social reform under the cloak of wartime emergency. "The Roosevelt administration chose early and probably almost by reflex," historian David Brody concludes. "It drew a sharp line between the tasks of making war and its commitment to domestic reform."[6]

The congressional climate turned even more sharply against FDR after 1936. At the end of 1937, "in the most smashing defeat Roosevelt had ever received in the House," a conservative Democratic-Republican coalition turned back the administration's fair labor standards bill by a vote of 216 to 198.[7] Conservative Democratic senators also unveiled a manifesto calling for an end to public spending as a response to the 1937 recession, a turn toward encouraging private investment, and the prohibition of sit-down strikes.[8]

In the 1938 primary elections, Roosevelt sought to regain power over Congress by purging as many as ten disloyal Senate Democrats and twenty-two House members.[9] Roosevelt particularly attacked the southern conservatives who had thwarted his labor, reorganization, and urban programs. However, the attempted purge was a complete failure and succeeded only in setting a major segment of his party more strongly against him. The November 1938 general elections gave the New Deal "its most painful beating," while Republicans "scored stunning gains throughout the nation."[10]

Republicans gained eighty House seats, mostly from midwestern and northeastern liberal Democrats. The 169 northern Democrats faced 93 southern Democrats and 169 Republicans. In the

Senate, six of the eight new Republican senators replaced liberal Democrats. The ensuing sessions of Congress investigated the WPA and the NLRB, slashed FDR's relief and public works appropriations, opposed his housing bill, and made it plain that the New Deal could no longer command congressional majorities.

As war engulfed the United States, Roosevelt's congressional position worsened. "In the crucial mid-war congressional elections in November, 1942, Republicans captured 44 additional seats in the House (13 short of a majority), nine in the Senate (nine short of a majority)." Northern Democratic losses strengthened the hand of southerners, whose "sense of independence was further enhanced by wartime prosperity and by suspicion of the administration's intentions on race relations."[11] The conservative coalition reached a peak in 1943–1944, and created a congressional climate diametrically opposed to the basic New Deal. Congressional resistance continued throughout the war and deepened when, in 1946, the Republicans gained enough seats to control the House and Senate.

War mobilization and the increasing tempo of production also enabled dominant private sector organizations to regain the initiative they had lost during the Depression. Federal urban agencies, including the WPA, subordinated their activities to defense production needs.[12] Such urban liberal forces as the labor movement and big-city mayors also found themselves swept into business-led mobilization efforts.

The labor movement adopted a "no-strike" pledge at the outset of the war. Though labor leaders had only a minor advisory role in the War Production Board and little influence on the shape of mobilization, they gained a great deal from wartime cooperation. Federal war contracts guaranteed union wage levels and union recognition and caused union membership to increase from nine to fifteen million between 1939 and 1945. Combined with rising real incomes for their members, these gains "acted wholly to reinforce the adherence of . . . labor to the existing framework."[13]

War mobilization also involved such urban champions as Fiorello La Guardia, who became head of the Office of Civilian Defense. La Guardia undertook a morale-building campaign; he

101

had no real resources or authority to shape local civilian mobilization. His direct contacts with local civil defense committees upset governors, however, and Roosevelt eased him out of the position. He symbolized the lack of impact which mayors had on the mobilization effort.[14]

Above all, the war removed the constituency which had motivated the construction of the New Deal coalition. After 1941, much of the central-city, unemployed, white working class was in uniform. The rest of it was working overtime in union shops, often in suburban locations, in the burgeoning wartime industrial apparatus. If Roosevelt chose not to press urban programs during the war, and if Congress was not likely to approve them, neither were central-city constituencies likely to press him to do so.

The Wartime Urban Development Program Delivery System

The conservative political environment in which war mobilization took place had both negative and positive impacts. Congressional conservatives dismantled the New Deal agencies which most irked them. While they could not roll back such fundamental New Deal reforms as the Labor Relations Board or the Social Security System, they did terminate the WPA, the CCC, and the National Resources Planning Board. They also ensured that remaining New Deal agencies like the PWA (which had become the Federal Works Administration) would be strictly subordinated to the war effort.[15]

In other respects, federal intervention tremendously accelerated its impact on domestic development. Through the War Production Board, the federal government increased private plant investment almost 60 percent over 1939 levels in just two years. This unparalleled new investment, more than $23 billion in new plants alone, doubled and in some cases tripled local economies practically overnight. These grants stimulated new patterns of investment, internal migration, and metropolitan growth for a quarter of a century after the war.

Trimming Old Programs

After the 1942 elections, programs closely associated with the New Deal's urban, liberal constituency base were in trouble. The Seventy-eighth Congress emasculated the Farm Security Administration and ended the Works Progress Administration, the National Youth Administration, and the Civilian Conservation Corps. It also shelved all public housing and all nondefense public works.

Congress steadfastly refused even to think about postwar urban policy during most of the war. Though Senator Robert Wagner and liberal California Congressman Jerry Voorhis introduced a resolution to establish a Post-Emergency Economic Advisory Commission in 1941, Congress never addressed it. During the war, the National Resources Planning Board considered how to resume and expand New Deal programs once the war ended. But "when President Roosevelt gingerly transmitted the board's reports to Congress in the spring of 1943, the legislators responded by cutting off funds for continuation of the agency's activities. Conservatives wanted no part of what they derisively called the American version of Britain's socialistic Beveridge Plan."[16] When Congress finally established committees in 1946 to take testimony on postwar conversion and reconstruction, they "seemed intent mainly on cutting short the kinds of programs in which New Dealers were interested."[17]

Wartime Federal Capital Investment

The demands and stresses of increased defense production meant that Congress could not adopt an entirely negative stance toward urban development programs. In June 1941, Congress passed the Community Facilities Act, also known as the Lanham Act, to aid war-boom communities with housing, nursery schools, child-care centers, clinics, schools, and other facilities. These were funded directly by the federal government through the Federal Works Agency, and targeted to areas experiencing the highest defense-related immigration. Since the war boom caused an internal migration of three million workers during the first eighteen months

103

alone, defense housing was badly needed. While the Lanham Act broke new ground, particularly in providing child care for the women working in war plants, it was clearly an emergency measure whose benefits disappeared the moment the war ended. Section 4 of the act required all defense housing units either be sold or demolished immediately after the war. In all, Congress appropriated $1.3 billion for public defense housing construction and $300 million to ensure privately financed defense housing. This money produced about 1.9 million new war-housing units.[18]

The most important urban development program conducted by the federal government during World War II was not in housing, however, but in the recapitalization of American industry for the war effort. Total additions to the U.S. physical capital plant between 1942 and 1944 amounted to $35.5 billion, almost equal to the entire 1939 value of the U.S. manufacturing plant. Almost all of the money came from the federal government. Approximately $10.1 billion went for military facilities, $4.0 billion for housing, and a total of $23.1 billion was spent on new manufacturing facilities.

Considering that the existing manufacturing investment was valued at only $39.5 billion in 1939, wartime investment amounted to an unparalleled expansion of the nation's productive capacity, far beyond anything the New Deal could have dreamed of achieving.[19] The War Production Board (WPB) summary report concluded, "The war-created facilities represent the greatest increment to manufacturing capital recorded in modern industrial history."[20]

The distribution of these new manufacturing facilities only roughly paralleled the distribution of existing facilities. The old, nineteenth-century northeastern manufacturing centers received less than their share while metropolitan areas in the Great Lakes, the South, and the West received more. Within these metropolitan areas, facilities were likely to be disproportionately located in the suburbs rather than the central cities. One review of WPB activities noted that "the larger factories were concentrated in a radius of 30 miles from the larger metropolitan areas."[21] The WPB spent over $100 million each, for example, to construct the Willow Run bomber complex 17 miles outside of Detroit and the Kaiser Steel plant in Fontana, 35 miles outside of Los Angeles.

Though the Detroit region received the largest absolute amount of plant investment because the automobile industry produced tanks and aircraft, California led in aircraft production (with 20% of all supply contracts) and shipbuilding, Texas led in synthetic rubber and petrochemical products, and the Gulf Coast area also led in shipbuilding. New military facilities were heavily placed in the South and West. World War II investments thus provided the basic, private capital stock for the postwar growth of Sunbelt cities.

Table 2 gives a detailed breakdown of previous and wartime industrial capital for central cities and suburbs of the major northeastern and southwestern metropolitan areas. While WPB investments roughly follow prior patterns, two relative differences stand out. First, wartime investments were often skewed toward suburban locations. In New York, Detroit, Baltimore, and Pittsburgh, for example, new investment was located outside the central cities twice or more as heavily as before the war (see suburban location index in Table 2). This pattern also held for such Sunbelt cities as Los Angeles, Dallas, Houston, and San Diego. Second, while more money was invested in the northeastern cities in absolute terms, the WPB financed much larger relative growth in the industrial facilities of the southwestern facilities. As Table 2 shows, cities from Los Angeles to Phoenix received from twice to nine times their prewar share of industrial investment.

Data on migration patterns and wartime housing shortages reinforce this conclusion. The war set loose migration patterns which operated throughout the postwar period: the South, especially the rural South, lost population to the urban centers of the North and West, while the West gained strongly relative to the North. Within this overall pattern, black migration was pronounced: between 1940 and 1943, fifty thousand black workers migrated to Detroit war plants alone. Los Angeles, San Diego, San Francisco, Denver, Dallas, and Houston were most hard-pressed by immigration along with Washington and Detroit.

Given the tremendous impact of the WPB, its decision-making

105

TABLE 2 The Distribution of War Production Board Plant Investments

City	1937 Manufacturing Wage Earners		1940–1945 War Plant Investment		War Investment Locational Indices*		
	CC	Suburbs	CC	Suburbs	CC	Suburbs	Suburbanality
New York	506	342	$380.5	$491.9	.31	.58	1.91
Chicago	391	148	699.4	233.1	.73	.64	.88
Philadelphia	214	132	311.0	97.1	.59	.30	.51
Detroit	235	172	325.7	712.6	.56	1.69	3.00
Baltimore	81	25	127.3	113.2	.64	1.86	2.90
Cleveland	132	31	355.3	64.4	1.09	.85	.78
Milwaukee	77	44	149.8	60.3	.80	.55	.69
Boston	59	189	81.0	181.0	.56	.39	.70
Pittsburgh	51	177	58.7	428.2	.47	1.19	2.11
Buffalo	57	49	148.3	169.4	1.06	1.41	1.33
San Francisco/ Oakland	57	31	$ 96.0	$ 86.5	.69	1.12	1.64
Los Angeles	86	59	$148.6	$664.9	.71	4.55	6.45
Dallas/Ft. Worth	23	3	100.9	42.9	1.82	5.80	3.22
Houston	17	11	252.5	197.3	6.02	7.55	1.25
San Diego	7	1	59.3	10.0	3.23	7.83	2.25

Denver	13	1	120.5	0.7	3.83	.33	.08
San José	6	5	2.8	55.9	.17	4.73	26.27
Phoenix	1	0	37.0	10.7	13.53	4.25	.32
San Antonio	6	1	2.4	0.0	.16	—	—
El Paso	2	1	3.2	0.0	.60	—	—
Tucson	1	0	6.5	0.0	62.00	—	—
Albuquerque	1	0	0.4	0.0	.33	—	—

SOURCE: 1937 Biennial Census of Manufacturing, Chapter 4, Table 2 (figures in thousands of wage earners) and Civilian Production Administration, "War-Time Manufacturing Plant Expansion, Privately Financed, 1940–1945" (1946), page 40 (figures in millions of dollars invested).

* Indices give the ratio of the area's wartime investment as a proportion of all wartime investment to area's 1937 manufacturing employment as a proportion of all 1937 manufacturing employment. Suburbanality index is the ratio of the suburban location index to the central-city index.

processes take on particular interest. The case of Detroit illustrates how different things might have been if New Dealers had controlled the WPB. In late 1940, Walter Reuther proposed that labor help to reorganize Detroit's automobile industry, converting existing idle plants to aircraft production. The head of the Office of Production Management, WPB's predecessor, was the former president of General Motors. Because of his and the industry's complete opposition, the government rejected Reuther's plan.

Instead, in January 1942, Roosevelt created the WPB by executive order. Its chairman had final say over procurement and production expansion and financing. To head the board, FDR chose former Sears Roebuck executive Donald Nelson. By separating the WPB from all other federal agencies, FDR "devised a radical form of industrial mobilization that contained no seeds of reform . . . so implemented as to give no alarm to the nation's industrial interests.''[22] Nelson staffed the WPB with over eight hundred "dollar-a-year" men drawn from the industries over which WPB had control. Labor was given only a minor advisory function. By bringing the chairman of the Army-Navy Munitions Board into the WPB, Nelson completed the marriage of the military-industrial coalition.[23]

Through the WPB, leaders of the largest industrial corporations could thus use government financing to reconstruct the private sector's capital base along new and more desirable lines. Instead of using Detroit's existing plants, it built new ones outside the city. The Production Executive Committee placed their new facilities largely beyond the reach of the unions, New Deal-leaning mayors, and the other constituencies which had fueled urban liberalism in the 1930s.

Although a liberal Democrat occupied the White House during World War II, this period thus clearly constituted a conservative counteraction to the urban liberal initiatives of the New Deal. Congress shifted strongly in a conservative direction, while business leaders retrieved the political initiative which they had lost in the 1929 Crash.

These conservative forces halted the momentum of New Deal urban development programs. Some, like the WPA and the NRPB, were simply terminated. Others survived, albeit in a much more cautious form. More importantly, in the WPB, congressional conservatives and private industry leaders created a massive reindustrialization program whose scale swamped anything attempted by the New Deal. This investment program had none of the New Deal's social reform characteristics. Instead, it emphasized industrial expansion outside the older central cities. Its housing element was designed to melt away rapidly after the war's end. It operated through the private sector rather than the public sector, and reflected choices sought by dominant private institutions. Finally, this investment program set loose forces which were to shape and constrain all subsequent efforts at urban liberalism.

THE EISENHOWER ADMINISTRATION AND THE IMPLEMENTATION OF URBAN RENEWAL

Not until twenty years after FDR's 1932 victory did conservatives get their first chance to organize both the executive and the legislative branches of the federal government. Dwight D. Eisenhower won the 1952 election with 57.4 percent of the presidential vote, the same margin which FDR had received in 1932. The Republican candidate won majorities in most of the fifteen largest metropolitan areas. Voters also gave Republicans a 1-vote majority in the Senate and an 11-vote majority in the House. For the first time since the Depression, Democrats, with their commitment to urban liberalism, had been nudged out of the key points of political control.

As Ladd and Hadley have noted,

> The Eisenhower years marked the transition point from the New Deal coalitions to those now emergent, just as it stands as a time of passage between the agenda of the industrial state and that of postindustrialism. [24]

Eisenhower's election gave conservatives a second chance to define an alternative to the urban programs of the Democrats. The conservative alternative to Democratic urban program delivery agencies proved mainly negative. Under Republican auspices, conservatives once more trimmed back programs like public housing, which deeply offended them. The Eisenhower administration stressed the control of public spending and emphasized the private sector as the proper channel for the delivery of housing and urban development.

The Eisenhower administration reorganized the programs which survived to meet more clearly the needs of the private sector. Eisenhower named HHFA officials who were close to the private housing industry and reformed the urban renewal program through the 1954 Housing Act to make it more commercially viable. The administration did not expand government intervention into the housing market by enacting new programs. To the extent that Eisenhower did mount an alternative program, it was embodied in the interstate highway system, which spent ten times more federal money than urban renewal to shape urban land-use patterns.

In sum, the Eisenhower administration provided conservatives with the chance to modify the Democratic urban program structure, but failed to consolidate a real alternative. This failure stemmed from conflict among conservatives about whether to have such an alternative at all, from the uneven success of such partial alternatives as the 1954 Housing Act, and from Eisenhower's recessionary fiscal policy. The Eisenhower administration's hostility toward Democratic urban program beneficiaries and its inability to develop alternative programs caused the president's urban policy to fail both economically and politically. Tight fiscal and monetary policy led to recessions in 1953–1954 and 1957–1958, which, in turn, caused housing starts to fall from their record levels of 1950–1953. In response to the Republican's recessionary policies, the voters returned substantial Democratic majorities in both houses of Congress in 1958, and in 1960, they narrowly elected a Democratic president.

The Political Context of the Eisenhower Years

The 1950s was an era which yearned to put the sacrifices of war behind it and reach for prosperity. Perhaps more than in any other era in American life, it succeeded. As Galbraith's *Affluent Society* and Reissman's *Lonely Crowd* noted, consumption replaced frugality and denial as America's organizing ethos during the 1950s. With government help, an increasingly concentrated and productive industrial apparatus gave both its unionized working class and its middle-class managers steadily rising incomes.

The expansion of the U.S. economy during the 1940s and 1950s had a tremendous impact on electoral demography. Between 1950 and 1960, metropolitan populations grew 26.4 percent. The overwhelming majority of this growth took place in the suburbs. When examined on the basis of 1950 boundaries, central cities grew only 1.5 percent in this decade, while suburbs grew 61.7 percent. This difference was even greater in larger metropolitan areas.[25] In the early and mid-1950s, housing production hit all-time highs and exceeded the rate of new household formation. (Almost all of this production was in suburban areas.) Homeownership rates rose from less than half of all households during the war to 60 percent by 1960; among AFL-CIO members, the figure reached 77 percent. Automobile production also peaked in 1950 and again in 1955. Consumer spending on cars swelled from an average of $7.5 billion in the thirties and forties to $22 billion in 1950 and almost $30 billion in 1955.

These trends produced what seemed at the time to be a permanent change in American urban life. The suburbanization of population and industrial employment, rising real incomes, and the development of home-centered life-styles during the 1946–1960 "baby boom" reinforced each other. While suburbanites from the central city brought their party affiliations along, their political concerns in 1950 differed greatly from those of 1932. Both Eisenhower and his Democratic competitors sought to capture this group during the 1950s. It was in this sense that Eisenhower's election marks a "transition point" from the alignments of the New Deal.

Because he did not trigger highly partisan feelings, Eisenhower got many of his votes from these suburban Democrats. His candidacy attracted not only the traditional northern, white, Protestant Republican bedrock, but also southern white Prostestants and

111

northern Catholics, both of whom had been central to the New Deal coalition.[26]

Kevin Phillips has characterized Eisenhower's appeal to the suburbanizing white ethnics of the North:

> Much of the new suburban middle class was Catholic: the sons and daughters of Al Smith supporters. Their large numbers usually reduced the power of old-guard suburban GOP machines; however, they were ardent supporters of President Eisenhower. . . . Once Eisenhower had proved that a Republican administration did not jeopardize the economic gains of the new middle class—most of whom had risen from the auspices of the New Deal and World War II—the party was able to profit enormously from Catholic preference for Republican anti-communism abroad and social conservatism at home in contrast to the suspect "egghead" liberalism of Adlai Stevenson.[27]

According to Phillips, these voters were "tired of Truman inflation, price controls and scandals," and liked Eisenhower's termination of the Korean War and the increasing prosperity of the early 1950s so much that they supported him even more heartily in 1956.[28]

Eisenhower's impact on the urban South is even more noteworthy than his suburban gains in the Northeast. Phillips notes, "The urban Deep South was strongly pro-Eisenhower and much readier to vote Republican than the rural Deep South."[29] In 1952, Eisenhower's candidacy brought Republican voting among metropolitan white southerners above 50 percent for the first time, where it has remained in every subsequent presidential election except Johnson's. Though the emerging professional and managerial stratum in the Northeast has become increasingly Democratic, this stratum became the vanguard of emergent Republicans in the South. In 1952, only 16 percent of this group identified themselves as Republicans, but they gave 68 percent of their votes to Eisenhower. By 1972, their Republican identification had doubled, while Democratic identification had been halved.[30]

Eisenhower's victories may have been more personal than ideological or partisan, but they did challenge traditional urban liberalism. In a halting, experimental, and none-too-conscious way, Eisenhower put together the first conservative alternative to the New Deal Democratic coalition's traditional northeastern, urban base. Eisenhower combined the northern suburban voters who had rejected the central city, the emerging southern and southwestern middle class, and traditional rural conservatism to build a majority against the nineteenth-century industrial central cities. It is hardly surprising that he modified Democratic federal urban development programs to respond to these constituencies.

Republicans won control of the House in 1946, but lost it again with Truman's victory in 1948. In 1950 and 1952, however, Republicans gained again, winning five Senate and twenty-eight House seats in 1950, and two more Senate seats and twenty-two more House positions in 1952. The Republicans in 1952 thus controlled the White House and both sides of Congress for the first time since the Hoover administration. As HHFA official Nathaniel Keith observed, "The Republican-conservative Southern Democrat coalition promised a working majority."[31] Only ninety northern Democrats, perhaps twenty-five Republican liberals, and no more than twenty southern Democrats could be counted on to favor urban legislation.

Republican control of Congress lasted only two years, but it put some of the most outspoken opponents of urban legislation into House leadership positions. In the Senate, Homer Capeheart of Indiana headed Banking and Currency, while Jesse Wolcott, whose opposition to public housing was "well-established and immutable," headed the counterpart House committee.[32] With this leadership, any urban and housing legislation capable of being reported out would be considerably more conservative than anything the Democrats enacted.

In 1954, control of Congress shifted narrowly back toward the Democrats, with margins of 49 to 47 in the Senate and 232 to 201 in the House. In 1956, despite Eisenhower's overwhelming victory at the polls, Democrats maintained their position in the Senate and gained 1 vote net in the House, for a 233 to 200 margin. Democratic committee chairmen were more favorably disposed to city legislation, but the balance of congressional power

113

remained with the conservative coalition which, according to Manley, appeared on over a quarter of all contested roll call votes and won over 90 percent of those it contested.[33]

Before the Democratic triumph in the 1958 election, "the votes of approximately 35 southern congressmen, most of whom came from districts comprised of small cities and towns, determined whether the housing measures crucial to the northern cities would be passed or defeated." As a result, it was "essential that statutes were written and that programs were administered so as to favor the interests of small cities, especially those located in the South."[34]

At the beginning of his first term, Eisenhower could thus count on strong conservative support within Congress for measures designed to trim the programs he inherited from the Democrats. Procity congressional forces remained strong enough to prevent Eisenhower from dismantling urban programs, and they had an impact on legislation such as the 1954 Housing Act. Indeed, Eisenhower sometimes needed their votes on such measures to overcome opposition from doctrinaire conservatives within his own camp. The balance of power, however, rested with conservative Democrats. Only after 1958, when Democrats won a 282 to 152 House majority and a 64 to 34 Senate majority, did the balance shift back toward urban liberals.

Eisenhower was the candidate of the Republican party's more moderate, northeastern, big-business wing. The importance of business sentiment to the administration was reflected in many of its actions, from cabinet appointments for corporation presidents to the stress on balanced budgets to managing federal programs in ways which favored the private sector.

Two of Eisenhower's presidential advisory committees exemplify the administration's efforts to tailor federal policy to business needs: the 1953 Advisory Committee on Government Housing Policies and Programs and the 1954–1955 Advisory Committee on a National Highway Program. Both of these committees, which paved the way for major changes in urban development legislation, were dominated by senior business officials from the sectors which this legislation would affect.

The Housing Advisory Committee, chaired by the new head

114

of the HHFA, Albert Cole, had twenty-three members, "largely from firms and professions closely aligned with the real estate lobby; ten were bankers and lenders, seven were in real estate, architecture, and building supply."[35] It also included a lawyer, an economist who had done a study for the Twentieth Century Fund advocating the use of renewal to enhance cities' "economic usefulness,"[36] two building trade union officials, and the Republican director of the Cleveland Housing Authority. "The Committee can be viewed," one observer has said, "as an assembly of interest groups, who had largely opposed the housing policies of the previous administration, whose task was to legitimize the housing programs of the new administration. The Committee's deliberations permitted those interests to bargain for the terms under which they would support the latter's programs."[37]

A primary concern of the committee was to shake up the urban renewal program, which had been slow to start under the Democrats.[38] Urban redevelopment had been under the housing administrator's office; the committee proposed changing the name to urban renewal, adding more funding, and setting it up as a separate Urban Renewal Administration with its own regional offices. With respect to land use in renewal areas, the committee advocated "its logical best use. Overemphasis on housing for reuse should be avoided and the land should be put to industrial, commercial, institutional, public, and residential use, or any combination thereof."[39] These recommendations would free urban renewal from the bureaucratic influence of housing-oriented constituencies and spur cooperation between City Halls and downtown developers. The committee's report provided the basis for the 1954 Housing Act.

Similarly, the Advisory Committee on a National Highway Program's report, "A Ten-Year National Highway Program," summed up the desires of the highway lobby. Its five members included two senior investment bankers, the president of the country's largest private construction firm, a manufacturer of road construction equipment, and the head of the Teamsters Union. As Altshuler and his colleagues have noted, the Eisenhower administration had "particularly close ties to the automobile and

115

oil industries,'' and while its domestic policy concentrated on reducing federal expenditures, including those for public works, ''nonetheless, it prepared and submitted to Congress the enabling legislation for the largest domestic public works program in the history of the world: the interstate system.''[40]

Like the Housing Committee, the Highway Committee proposed a new and separate federal bureaucracy to advance the construction over ten years of a federally funded, but locally planned and built, limited-access highway system. It stressed that this system should be free to users and financed through $23 billion in federal gasoline tax revenues. While the proposal appealed to rural states, it also stressed the development which interstates would stimulate in metropolitan areas. The highway program would be administered through the then-predominantly Republican state governments.[41] This report provided the basis for the passage of the National Interstate and Defense Highway Act in 1956 and its companion, the Highway Revenue Act of 1956.

These committees and their proposals show how Eisenhower sought to reorganize the ''partnership'' which was evolving among local interests. In contrast to the New Deal, the Eisenhower administration sought an exclusive focus on assistance to dominant private sector organizations. It relegated public housing and its constituency among the central-city poor to its lowest postwar priority. Development agencies with the least political accountability to central-city constituencies, such as state highway departments, by contrast, gained the most during the Eisenhower years.

Eisenhower-Era Changes in the Program Delivery System

During the Eisenhower administration, three basic changes took place. First, congressional conservatives sought to eliminate public housing and managed to reduce the rate of construction to a small fraction of the numbers contemplated in the 1949 Housing Act. Second, the Housing Act of 1954 reinvigorated the urban renewal program, which had been stalled by a variety of organizational design problems. Finally, with support from northern urban Democrats as well as conservatives, the administration passed the interstate highway program and set up the highway trust fund to finance it.

The 1950s were not kind to public housing. Foes of the program occupied key congressional leadership positions which controlled housing legislation and appropriations. Eisenhower appointed a former Republican congressman who had voted against the 1949 Housing Act because of its public housing provisions to head the HHFA and a NAREB member to head the public housing program.

In a pattern which was repeated almost yearly, House conservatives chafed against the administration's modest construction proposals (35,000 units per year) and allowed them to remain only because the Senate would not pass omnibus housing legislation without them. Eisenhower, who wanted some units for relocation purposes, had to get northern urban Democratic votes to overcome the opposition of his own party's rank and file. In order also to get the votes of key, swing southern Democrats, the public housing program was altered over time to favor their districts. In contrast to these difficulties, FHA assistance to private, single-family housing construction expanded rapidly.[42]

Congress also thoroughly reorganized the urban renewal program through the Housing Act of 1954. Legal challenges, the difficulties of achieving complete clearance of urban sites, constraints on allowable reuses, and lack of private financing had hobbled the program since its enactment in 1949. By 1953, it had obligated only $53 million of its $300 million authorization. Eisenhower's 1953 Advisory Committee emphasized the need to get this program underway on a much larger scale.

The 1954 Housing Act shifted urban renewal from a nationally directed program focusing on housing to a locally directed program which allowed downtown businesses, developers, and their political allies, who had little interest in housing, to use federal power to advance their own ends.

The 1954 Act made the urban renewal program independent of other housing programs in HHFA, renamed it the Urban Renewal Administration, and decentralized its operations into seven re-

117

gional offices. It also provided an exemption from the "predominantly residential" use requirement, emphasized rehabilitation over clearance, and required the establishment of local advisory committees which would develop a "workable program." Finally, it also provided smaller cities with funds to hire planners, increased authorized funding by an additional $400 million, and made FHA and FNMA financing available especially for the residential structures to be built in renewal areas.[43]

In its initial phase, DSCUR had no field offices, and its location directly under the housing administrator had hampered the program's dealings with local redevelopment officials. By gaining status equal to the FHA and establishing seven regional offices, urban renewal officials could have much more extensive and responsive contacts with local developers and renewal agencies and would suffer correspondingly less oversight from housing-oriented central administrators. (By 1958, more than two-thirds of the agency's personnel was located in the field.)[44]

The requirement for establishing local, blue-ribbon, citizens' advisory committees also focused the program on the needs expressed by dominant local institutions. As Keith has pointed out, in the postwar years there was a significant

> emergence of associations of the power structure in major cities . . . dedicated to the revitalization and redevelopment of the urban centers. The forerunner of this trend was the Allegheny Conference in Pittsburgh . . . established primarily on the initiative of the Mellon interests. . . . Comparable organizations . . . began to appear in other cities like Philadelphia, Chicago, Cleveland, Detroit, St. Louis, San Francisco, Washington, Buffalo and New Haven.[45]

The 10 percent exemption from the "predominantly residential" requirement gave further notice that the Urban Renewal Administration would not ignore the interests of such groups. After the 1954 Act's passage, the URA sent out special teams to cultivate these new clients. Business supporters formed a national advocacy organization, ACTION, to propagandize on behalf of renewal.

With the deepening of urban renewal's central-city business

118

constituencies and its broadening to smaller cities, especially those located in swing southern congressional districts, its funding mounted steadily. The 1954 Act increased authorizations to $400 million for two years, while subsequent reauthorizations increased that amount by $350 million in 1957 and then into the billions by the early 1960s. (Democratic Congresses also widened the "predominantly residential" exemption again in 1959 and 1961.) The 1954 Act also established new FHA financing vehicles to deal with the reluctance of established financial institutions to invest in urban renewal areas.

The Eisenhower administration thus reformed the renewal process to make it more effective and responsive to local private sector needs and to widen its congressional support from districts containing small cities. Important political imperatives lay behind the changes. "The price paid for the increased interest and support of these elite groups," notes Feinstein, "was a further skewing of the renewal program away from a worst-first attack on slum areas . . . [toward] a focus upon downtown . . . upon hospitals and educational institutions . . . and upon aggregations on the order of New York's Lincoln Center."[46]

The enactment of the 1956 Interstate and Defense Highway Act and the 1956 Highway Revenue Act represented an even stronger and clearer step in the same direction. In 1955, only 22 percent of national highway expenditures went to urban highways; seven years later, the urban share had increased to 35 percent of a total amount which had tripled to $2 billion annually. As a result of the interstate program, "substantial highway investment was being focused for the first time on the inner, intensely developed portions of large urban areas."[47] Previous to 1956, most states spent little on urban highways and in many cases state legislation forbade state highway agencies from spending money in urban areas.[48] The 1956 Act permanently changed this situation and made state highway departments a major force in metropolitan development.

The interstate highway idea, like federal intervention into housing and urban renewal, had its origins in the New Deal. PWA and WPA funds had built a number of urban highways. The 1938 Federal Aid Highway Act had mandated a Bureau of Public Roads study called *Toll Roads and Free Roads*. The study concluded that a national system was necessary, that tolls would not and should not support it, and that therefore a major federal initiative would be required. The 1944 Highway Act had taken a small step in this direction by establishing the ABC system of ranking highways that took effect immediately after the war. This system set out not only the "U.S." routes which became the basic interstate routings (the "A" part of the system), but also mandated federal aid for urban highways for the first time (the "C" part of the system). To improve these designations, the Bureau of Public Roads released a detailed route map in 1955 which contained individual maps for one hundred urban areas, showing the approved interstate route locations. This document, known as the "Yellow Book," became an invaluable tool for convincing congressmen of the program's merits.[49]

Given tremendous interest group support, favorable public opinion, the previous studies, and Eisenhower's advocacy, enactment of the program was not really in question. The key issues concerned who was to get what and how it would be financed. It took Congress two years to sort out these details. Highway industry leaders who objected to increased highway user taxes and southern Democrats who opposed increased federal indebtedness initially defeated the measure by narrow margins in both houses during 1955.

In 1956, these problems were ironed out by financing the system on a pay-as-you-go basis out of dedicated federal taxes on gasoline, tires, and vehicle weights. The Yellow Book's guarantee that a majority of districts would get something from the Act also encouraged votes. The bill passed the House by 388 to 19 on the key vote, and the Senate by 89 to 1. The " 'highway lobby swarmed, trade association by corporation president, all over Capitol Hill' in support of the highway bill, and not a single major interest group actively lobbied against the legislation."[50] Thus the Eisenhower administration launched a program continued by subsequent Democratic administrations, which had as strong an impact on metropolitan form as any other federal urban program.

When completed in about 1990, the system will have cost over $114 billion, 90 percent of which will have been federal funds.

Eisenhower apparently discovered that nearly half the interstate funds would be spent in urban areas only by accident in 1959.[51] The Bureau of Public Roads and congressional advocates of his program, however, suffered under no such illusions. The interstate highway program provided extremely attractive federal financing from a dedicated trust fund whose revenues automatically grew as a result of the construction it financed. This new program worked through state highway agencies, which were typically biased against urban areas and dominated by civil engineers rather than socially oriented planners. These agencies worked through local elected officials in placing construction contracts, siting interchanges, procuring land, and the like. In contrast to the New Deal programs, the Eisenhower highway program thus built local political alliances based on dispersing population and physical investment away from the older central cities.

Within central cities, highway departments typically aligned interstates to create barriers between minority neighborhoods and areas they wished to preserve. For many years, they gave no relocation assistance to displaced tenants. They did, however, assist the growth of central business districts. Even more, they promoted the growth of suburban and new metropolitan areas. As a result, the interstate program provided a clear, conservative alternative to the New Deal urban development programs.

The Eisenhower administration did not dismantle the New Deal program structure, nor did it present a well-worked-out conservative alternative. But it did make significant changes in the overall program delivery structure. It reduced the housing commitment to central-city working populations, which had characterized the Democratic programs, and spread development benefits toward the suburbs and smaller, newer cities. Through the 1954 Housing Act, it oriented the urban renewal program toward central-city business interests and the needs of other dominant institutions like hospitals and universities. While this change had begun under the Democrats and was supported by them, Republicans hastened and completed it. With these changes, Eisenhower and his conser-

121

vative congressional allies sought to tailor Democratic programs to their own sources of electoral support. Given the Democratic control of Congress after 1954, Eisenhower's antipublic spending attitude and his lack of a clearly conservative urban strategy, his achievements were remarkably substantial.

THE NIXON-FORD ADMINISTRATIONS AND THE CONSERVATIVE ALTERNATIVE

As the previous chapter has shown, the development trends of the 1950s culminated in increasing division and conflict within the major cities during the 1960s. In response to these conflicts, the Great Society political entrepreneurs attempted to use new kinds of federal programs to bring formerly excluded constituencies into the Democratic party alongside the constituencies which had traditionally benefited from past Democratic federal urban programs. In the process, they sparked new kinds of conflict within the Democratic coalition, and not only on issues of racial justice, citizen participation, and Great Society legislation.

With his earlier training in anti-Communist invective, Richard Nixon was uniquely endowed with the skills required to mobilize conservative resentment against these conflicts. Just as Democrats had formulated new programs during their years out of power in the 1950s, Nixon and his conservative allies had developed a penetrating critique of liberalism during the 1960s. Nixon's New Federalism was a powerful and thoughtful attempt to reorganize federal intervention into urban development along conservative lines. It may have been, in Richard Nathan's phrase, a *Plot That Failed*, but it did have a remarkable impact on the federal program structure.

The Political Context of the Nixon-Ford Years

Like Eisenhower's 1952 and 1956 triumphs, Richard Nixon's wins in 1968 and 1972 "occurred largely in the context of candidates and issues, not parties."[52] The accumulation of conflicts within Democratic ranks weakened Humphrey against Nixon in

1968. Just as the Korean War hurt Stevenson's 1953 candidacy, the Vietnam War cut into Humphrey's support both from blue collar ranks and from educated professionals. Even more crucially, black protest and the inability of the Great Society to bridge the gap between blacks and whites pushed many descendants of the New Deal blue collar urban ethnics into the arms of Nixon and Wallace. It also put Nixon in a strong position in the South.

As Gary Wills has pointed out, Richard Nixon has been a genius at winning elections by mobilizing fear and resentment. In 1968 and 1972, he capitalized on the conflicts vexing the Democrats. He spoke out forcefully against those who wished to speed social change. As Ladd and Hadley have pointed out, "Large segments of the white bourgeoisie, including many who in the 1930s were associated with the Democratic working class, have adopted a position of resistance if not reaction."[53] Nixon combined these "positional conservatives" with traditional rural, southern, and upper-class sources of conservatism to compile first a narrow and then an overwhelming majority.

In 1968 and 1972, Nixon constructed an urban counterstrategy which gave him considerable support from major urban areas. Nixon combined an appeal to the white, Catholic, blue collar ethnics of the northern suburbs with an appeal to the middle-class whites of the newer southern and southwestern cities. From the first group he won enough votes to reduce the traditional Democratic majorities in the large, old central cities, and from the second he won absolute majorities.

Kevin Phillips has mapped the appeal of Nixon's conservative urban strategy in considerable detail, although he mistakes ideology for partisanship.[54] In the New York suburbs (Westchester, Nassau, and Suffolk counties, as well as Middlesex County in New Jersey), Democrats won considerably less than half the votes, and lost ground from the 1960 elections. In the Midwest, "the fast-growing middle class tracts surrounding Columbus, Cincinnati, Indianapolis, Chicago and Milwaukee gave Nixon better majorities in 1968 than they had in 1960."[55] These majorities canceled out Humphrey's central-city majorities sufficiently so

123

that with exurban votes, Nixon carried all the upper midwestern industrial states except Michigan.

Below the Mason-Dixon line, from Virginia to Southern California, the combination of Wallace and Nixon votes overwhelmed the Democrats, and in many instances Nixon won outright urban majorities (solidified in 1972 by Wallace's absence from the race). In 1968, Nixon "amassed considerable leads . . . in most of the major urban areas of Florida and Texas." Nixon lost Texas to Humphrey only because Wallace also got many urban Texas votes.[56] In the Southwest, Nixon won majorities in nearly every major city, including Los Angeles. By beating Humphrey 63 to 30 percent in Orange County and 57 to 36 percent in San Diego, Nixon overcame his losses in the northern part of the state. In the rest of the Southwest, metropolitan Phoenix and Albuquerque made their two states among the most pro-Nixon in the nation. As in other areas, the elimination of Wallace as a contender and the liberal candidacy of George McGovern in 1972 confirmed and extended these trends.

Richard Nixon thus entered the White House in 1969 with a well-established position against urban dissidence and a political obligation to the metropolitan constituencies which had given him the majority over Hubert Humphrey. Especially after 1972, this resonance between constituency and ideology, as vibrant in its own way as that between the central cities and the New Deal, provided Nixon with a mandate to square off against Democratic urban programs.

Like Eisenhower, Nixon faced a nominally Democratic Congress in which the conservative coalition gave him a "working majority." After the Republican low point of 1964, that party's delegation climbed almost fifty seats in 1966 and again in 1968, but remained about twenty-five seats shy of a majority. After a slight Republican dip in the 1970 off-year elections, Nixon's 1972 landslide reelection left the House with a balance between 192 Republicans and 243 Democrats.

Two-thirds of these Republican gains over the Great Society's Eighty-ninth Congress came from northern Democratic losses. Although eighteen southern Democratic seats shifted to the Republicans, their ideological outlook remained stable. Democratic Rules Committee chairman William Colmer of Mississippi, who had repeatedly thwarted urban legislation, was succeeded in 1972, for example, by his administrative assistant, Trent Lott, who ran as a Republican. The loss of three dozen northern Democratic seats to the Republicans was far more damaging than erosion in the South to Democratic urban programs' legislative base.

Between 1968 and 1974, therefore, President Nixon could count on the conservative coalition to give him majorities. Manley's analysis shows that "during Nixon's first term, in both the House and Senate, the Coalition's appearance reached all-time highs, and Coalition victories approached the high levels of the 1940s and 1950s."[57] The conservative coalition appeared on roughly four out of ten contested roll calls in both houses, and won over three-fourths of these votes.

But just as Eisenhower faced an increasingly resistant Congress after 1958, the 1974 off-year elections cost the Republicans almost fifty seats. Spurred by Watergate and the recession, northern and western Democrats picked up almost all of these seats. These victories gave the Democrats a 291 to 144 margin over the Republicans, producing a more Democratic House than even in 1964. More importantly, nonsouthern Democrats held 204 votes against 231 for Republicans and southern Democrats. Since thirty-seven southern Democrats and Republicans represented city districts, the 1974 elections were sufficient to give prourban legislators a bare majority in Congress. This abrupt and adverse shift forced the Ford administration to abandon legislative advocacy in favor of vetoing unwanted Democratic measures.

When the Nixon administration came into office in 1969, it faced an urban political arena populated with a host of federally inspired entities. The Great Society programs bypassed local government to create new organizations which it used as a lever to reform traditional local coalitions. In the process, the urban development agenda of the 1950s and early 1960s had been called into doubt in the older northern cities.

Floyd Hyde, Nixon's appointee to head the Model Cities Program, expressed concern about this impasse early in the new

125

administration: "The Federal government has undercut city government's authority by funding programs through independent agencies . . . or other non-city institutions, thereby sapping city government's capacity and discouraging it from assuming responsibility for most of the physical, social and economic problems of its residents." Hyde echoed the feelings of Domestic Council chief Patrick Moynihan and Nixon himself when he asserted the need to "reverse this trend."[58]

From the Nixon administration's political perspective, the Great Society programs had several defects. Obviously, they reinforced politically unfriendly constituencies. While central-city neighborhoods had given local and even national Democratic politicians many uncomfortable moments, they clearly voted for the Democrats. In both the South and the central cities, black activism of the 1960s has been highly correlated with subsequent Democratic voting behavior. Almost a quarter of the blacks elected to local office in the 1970s received their initial political training in the Community Action Program.[59] Many of the programs which Nixon inherited were therefore candidates for termination. Nixon also wished to remove the project area committees, environmental impact reviews, citizen participation mechanisms, and new social planning programs like Model Cities, which encumbered the development process.

Even more importantly, the Great Society federal programs had brought unwanted constituencies into the higher reaches of the federal government itself. The Nixon administration was openly hostile toward the various federal agencies which had "gone native." Not only OEO, but major portions of HUD, Labor, and other old-line cabinet departments were viewed as excessively under the influence of unfriendly—and uncontrolled—interest groups. Whatever legislative moves the administration made to alter the balance of power among local political interests would thus have to be accompanied by "a program designed to take power away from Federal government bureaucracies."[60]

The Nixon administration also had its own friendly local constituencies to reward. The categorical grant programs enacted during the 1960s had a strong, northern, big-city distributional bias. The Nixon administration wished to shift the focus of federal largesse toward more politically supportive regions, including the suburbs and southern and southwestern metropolitan areas. Although it is not known whether the White House used a computer terminal and detailed local voting data to devise its new aid formulas, such an effort would be quite consistent with the observed results.

The New Federalism: Reshaping the Intergovernmental Urban Program Delivery System

To restructure the federal grant-in-aid system, the Nixon administration had to overcome the opposition of those who benefited from the *status quo*. It did so by using a number of sticks and a number of carrots. To create a demand for new administration initiatives, it terminated some programs and impounded funds for others against the background of recessionary national economic policy. The moderate 1969–1970 recession and the severe 1974–1975 recession hit large central cities hard and aggravated their financial condition. While the administration felt these recessions were necessary to restrain inflation, they also had the effect of reasserting market discipline over groups seeking political control over urban development.

In this context, urban constituencies came to support any new federal program. Believing President Nixon's promise that general revenue-sharing money would not come at the expense of existing program titles, mayors thus lobbied for a measure which the administration wanted as the opening wedge for changing the whole intergovernmental grant process.[61]

The Nixon administration also offered inducements, termed "spreading" in Nathan's studies and "distributive localism" by Professor Samuel Beer.[62] Both general revenue sharing and the Community Development Block Grant (CDBG) Program "increased support for smaller city governments in general and also for larger cities in the South and West that were not active participants in the older categorical programs."[63] The New Federalism thus terminated some programs, established a climate ame-

127

nable to alternative programs, and sought to use them to redefine grant-system politics at both the local and Washington levels.

Terminating Great Society Programs

Richard Nathan has observed that "Nixon spokesmen often took a hard line" when they "opposed reliance on the kinds of quasi-governmental antipoverty agencies that had been established in the Great Society."[64] When the administration undertook a government-wide reduction in employment force, all of OEO's cuts came out of its community organizing manpower. As a congressman, the new OEO director, Donald Rumsfeld, had attacked the establishment of HUD as "another bureaucratic maze which would merely confuse the public, employ the faithful, and further waste taxpayer dollars."[65] He transferred such widely accepted OEO programs as Head Start and manpower training to other agencies. Congress resisted, however, specifying in the 1971 OEO reauthorization that "the administration could make no further transfer of programs. Funds for all 15 OEO categorical programs were earmarked to impede budgetary shifts or cutbacks by the White House."[66]

Congressional opposition only redoubled Nixon's desire to terminate the agency. Bolstered by the size of his 1972 reelection majority, Nixon announced that his budget for FY 1973 would contain no funds for OEO, and appointed a new OEO director "committed to physically dismantling the agency and thoroughly discrediting its programs."[67] Though Congress narrowly averted the actual termination of OEO, it was dismembered and the surviving local CAAs became largely service-providing agencies.

The Model Cities Program faced a similar fate. Nixon sought to strengthen mayoral control over wayward, federally funded activities. In some respects, Model Cities had sought to help mayors coordinate fragmented federal programs. The problem, of course, was that the Johnson administration had focused on the urban poor as consumers of federal policy, while Nixon had an entirely different set of constituencies in mind. As an aide to the new HUD assistant secretary for Model Cities put it, "We've got the right constituency and the wrong process for the liberals, and we've got the wrong constituency and the right process for the conservatives."[68] As a result, the effort by some new HUD officials to "scrape away the Johnsonian rhetoric and show that there's a lot of Republicanism in it" was ultimately doomed.[69]

By 1972, with community development revenue sharing clearly in the offing, the president blue-penciled HUD's Model Cities budget request. Congress appropriated $150 million to close out the program, and it became one of the ten HUD programs folded into the Community Development Block Grant.[70] Though the original Great Society commitment to spend $2.3 billion on the Model Cities was kept, most local jurisdictions chose not to continue the program from their CDBG funding.

After his landslide reelection, Nixon also suspended all federal housing subsidy programs in January 1973. He had previously vetoed HUD appropriations for these programs, but housing producers and their congressional allies had successfully expanded funding for the new programs contained in the 1968 Housing Act. Between 1969 and 1973, 1.6 million new households received federal housing assistance, more than had been received in the entire previous thirty-two-year history of public housing. A mounting scandal in Section 235 allowed Nixon to stop this trend by fiat for sixteen months pending the passage of his community development revenue-sharing bill.

Nixon's FY 1974 budget proposals also threw down the gauntlet. This budget proposed "significant reductions in federal expenditures on a host of categorical grant programs" and confirmed the mayors' "worst suspicions when it repeatedly indicated that the antipoverty program, public service employment, library assistance, and a host of social service programs were specified for phase out or reductions."[71] The administration had earlier promised that the $5.3 billion annual general revenue-sharing program would not be financed through cuts in other programs. By cutting $6.5 billion in one hundred programs, the FY 1974 budget infuriated the mayors and urban interest groups which had lobbied for the passage of general revenue sharing in 1972.

If urban interest groups thought Nixon's 1974 and 1975 budget

129

proposals were a "gigantic double cross," they found administration economic policies even more disturbing.[72] The administration's tight fiscal and monetary policies engineered a recession in 1969–1970, with recovery taking place in time for the 1972 landslide reelection. The second recession took place from late 1973 through 1975, and was the deepest economic decline since the Depression. Nixon's conservative economic advisers felt that only a steep recession could break the inflationary cycle.

These recessions hurt the northern central cities (many Sunbelt cities were unphased), increased unemployment as well as the demand for locally funded social services, and decreased local revenues.[73] The recession's impact was particularly severe in the biggest, oldest, northeastern central cities. These heartlands of the Democratic vote suffered substantial employment and population losses between 1970 and 1975. A number of them, like New York, narrowly skirted bankruptcy. Against this background of austerity and budgetary reduction, the administration proposed its "New American Revolution."

Implementing the New Federalism

While growing conflict between Congress and the president and the deepening Watergate affair prevented complete enactment of the New Federalism, several key components were passed between 1972 and 1974. Among them were general revenue sharing ($5.3 billion in its first year), the CDBG Program ($3.1 billion), CETA ($2.6 billion), and the Title XX Social Services Program ($2.2 billion). The Democratic landslide in the 1974 congressional elections and Carter's narrow victory over Ford in 1976 closed off this period of conservative reform. Nevertheless, substantial changes were made before it was over.

The General Revenue-Sharing proposal of 1972 was the flagship of Nixon's New Federalism. Although he could count on some conservative support for this measure in Congress, he faced opposition from the traditional lobby groups, like the AFL, NAHRO, the National Housing Conference, USCM, and NLC, which had a considerable stake in the existing grant programs. While these groups could all agree on the desirability of new money with no strings, they could not agree on an allocation formula for the funds. Combined with the resistance of key congressmen like Wilbur Mills, this was sufficient to stall the measure in 1970 and 1971.

Given mounting fiscal distress within the big cities, the appeal of Nixon's anti-Washington, prolocal government rhetoric, and the approach of the 1972 presidential primaries, pressure increased on the Democrats to support some form of revenue sharing. (Mills' presidential aspirations made him a convert.) The Democrats favored a program targeted to needy cities, not states. The two sides worked toward a compromise bill containing elements desired by both. With strong lobbying from the mayors, the resulting bill obtained a closed rule and passed with bipartisan support. In the crucial House vote, 223 favored the measure and 185 opposed it. This margin was achieved by combining Republicans (who favored it 113 to 57) and northern Democrats (89 to 69). Two-thirds of the southern Democrats opposed the measure. It thus passed because liberals and conservatives both supported it.[74] The measure drew liberal support despite the fact that it favored suburban jurisdictions, the newer cities of the South and Southwest, and state governments, all of which were largely Republican in the late 1960s.

The 1974 Community Development Block Grant Program carried this distributional change even further. With the impoundment of $12 billion in appropriated housing funds and a deepening recession in 1973 and 1974, housing starts (which had been over two million annually between 1971 and 1973) fell to 1.34 million in 1974. Despite its drawbacks from the point of view of categorical grant constituencies, the 1974 Housing and Community Development Act, with a three-year, $8.4 billion authorization, thus held an undoubted attraction. The 1974 HCDA folded ten categorical programs, including urban renewal, Model Cities, and water and sewer grants, into one single "pot" distributed according to a formula which favored population, poverty, and housing crowding. Another title reorganized and refunded the subsidized housing system.

131

As with the General Revenue-Sharing proposal, the president, Congress, and categorical grant interest groups disagreed over a number of issues. Differences included whether local entitlements would be granted automatically or be subject to HUD review, whether a "hold-harmless" provision would protect cities which had done well under the old grant system, and the manner in which the formula would be constructed. These disagreements thwarted congressional action in 1972 and 1973.

After winning concessions from the White House on many of these issues, urban lobby groups and congressional Democrats swung behind the measure. A "hold-harmless" provision ensuring that past beneficiaries would not face sharp reductions was the key to getting this support. (The hold-harmless provision would lapse after the 1976 elections, and the CDBG formula was thus obviously subject to revision depending on the outcome.) The Senate passed the measure 76 to 11, while the House voted 351 to 25. President Gerald Ford, an inveterate foe of urban programs, signed the measure two weeks after Nixon's departure, and soon some $3.1 billion annually was being distributed to twenty-five hundred cities with populations over fifty thousand.

Congress also passed two other block grant programs—the 1973 Comprehensive Employment and Training Act and the 1974 Title XX social services consolidation. Like CDBG, these programs did not go as far toward the "no-strings" automatic allocation as the Nixon administration would have liked. While formulas based on such factors as population, unemployment, and welfare case loads set target entitlements, local jurisdictions still had to submit grant applications subject to federal review to get the money. Both programs retained a diversity of program titles, each with its own eligibility requirements, funding and planning cycles, and reporting mechanisms.

Congressional majorities for these reforms to the grant system were achieved only after Republicans made significant concessions to central-city interest groups. Further, the impoundment issue polarized relations between President Nixon and Congress, as did the recession. According to one analyst, "Nixon's New Federalism had in many cases gone too far, too fast, and demanded too much from state and local chief executives. . . . It had provided too few incentives and guarantees . . . [thus] faltering as a domestic strategy."[75] More fundamentally, Watergate and the 1974 elections aborted further New Federalist initiatives. Ford spent the remainder of his term vetoing Democratic efforts to expand various urban program categories.[76]

Increasing White House Control over Cabinet Departments and Shifting Bureaucratic Conflict to the Local Level

The New Federalism also sought to wean the domestic cabinet departments from their urban clients and bring them under White House control while simultaneously shifting the locus of bureaucratic conflict from Washington back to the local level. Nixon thought that the departments resisted White House direction because they had become captives of their local—typically Democratic—clients. This tension was particularly apparent in Nixon's conflicts with Secretaries Romney at HUD and Finch and Richardson at HEW.

In his campaign against these conditions, Nixon enlisted the growing antipathy against unaccountable federal bureaucrats and their maze of fragmented, overlapping, and wasteful programs. His speeches repeated such ideas as "Good people cannot do good things with bad mechanisms, but bad mechanisms can frustrate even the noblest aims," "it is important that we move boldly to consolidate the major activities of the government," "local leaders often find it virtually impossible to relate Federal assistance programs to their own local development strategies," "we must 'shuck off' and 'trim down' social programs from the 1960s which have been failures largely because they 'threw money at the problems,' " and "the time has come to reverse the flow of power and resouces from the states and communities to Washington."[77] A clear political motive lay behind these sentiments. Nixon wanted to evict the constituencies he opposed from positions of influence in the federal bureaucracies.

His efforts met with only partial success. By shifting the decision-making power over federal urban development funds to the

133

local level, Nixon shifted conflict over resource allocation back onto Democratic big-city mayors. The 1973 mass transit amendment to the Highway Trust Fund, often pictured as a victory for urban liberals, had the same effect: it made no new funds available to local jurisdictions, but shifted the conflict over how to use existing funds onto local officials, thereby preserving the dominance of highway-oriented interests over national policy.[78]

Nixon's revenue-sharing proposals also effectively altered the constituency base to which HUD and other federal departments responded. The CDBG Program doubled the number of HUD client cities to include suburbs and the rapidly growing cities of the South and Southwest.

Nixon's efforts to exercise political control over the cabinet departments proved less successful.[79] By centralizing control over domestic policy in the White House, Nixon only increased the size of the Executive Office and bogged it down with operational decisions. Nixon's subsequent reaction, stillborn because of Watergate, was to reduce the White House staff and place trusted political agents into key department positions. Simultaneously, he proposed to reorganize the existing departments into a number of "super cabinet" areas. Both of these efforts were washed away, however, by the growing controversy over Watergate.

The cloud of Watergate has tended to obscure Nixon's tremendous legislative achievements. He had as much impact on the logic, politics, and distribution of federal urban development program grants as any Great Society liberal. Over seven years, Richard Nixon largely undid their work, killing or severely restricting most of the new agencies the Great Society created.

Nowhere was his success more evident than in the Community Development Block Grant Program. Great Society measures shifted the focus of urban renewal from downtown development toward neighborhood rehabilitation and subsidized housing construction. In many cases, local development agencies became more involved with neighborhoods than with downtown. In one swift move, CDBG removed federal support and legitimacy from many of these suspect policy directions.

The 1974 CDBG distribution formula was also significant. The original formula stressed qualities—poverty and population growth—which were more abundant in southern and southwestern cities than in the Northeast. If it had not been amended in 1977 and the "hold-harmless" provisions had expired, New England would have lost 37 percent of its funds while the West South Central region would have increased 203 percent. The share of funds going to large central cities would have dropped from 71.8 percent of HUD grants to 42.2 percent. In addition, various studies of urban "hardship" conditions showed that CDBG allocations were poorly correlated with need. Newark, New Jersey, which topped the list with a Nathan-Adams hardship index of 422, would have lost half its funding under the old formula, while Fort Lauderdale, with an index of 64, would have quadrupled its aid.

Despite the 1977 formula modification, cities which had not benefited from the categorical programs but which voted heavily for Nixon in 1972 made major gains under CDBG. Between 1971 and 1974, for example, grants to Dallas increased tenfold, Houston fourfold, Phoenix fourfold, and Birmingham fivefold, while most northeastern cities made little gains.[80] While the general revenue sharing, CETA, and Title XX formulas differ in their specifics, they had a similar impact.

CONCLUSION: THE CONSERVATIVE COUNTERPOINT TO
DEMOCRATIC URBAN PROGRAMS

The conservative counterpoint to Democratic urban liberalism had three impacts on the federal urban program delivery system. First, conservatives successfully undermined Democratic efforts to mobilize and channel central-city constituencies through federal intervention. From the termination of the WPA during the war years to Nixon's assaults on OEO and the Model Cities Program, even when conservatives have not been able to kill these programs, they have crippled their effectiveness as vehicles for political participation and political advocacy.

Second, conservatives have reorganized the remaining elements of the federal urban program delivery system to respond more effectively to the needs of dominant local institutions, particularly private sector institutions. Their efforts to do so have taken many forms. At some points, such as the War Production Board's massive recapitalization of the U.S. economy during World War II or FHA assistance to suburban housing construction, conservative intervention has worked directly through private sector institutions. At others, such as the 1954 Housing Act's reform of the urban renewal program, conservative efforts have redesigned government agencies to serve the needs of dominant private institutions and to remove claims from other constituencies.

Finally, by developing new components to the federal urban program delivery system, conservatives have shifted its center of political gravity away from central-city constituencies and toward more conservative constituencies in the suburbs and new metropolitan areas. This has constrained the former and stimulated the growth of the latter. In a sense, conservative national political entrepreneurs adapted the Democratic urban strategy to their own political ends by developing an antiurban thrust within the delivery system. WPB investment patterns laid down the basic physical capital investment which made possible the growth of suburbs and new metropolitan areas after the war. The interstate highway system, the pattern of FHA-assisted housing construction, and the CDBG allocation formula, not to mention the incidence of defense procurements, reinforced this pattern of growth. In contrast to the emphasis which urban liberal Democrats developed, conservative Republican political entrepreneurs used federal urban programs to favor growth in conservative constituencies.

In reaching toward these goals, conservatives faced the same kinds of constraints which governed the efforts of the urban liberals. Just as liberals had to compromise their programs to get support from Republicans and southern Democrats, or, at any rate, reduce their opposition, conservative entrepreneurs have also had to engage in horse trading with liberals to get majority votes. One consequence of this fact was that, contrary to what might be expected, the federal urban grant system did not contract under conservatives. Indeed, under Richard Nixon, an ambitious conservative innovator, federal urban program expenditures rose even more rapidly than during the Great Society. He was willing to spend money to implant fundamentally new concepts.

Conservative successes made matters difficult for the Democrats in a number of ways. Obviously, they reduced the political efficacy of federal urban programs for Democrats, and made urban program reform a high priority for in-coming Democratic administrations. Conservative successes also made the internal conflict within the Democratic coalition more acute by preventing Democratic programs from delivering what urban liberal Democrats had promised to their central-city working-class constituents. Conservatives made sure that public housing would never provide ''a decent home and suitable living environment'' for central-city families and that urban renewal would spur downtown development rather than neighborhood rehabilitation. The search for support from powerful local program beneficiaries might have pushed Democrats in these directions in any case, but the conservative swings in national politics certainly hastened the speed with which they embraced these interests.

By fostering metropolitan development trends which dissolved the core constituencies which had made the New Deal possible, the conservative counterpoint also aggravated the long-term developmental crisis facing the Democratic party. The gradual emergence of a conservative urban counterstrategy based on aid to the suburbs and newer metropolitan areas directly challenged the viability of the Democratic urban strategy and indeed of the older central cities themselves. Conservative policy initiatives have heightened the competitive advantage of the suburbs and new metropolitan areas. This worsened economic conditions in the older central cities, heightened their fiscal distress, and limited the scope of action open to liberal political leaders within them. Conservative programs also reinforced the private sector movement away from jurisdictions where challenges arose to progrowth politics, to those, like the southwestern cities, where they did not. Conservative political gains thus came at the cost of heightened economic and fiscal distress for the system of cities as a whole.

The conservative counterpoint also added to the irrationality, internal inconsistency, and lack of political accountability of the

137

federal urban program delivery system. By undercutting Democratic programs, conservatives reduced the delivery system's responsiveness to the beneficiaries for whom it was initially designed. Since conservatives added new programs more easily than they could terminate old ones, programs increasingly worked at cross purposes. During the periods of conservative ascendancy, the number of demoralized and crippled programs also increased, subsequently burdening Democrats as well as Republicans. Over time, this build up of bureaucratic ineffectiveness and lack of accountability has become one of the system's primary problems and one that, despite considerable rhetoric about efficiency and reorganization, neither liberals nor conservatives have been able to resolve.

While the conservative urban counterstrategy debilitated Democrats and helped Republicans win the presidency, it has not enabled them to consolidate a permanent national majority. A principal reason is that Republican policy initiatives have done for the Democrats what they have not been able to do for themselves, namely, unite the diverse and conflicting constituencies within the Democratic party. Attacks on program beneficiary groups and recessionary national economic policy have repeatedly mobilized the central-city voters needed for Democratic victories in national elections. Truman, Kennedy, and Carter all benefited from the tendency of conservative political entrepreneurs to provoke a liberal urban reaction.

Forging Progrowth Coalitions in Urban Politics: Boston and San Francisco

1. INTRODUCTION

If the analysis of how progrowth coalitions came to be an organizing force in local and national Democratic politics must begin with why national political entrepreneurs used federal programs to intervene in local politics, it must end with how local political entrepreneurs put them to use.

Under the Democrats, federal intervention was focused on building new kinds of local Democratic political coalitions around new kinds of government institutions and practices. Democratic political entrepreneurs hoped by this means to strengthen their national power. Local cases must obviously be examined to see how this strategy of intervention worked out.

The highly decentralized method of intervention also requires the examination of local cases. The federal government did not—indeed it could not—intervene directly. Instead, it operated indirectly, as a kind of "banker government," funding local agencies to conduct national programs. The federal government therefore ceded a tremendous amount of discretion and control over its programs to local political actors who, in a sense, completed the construction of the intergovernmental program delivery system. The federal government provided some powerful tools, and designed them to achieve political as well as economic change at the local level, but in the final analysis local actors were the ones who put these tools to use. Their distinctive concerns and interests had considerable impact on the shape and effect of these programs. These local concerns led to outcomes which differed from those

139

which national advocates of federal urban development programs had in mind.

This leads to the final reason for descending to the local level. So far, we have looked only at the federal penetration of the urban political arena. Only by looking at the consequences can we begin to see how local politics, aggregated across the system of cities, had a reciprocal influence on national politics and national policy.

Boston and San Francisco typify those large old cities which, though once dominated by blue collar economies and ethnic politics, federal programs have helped to transform into postindustrial administrative centers. This was the class of cities for which these programs were designed. The two cities differ in many ways, of course. Boston developed long before San Francisco, was more heavily influenced by waves of Irish and Italian immigrants during the second half of the nineteenth century, and built up a larger manufacturing base than San Francisco. As a result, Boston developed a strong tradition of machine politics while the other Bay Area has had a reform political tradition.

The similarities between the two cities dominate these differences, however. Both cities served as major ports and built up the warehousing, wholesaling, and processing activities associated with that function. Both absorbed streams of immigrants who went to work in these industries and became blue collar ethnic cities. As a result, these two cities shared many characteristics with other old cities of the Northeast. Because they were early centers of trade and commerce, both cities also developed strong banking, business service, and corporate headquarters institutions. Boston and San Francisco are also richly supplied with the nonprofit and public service institutions which have become increasingly economically dominant since World War II.

Boston and San Francisco thus represent outstanding examples of the transformation of old cities into postindustrial administrative and service centers. This fundamental similarity reflects a remarkably parallel sequence of political developments in the two cities between the Depression and the late 1960s. Both cities experienced declines in blue collar employment and residential population between 1930 and 1958, which, in turn, caused real

140

estate values to decline. The prevailing political leaders in both cities seemed unwilling or unable to respond to these and other signs of "blight." Although Boston was more clearly marked by patronage politics and partisanship, the political systems of both cities seemed to be experiencing a kind of political exhaustion.[1]

In both cities, a progrowth political coalition emerged out of these conditions which engineered the land-use changes and public investments necessary for new kinds of institutions to become dominant. Both in Boston and San Francisco, business leaders formed a consensus about the kinds of changes needed in the local government development agenda, and joined forces with innovative political leaders to put these changes into effect. After 1958, these joined economic and political forces built powerful new development agencies in both cities, attracted nationally known development administrators to head them and outside capital to fund them, and implemented ambitious plans for redeveloping central business districts and the adjacent strategic neighborhoods.

These progrowth coalitions brought together a variety of constituencies into what Robert Salisbury has called "a new convergence of power."[2] Among them were downtown business elites, ambitious political leaders seeking to modernize urban politics, middle class, good government reform groups, the professional city planners to whom they turned for advice, a powerful new stratum of public administrators, and private development interests, including developers, lenders, builders, and the construction trades.

Many differences divided these constituencies, and they came into conflict with each other almost as often as they cooperated. In the case of downtown business interests, for example, it took years in both cities even to develop an internal consensus on the need for public intervention and the kinds of projects to be undertaken. It was even more difficult to negotiate a joint agenda which could unite different constituencies. Yet on the crucial points, this agenda was ultimately forged.

Political entrepreneurs in Boston and San Francisco gradually overcame the disagreements among these constituencies and constructed progrowth political coalitions during the 1950s. These coalitions came to power in both cities in the late 1950s. Following Robert Moses' dictum that city-building should not be undertaken "by the Vestal Virgins of long-haired planning but by administrators driving persistently at limited objectives and reaching them,"[3] both these cities began ambitious urban renewal programs headed by two nationally known development administrators, Edward M. Logue and M. Justin Herman. While they successfully executed these programs, they also triggered new conflicts in urban politics which ultimately undermined progrowth politics.

2. THE FORMATION OF A CORPORATE DEVELOPMENT AGENDA AGAINST A BACKGROUND OF ECONOMIC DECLINE AND POLITICAL EXHAUSTION

Economic Decline

Between World War II and 1960, Boston and San Francisco were characterized by rapid suburban growth, declining central-city population and employment, stagnant central-city real estate values, and an influx of minorities, particularly blacks, into central-city neighborhoods.

As peninsulas, Boston and San Francisco were prevented from annexing peripheral growth even sooner than other old cities, and thus both contain only small fractions of metropolitan area population. While these centers declined between 1950 and 1960, the surrounding areas grew rapidly.

In Boston, suburban population increased by 50 percent, from two to three million persons, during the 1950s. Much of this population growth was spurred by Route 128, a key circumferential freeway, constructed between 1949 and 1952 as the first element of the region's projected freeway system.[4]

Route 128 attracted the region's growing electronics industry, including the Mitre Corporation, Raytheon, and branches of such firms as AVCO and General Electric. Between March 1954 and June 1956, sixty-eight new plants with 4.5 million square feet of space were built along Route 128. By 1963, the number had grown to 400 new plants. Much of this growth was spawned from MIT's

142

federally funded research activities at the Lincoln Lab and the Instrumentation Lab, also located along Route 128.[5] MIT, the individual companies, the old-line Brahmin banks which financed them, and development companies like Cabot, Cabot and Forbes found such locations preferable to central Boston.

As a result, suburban employment grew 22 percent to three-quarters of a million, while Boston's employment dropped 7.7 percent from 312,000 to 288,000. More than a quarter of this metropolitan growth occurred in the electronics industry, and 21 percent of the jobs in this sector went to professional and technical workers. Printing and publishing, Boston's leading industry, lost ground slightly during the decade, and other industries, such as food processing, plummeted.

The San Francisco Bay Area experienced an even stronger thrust toward suburban development during the 1950s. The New Deal constructed two key elements of the regional transportation infrastructure, the Bay Bridge and the Golden Gate Bridge, while War Planning Board investments doubled the region's employment in just five years.

The wartime experience with central-city plants convinced Bay Area business leaders that postwar industrial expansion should be located in the suburbs. A 1946 pamphlet produced by the California State Reconstruction and Reemployment Commission captured their sentiment. Managers of small new plants in the Santa Clara Valley, it noted, "testify that their employees are more loyal, more cooperative, more productive workers than those they have had in the big cities." As a result, major firms found "they could work better in a dozen small country factories than in one immense big city plant."[6] In a 1948 debate before the Commonwealth Club, a San Francisco banker echoed this sentiment: "Labor developments in the last decade may well be the chief contributing factor in speeding regional dispersion of industry. . . . Large aggregations of labor in one [central city] plant are more subject to outside disrupting influences, and have less happy relations with management, than in smaller [suburban] plants."[7]

The 1950s translated these beliefs into action. While San Francisco's employment remained constant at 331,000, the Bay Region's suburban employment grew 38 percent to three-quarters of a million. Major auto production plants moved from increasingly black Richmond and Oakland to rural, white Fremont; across the Bay in Santa Clara Valley, acres of orchards disappeared under the rapid expansion of the electronics industry and defense plants, many of which had begun during World War II. Stanford's Dean of Electrical Engineering, Frederick Terman (former head of the World War II MIT Radiation Laboratory), lured government contracts to such university-spawned firms as Fairchild Semiconductors and Hewlett-Packard. The University of California operated classified military research in its Lawrence/Livermore facilities in the East Bay suburbs.

The central-city economies of Boston and San Francisco contrasted markedly with this suburban boom. The 1950s provided a picture of commercial and industrial decline with the increasing presence of "blighting" lower-class minority groups and a lack of business confidence and investment even in the central business districts. Boston proper did not really recover from the Depression until the 1960s. Between 1950 and 1960, the city's population declined 13 percent from 801,000 to 697,000. Its employment also dropped 8 percent to 288,000. The 1965 General Plan tried to put the best face on these numbers by noting that "postwar blight and decline in Boston's population have temporarily, at least, weakened the growth potential of Downtown retail."[8]

This economic decline influenced both the Boston central business district (CBD) and the inner ring of old, dense, ethnic neighborhoods, such as Roxbury/North Dorchester, the South End, Charlestown, and South Boston. About half the city's population decline came from these four neighborhoods. Roxbury and the South End experienced an influx of blacks, which hastened the whites' departure and raised fears of declining property values. According to Boston's 1950 General Plan, 1,100 of Boston's 16,000 acres of residential land were severely substandard and deserving of clearance. These acres were concentrated in the South End, Roxbury, Charlestown, and South Boston. Remarking on the West End, which became the city's first slum clearance project, the 1950 Plan observed that "such an environment undoubtedly impairs the mental and physical health of its inhabitants."[9]

The South End provided a compelling example of neighborhood blight in Boston. Its total population fell by almost half between 1950 and 1960. In 1950, the population was 74 percent white and highly ethnic; 18 percent of the population had been born outside the United States. By 1960, the population was only 60 percent white. Located near the CBD, it was the densest and poorest neighborhood in Boston. Many of its residents lived in the neighborhood's 1,350 rooming houses. One contemporary profile described the neighborhood housing stock as

> consisting of small apartments or single rooms on upper floors of dingy, century-old buildings in which a single bathroom and toilet are shared by from two to ten other tenants. Yard space is at a minimum. . . . Parking is scarce. . . . High volumes of through traffic and truck traffic, excessive crime and vice, excessive alcoholism, juvenile delinquency . . . and dirt, filth, disorder, irresponsibility, and social abnormality everywhere are in evidence.[10]

Eight out of ten structures had been built before 1900; 22 percent were described as dilapidated, and another 43 percent needed major repairs.

The advancing decay of neighborhoods like the South End made the future of the central business district somewhat questionable. As the 1950 General Plan noted, construction had fallen off sharply in Boston. "Nothing since 1931 can approach the volume of new work undertaken annually during the boom period of the 1920s."[11] Between the 1920s and 1959, not a single office building was constructed.

Boston's antiquated mixture of wholesaling and retailing activities and nonconforming uses impeded CBD investments. "The proof of this contention," a city administrator noted, could be found in "the constantly decreasing valuation of real property, the loss of population and the lack of new construction to offset the deterioration of the uneconomic types of space built for the needs of another generation."[12] Boston's total real estate valuation declined 28 percent from a pre-Depression high of $1.8 billion to $1.3 billion in 1960.[13]

San Francisco did not present as uniform a picture of decline during the 1950s. Its population declined from 775,000 to 740,000 during the decade, while its labor force remained constant at 331,000 jobs. The number of whites dropped 13 percent, however, while the number of minorities increased 43 percent. In employment, the city's traditional manufacturing industries, wholesaling, and the waterfront declined heavily, but were offset by CBD gains. Banking employment, for example, nearly doubled during the 1950s, but maritime employment dropped by one-quarter.[14]

San Francisco's oldest and most centrally located ethnic neighborhoods reflected this decline in blue collar employment. In 1945, the San Francisco City Planning Commission analyzed the housing stock data which had been collected by the WPA real property inventory in 1939 and 1940, and found that in large parts of the districts around the CBD, almost the entire housing stock was blighted. "The future of this once valuable property will be dark and uncertain," their report warned, "until the old structures can be scrapped and attractive new buildings adapted to modern needs can be built on the land."[15] (This statement captioned a picture of two magnificent examples of Victorian "carpenter's gothic.")

Because it was ideally located on a rise just to the west of the Civic Center and the city's commercial core, and because it had become the focal point for black and Japanese migration to San Francisco, the Western Addition drew particular attention as a center of blight in San Francisco. A 1947 pamphlet produced by the San Francisco Planning and Housing Association unwittingly revealed the middle-class bias against the Western Addition. The study, entitled "Blight and Texas," contrasted it against the middle-class Marina district, which it found "clean and bright." The Western Addition, it charged, "is not white. It is gray, brown, and an indeterminant shade of dirty black." The area constituted "an unfortunate blot on a proud escutcheon."[16]

A more careful 1947 study by planning consultant Mel Scott found that the Western Addition had "rapidly deteriorated into a low-rent, substandard area" where assessments had "dropped an average of 50 percent in many residential blocks.'' It was populated by ''a mixture of races and nationalities,'' although ''during World War II the Negro population of the area increased so rapidly that many persons now refer to it as a colored district.'' Scott's report objected to the area's ''indiscriminate mixture of commercial, industrial, residential, and institutional uses,'' the ''rear dwellings, sheds, and all kinds of odd structures filling the backyards,'' and the 35 square blocks ''in which more than half of the dwelling units were in need of major repairs or were unfit for use.'' The report detailed many social pathologies, including juvenile delinquency, infant mortality, and vice which it held stemmed from these ''squalid, dispiriting'' physical conditions.[17]

As in Boston, neighborhood conditions in the area around the San Francisco CBD slowed investment within it. Immediately adjacent to the CBD sat a wholesale produce market. It was a congested, filthy, low-rise impediment to the CBD's expansion. As the port had declined as a break-bulk point for shipping, the many warehouses ringing the downtown area had also become obsolete. As in Boston, central-city construction was slow in the 1950s. Only one major office was built between 1930 and 1958.

San Francisco, like Boston, thus suffered both blight and decline in its inner neighborhoods and obsolete land uses which impeded CBD investment. Though San Francisco's blight was not as severe as Boston's, it was similar. As in Boston, San Francisco's real estate values fell 32 percent from their height in the 1920s to their low point in 1950. Although San Francisco's real estate values rebounded before those of Boston, it contained a seriously undermaintained and often dilapidated housing stock, increasingly inhabited by minority groups, in close proximity to downtown. Despite concerns about these conditions, neither city's elected officials seemed capable of responding to them.

Political Exhaustion

Three conditions impeded the ability of city government in Boston and San Francisco to reshape city land-use patterns and stimulate new private investment in the years after World War II. Government in both cities was fragmented, weak, and mired in

147

patronage politics. This political culture produced leadership which was not likely to champion an aggressive new development agenda. Second, though the tax base which financed city government contracted between 1930 and the 1950s, city payrolls and the demand for public investment were expanding. Just when the deferred needs of two decades were being faced, city finances took an unpromising turn. Both cities, and particularly Boston, already had high tax rates, which came under attack from the business community. Thus even if local political systems had produced political leadership supportive of a new development agenda, the prevailing fiscal resources could not finance it, at least without severe cuts in other budget components.

Finally, postwar Boston and San Francisco inherited a tradition in which government bowed to private-market land-use decisions. City government lacked the organized capacity to intervene in the land market. The early efforts to implement the 1949 Housing Act had bogged down in inexperience, legislative imperfections in program design, and the absence of separate renewal authorities.

In Boston, the urban renewal program was initially lodged in the Housing Authority, with an interdepartmental coordinating committee making many important decisions—or rather nondecisions. In San Francisco, urban renewal activities were initially undertaken by the poorly staffed Department of City Planning, and later by a Redevelopment Agency which conducted its activities through work orders to other departments which saw it as a competitor and, consequently, were often uncooperative.

These three conditions—lack of political leadership, lack of fiscal capacity, and lack of a powerful and independent development agency—added up to a political analog to the "obsolete" land-use patterns which hindered new development in central Boston and San Francisco. Indeed, both cities entered the 1950s with considerable mutual suspicion between Downtown and City Hall.

Boston

In Boston, the Brahmin business elite commanded the high ground from their State Street banks and the state capitol on

Beacon Hill. Republicans controlled the governorship and both houses of the Massachusetts legislature, with few exceptions, from the Civil War to 1949. During these years, Boston's Yankees had conducted political guerilla warfare on their Irish adversaries down the hill at City Hall. State legislation had removed City Hall control from the police department, auditing power over city finances, sewer and water system construction, the port, and the Boston transit system, vesting them in special bodies over which the Republicans governor had appointive influence.

In 1949, the legislature also reformed the city's charter, giving Boston's citizens the choice of city manager government or mayoral government with a primary election for that office. (Previously, Boston lacked a primary, and Mayor Curley had won repeatedly by pluralities rather than majorities; he had even put up false candidates to split his opponents' votes.) Boston chose to retain strong mayoral government. The 1949 reform continued the nonpartisanship first enacted in 1909 and abolished district election of city councillors, thus further weakening the centralized political organization.[18]

Boston's fragmented political system produced an individualistic one party, or nonparty, politics in which each elected official curried his own following with whatever perquisites his particular office afforded. For Mayor Curley, this included the property tax "abatement racket," in which "Curley used to order his assessors to add a million or so to the assessments of various large properties." The owners would then apply for an abatement through a lawyer well connected at City Hall, who would receive an ample fee for successfully handling the case. Much of this fee, in turn, would fuel Curley's political operations.[19] Such practices obviously poisoned relations between the mayor and the business community.

In 1947, Curley went to jail after being convicted of mail fraud, and the state legislature passed an act making John Hynes, then city clerk, acting mayor. (As the city council president was also under indictment at the time, he was passed over.) Hynes defeated Curley in 1949, and was reelected over Curley in 1951 and Senator John Powers in 1955. Hynes "created the impression that he was an efficient, devoted, and honest mayor," and took steps to initiate

149

Boston's urban renewal process.[20] Hynes made certain the West End project, which Italian-American city councillors opposed, moved through the demolition stage, and was also instrumental in convincing the Prudential Insurance Company to undertake the first major commercial redevelopment project in Boston, the Prudential Center. These efforts encouraged financial support from the Boston business community for Hynes and votes from middle-class Republicans, who were enough to tip the balance in a race between two Democrats.

Though Hynes favored the kinds of redevelopment projects sought by major Boston businessmen, he did not entirely depart from the patterns Curley had established. A young lawyer, Jerome Rappaport, had organized the New Boston Committee to generate business support for Hynes in 1951. The committee's efforts were undermined, however, "when Rappaport, the idealistic young lawyer, began appearing in tax abatement cases," which caused "cynical comment and further loss of morale."[21]

Rappaport was subsequently named developer of the West End renewal project, and was sold land which had cost the city $7.39 a square foot for only $1.37 a square foot. This gave renewal a bad political smell. Although Hynes established a Redevelopment Authority in 1957, it had only seventeen employees and a budget of only $260,000. Its activities continued to be mired in interdepartmental conflict. The city's fiscal condition also continued to deteriorate through the 1950s. In 1957, when Hynes sought to refinance the city's debt with a $45 million loan from the state, the banking community required him to reduce the number of city employees and begin to equalize business property assessments.

In 1959, Hynes announced that he would not run for reelection. Senator John E. Powers, recently elected president of the state Senate, became the leading candidate to succeed him. Powers had served twenty-one years in that body as a strong advocate of organized labor; in 1957, he had led the campaign which defeated Governor Furcolo's proposal for a state sales tax which the business community strongly wanted. As a powerful, regular Democrat, Powers gave every indication of being as dominant—and some charged as corrupt—a mayor as Curley had been. At the end of the 1950s, after a decade of central-city decline and at best halting efforts by a relatively friendly mayor to launch a redevelopment program, the Boston business elite was dismayed by the prospect of Powers' election.

San Francisco

Though San Francisco's political history during the 1940s and 1950s was more conservative—the electorate put Republicans rather than Democrats into the nonpartisan mayor's office—it was surprisingly similar to Boston's. "Sunny Jim" Rolph, mayor between 1912 and 1931, was cut from the same kind of old-fashioned mold that produced Curley. He was a populist who attacked the Southern Pacific and other big businesses while building public works and handing out patronage to his supporters. His successors Angelo Rossi (1931–1943) and Elmer Robinson (1947–1955) cared little for modern management and instead built power by closely supervising (and some charged benefiting from) the city's vice interests.

According to one observer, Mayor Robinson, formerly a judge, "was a professional politician of the smoke-filled-room school," who "didn't do the town any harm, [but] didn't do it much good either." George Christopher, a city councilman who challenged Robinson's reelection in 1951 but lost by a small margin, attacked Robinson for "more politically-inspired expenditures than any other administration . . . the result [of which] is an all-time high in the city tax rate. . . ." The closeness of Robinson's win prevented him from running for governor, and in 1955, Republican George Christopher, owner of a dairy company and member of the Board of Supervisors, decisively beat Democrat George Reilly, "an old-time fixture at the city's political trough," by 162,280 to 77,084—with help from many of the city's leading business contributions.[22]

Robinson had given one of the board seats on the San Francisco Redevelopment Agency (SFRA) to an optometrist who had threatened to run against him in 1951. Another of his appointees was a private detective. (The SFRA had been established in 1951 to

151

begin work on the Western Addition project as recommended by Mel Scott's 1947 report to the city.) In 1953, according to Allan Temko, architectural critic for a San Francisco newspaper, "a political quarrel erupted between political hacks and planners which resulted in the resignation of James E. Lasch, director of the Redevelopment Agency."[23] Lasch went on to head ACTION, which national business leaders had set up to propagandize for urban renewal. At the time, Supervisor Christopher had chided Robinson's "refusal even to investigate the circumstances behind the Agency's chaotic action or to listen to the appeals of responsible San Francisco business and civic organizations that he sweep his appointed troublemakers off the Agency."[24] Instead of heeding this challenge, Robinson appointed "Eugene J. Riordan, an elderly appraiser and a gentleman of the old school but with no evident qualifications for so demanding a post," new director of the Agency.[25]

Two examples show, however, that urban renewal continued to be "snarled in the same net of red tape, incompetence, and apathy" during George Christopher's first term (1955–1959) as under the Robinson administration. (Christopher did not replace Riordan.) In 1956, James D. Zellerbach, head of the Crown-Zellerbach paper products company, had joined with stockbroker Charles Blyth to form a committee to promote urban renewal. The Blyth-Zellerbach Committee's first priority concerned the produce market adjacent to the financial district. According to Temko, this "badly blighted nest of low buildings belonged to the nineteenth century in mood and location." It was rat-infested and jammed with trucks, and yielded only $250,000 in property taxes for 50 prime acres in the heart of the city. The B-Z Committee financed an initial study to redevelop the area which the Redevelopment Agency and Mayor Christopher heartily endorsed.[26]

In the event, numerous problems cropped up. Some of the city's leading citizens, including Temko, strongly objected to Skidmore, Owings and Merrill's preliminary designs. Some produce merchants did not want to be displaced, and the rest could not agree on an alternate site for the produce market (Christopher wanted it to remain within the city limits, while others wanted to move it out). In 1956, holdover Redevelopment Agency appointees from the Robinson era refused to issue bonds which Christopher sought to finance the market's relocation.

New York developer William Zeckendorf had promised to finance all further planning costs for the project in return for control over the development rights. Redevelopment Agency chairman Joseph Alioto had publicly backed Zeckendorf, feeling that neither the city government nor its local developers were likely to provide the money on their own. (The SFRA had only a few staff members and was relying on other departments to do its work.) The planning director and the Planning Commission chairman strongly opposed giving an outsider control over a project which was so vital to the city, however, and Christopher ultimately sided with them. Thus the redevelopment project that was physically and politically closest to downtown remained tied up in political entanglements.[27]

Red tape and scandal also stymied the city's other project, the Western Addition A-1 renewal area. Though the Board of Supervisors had approved the project before the passage of the 1949 Housing Act, The SFRA had moved slowly in acquiring properties. California's enabling legislation hampered land-taking by eminent domain, and the SFRA could not get the city attorney's office to expedite its condemnation suits.

In this environment, speculators moved into the Western Addition, acquiring property from elderly absentee owners and then negotiating favorable settlements from the city. Realtor Chester MacPhee, who, as supervisor, had chaired the urban renewal committee which designated the A-1 project and who had lobbied for the passage of the state redevelopment act, turned out to be one of the speculators. MacPhee had been a strong ally of Christopher's on the board, and when the office came open in 1958, Christopher appointed MacPhee to the powerful position of chief administrative officer. MacPhee, therefore, would control such departments as public works, building inspection, and real estate, and would sit *ex officio* on the Planning Commission. Unbeknown to Christopher, MacPhee was a stockholder and director of the Del-Camp Investment Corporation, which "had systematically

153

acquired some 45 buildings in the [Western Addition project] area and was demanding exorbitant prices from the city."[28] The disclosure of these ties forced MacPhee's resignation in late 1958.

These events justified the *San Francisco Chronicle*'s characterization of the SFRA as the firm of "Dawdle, Dawdle, Bumbling and Pokery, specialists in deceleration."[29] In 1958, on the eve of his reelection campaign, Christopher finally gained control over the Redevelopment Agency. In the same year, the Agency's elderly director, Eugene Riordan, also retired, setting the stage for reorganizing the Agency. Just as in Boston, with the end of Mayor Hynes' tenure in office in 1960 and the threatening candidacy of John Powers, the San Francisco business leadership faced a crucial political turning point for its redevelopment agenda in the 1959 Christopher reelection campaign.

Formation of a Business Consensus

Boston and San Francisco have relatively tightly knit business communities, with the major corporations interlocked through the largest banks and tied to old-line law firms. Typically, the descendants of the families that acquired industrial wealth during the nineteenth century have moved away from management of the industrial firms to become stockbrokers, investment bankers, lawyers, and philanthropists. From these positions, and from the boards of trust companies, insurance companies, and other capital pools, they and their trust managers have preserved old family wealth and extended it into new directions.

In Boston, for example, Charles Coolidge, a partner in the law firm of Ropes, Gray, and a former member of the Harvard Corporation, served as the board chairman of the Mitre Corporation, while Charles Francis Adams, whose provenance extends back through the founder of the Atchison, Topeka, and Santa Fe to the nation's early presidents, served as chief executive officer of Raytheon, one of the first firms to develop along Route 128. Cabot, Cabot and Forbes, which developed almost half the sites around 128, was also closely associated with old wealth.

In San Francisco, "business and civic activities are concen-

154

trated within a few square blocks of the downtown area. Most of her leaders are on a first-name basis with each other.''[30] Just as Boston's elite revolves around the Somerset and other such clubs, the Pacific Union Club and the Bohemian Club bring together San Francisco's business elite. The downtown area houses the nation's first, eleventh, twelfth, and twenty-third largest banks, its largest public utility (Pacific Gas and Electric), one of its largest railroads (Southern Pacific), and more than a hundred large national corporations, including Levi-Strauss, Del Monte, Standard Oil of California, Bechtel, and Crown-Zellerbach.

During the 1950s, Boston and San Francisco business and nonprofit institutional leaders slowly organized a central-city development agenda on a number of levels. They formed elite and mass advocacy organizations, such as the "Vault" and the Boston College Citizen Seminars in Boston and, in San Francisco, the Blyth-Zellerbach Committee and the San Francisco Planning and Urban Renewal Association (SPUR). They also created broad support within "informed opinion" by conducting numerous planning studies. By the end of the 1950s, these efforts had generated a clear critique of the urban development impasse, an action agenda, and organizations capable of advocating that agenda.

Boston

In Boston, the dean of Boston College's School of Business Administration took the lead in conducting a dialogue among diverse elements of that city's business community. BC's Citizen Seminars began in 1954, and brought together business and political leaders to discuss Boston's fiscal, economic, and political problems. Funded by a Ford Foundation grant, these seminars continued bimonthly for over a decade; several hundred leading business and political figures steadfastly attended them. Governor Christian Herter, addressing a 1955 gathering, noted:

In this audience is much of the stuff of effective leadership in Boston and in Massachusetts. Indeed, I have seldom if ever seen in one room so many people whose political and economic

155

attachments have such capacity for directing great and good forces.

The function of the seminars, in his view, was to let the gathered notables "express freely and fully what has been on their minds," "fraternize at the informal social hours and dinners which follow the discussion," explore the "large and complicated political problems involving all kinds of tensions and countertensions," and, finally, "find the means of correlating and giving unity to all the things of value said here," and to "unite the forces we represent in a program of action."[31]

In a series of addresses by Democratic public officials, Republican business executives, and business experts on economics and development, the BC Citizen Seminars did indeed fashion a consensus on a number of issues, including reforming the operations of Boston government, the city's urban renewal program, and the need for a coalition between businessmen and public officials to carry out these plans. Their critique of Boston's government was clear: it constituted an excessive tax demand on business property, which, in turn, impeded new investment. The remedy involved broadening the tax base, trimming the Boston payroll, and creating a more favorable political climate for the private sector.

Mayor Hynes himself conceded many of these points in his address to the inaugural BC session in 1954. After describing the difficulties in trimming services and the declining tax base, which resulted in a climbing property tax rate which disproportionately fell on business property, he concluded that this discouraged further investment. "Until the existing log-jam is broken, until we reach the point where Boston is once again attractive to new businesses, and until we reach the point where present Boston business will reconstruct or expand," he concluded, "we will not be out of trouble."[32]

These views paralleled those of major business leaders. Robert Ryan, vice-president of Cabot, Cabot and Forbes, noted at a 1957 session that "Boston has reached the point where private funds cannot be invested in Boston in any amount equal to filling the need until those funds can be assured a chance of return on investment.'' Boston's high tax rate, its reliance on the property tax, and its relative overassessment of business properties prevented this return.[33] Charles Francis Adams, Jr., president of Raytheon, added: "We have been in a sense living beyond our means. Our social legislation outstrips the rest of the nation, while our economic structure each year groans more audibly under the additional burdens imposed upon it.'' Slowing the growth of the public sector and easing the tax burden on business were, Adams argued, "surely indicated."[34]

This business sentiment made itself felt in the Massachusetts state legislature in 1957. In return for the passage of a $45 million refunding loan to bail out Boston, Mayor Hynes was forced to agree to reduce the number of city employees by 5 percent, reduce temporary personnel by 15 percent, and conduct a property tax equalization survey. Even after passage of the refunding bill, significant revenue shortfalls remained likely. This became an issue in the 1959 mayoral election because the leading candidate, John Powers, had opposed a new revenue source, the sales tax, which would have eased the burden on business properties.

At an early 1959 session of the Citizen Seminars, Richard Chapman, president of the Merchants National Bank, attacked Boston for "unchecked extravagance" and dismissed Hynes' actions on his refunding bill promises as "so tardy and trivial that it now becomes necessary to step up the tempo to far more urgent action."[35] These sentiments were confirmed in a 1960 survey of businessmen's views about the political climate in their cities. Of the five cities examined, Boston received the worst ratings on "political climate" and "tax situation"; 37 percent of the sample thought Boston was "corrupt to the point of inhibiting growth."[36]

The Seminars also presented a clear agenda for implementing urban renewal in Boston. Mayor Hynes presented this view: "The only way that decay and blight may be uprooted," he said, "is by a complete physical change in the affected neighborhood or area."[37] Business leaders attending the Seminars applauded these ends. In 1956, a senior Arthur D. Little official stressed the role of "Boston as a headquarters city" and the need to follow through on the Chamber of Commerce's recommendation that "a full-

157

time, professional coordinator bring together the several parts of Boston's redevelopment program.'' He also stressed the Municipal Research Bureau's call for ''an independent Urban Development Authority which would be separate from the Housing Authority.''

Cabot, Cabot and Forbes official Robert Ryan reiterated these demands in 1957. He asked the mayor to form a committee of ''the best brains and the most effective leaders in the community,'' ''persons who represent the highest level of economic power in the community,'' to push the program.[38] A vice president of New England Telephone, also president of the Greater Boston Chamber of Commerce, repeated essentially the same demands in late 1957, applauded the legislature's creation of the Boston Redevelopment Agency in that year, and urged the appointment of a strong director.[39] Like the mayor, these gentlemen knew that blighted neighborhoods needed ''complete physical change'' and wanted action.

By 1959, the legislature had provided a legally distinct entity, but it lacked a sufficient staff and funding, and, in particular, a vigorous director. The Agency's board chairman, Joseph Lund, was well suited for the job from the business community's point of view. Vice president of the R. M. Bradley real estate development company, he was a former president of NAREB, board member of ACTION, trustee and chairman of the Urban Land Institute's research committee, and executive committee member on Boston's Committee for Economic Development, which prepared a study of the city's economic future. Lund sought to emulate the ''sparkling leadership of Robert Moses,'' and quoted him to the effect that renewal must not be ''subject to unnecessary delays by carping armchair critics and constipated comma-chasers.''[40]

The business leaders speaking at the BC Citizen Seminars also understood the political coalition needed to implement their agenda. Their model was provided by Pittsburgh, ''a city where a Democratic mayor recognized that the salvation of a city is good politics and where Republican businessmen recognized that where a city's future is at stake, petty differences must be cleaned out with the slums.'' Like Philadelphia and New Haven, which had sent emissaries to the BC Seminars, Boston needed ''effective leadership by a small, nonpartisan group of principal citizens, wielding their personal influence and economic weight to get a coherent program framed and carried into execution.''[41]

Out of the Seminars grew a much more exclusive group which was later called ''The Vault'' because it met in the Boston Safe Deposit and Trust Company boardroom. Formed in 1959 to support John Collins against Senator John Powers, the group had about sixteen members, including the chief officers of the four largest commercial banks, the two largest retailers, the two largest industrial firms, the leading law firm, the city's public utility, and its third largest insurance company. These individuals were in turn interlocking members of the boards of the most important firms, civic associations, and nonprofit educational and medical institutions.[42] The Vault met monthly with Collins after his victory, provided the ''highest level of economic power'' in behalf of his renewal administrator's efforts, and supported his reelection in 1963. It also subsequently supported Mayor Kevin White's first general election campaign after its initial favorite, Edward Logue, had been defeated.

San Francisco

In the immediate postwar period, the Bay Area Council (BAC) provided the strongest high-level corporate initiative for the region. A planning and advocacy body organized by the region's top corporations in 1946 to promote regional planning and government, the Bay Area Council played a catalytic role in creating the Bay Area Rapid Transit system. It lobbied the state legislature to establish a planning body for the system, financed the campaign to pass the construction bond issue, and its leading members, such as Bechtel Engineering and Kaiser Industries, designed the system and received most of the construction contracts.[43] Of the twenty-seven *Fortune* 500 industrial firms in the Bay Area, twenty-three have top executives represented on the BAC; these include Southern Pacific, Pacific Gas and Electric, Lockheed Missiles and Space,

159

Hewlett-Packard, Kaiser, Crown Zellerbach, Utah International, Standard Oil of California, as well as four major banks, the two newspapers, Berkeley and Stanford, and such nonprofit organizations as the Stanford Research Institute. While BAC did not get the regional super-government it wanted, its other successes, like BART and the Metropolitan Transit Commission, helped to shape regional growth patterns.

Early in the war, a number of leading San Francisco citizens, including architects like Donn Emmons and Theodore Bernardi, future planning commissioners Morgan Gunst and Julia Porter, and BAC member Jerd Sullivan, also formed the San Francisco Planning and Housing Association (SFPHA). Dedicated to "building, labor, financial, industrial, civic and welfare interest," the SFPHA published a number of studies advocating urban renewal, including the 1945 study "Blight and Taxes," which identified the Western Addition as a prime candidate for urban renewal.

Members of this group served as an advisory commission to the City Planning Commission on its first urban renewal neighborhood designations in 1947. Mayor Roger Lapham (1943–1947) also appointed Gunst and Porter to the commission. Gunst was later named to head the Redevelopment Authority. The public studies undertaken during these years make plain the assumptions and goals of the city's development program. As one wartime study observed, "San Francisco is a city not only of California, or of the United States, or of North America, but of the World. . . . The central commercial and administrative core of this large urban and rural complex is centered and concentrated in Downtown San Francisco."[44] The first City Planning study on renewal also stated that "San Francisco is to the Bay Region what the Island of Manhattan is to the New York Region," that the Western Addition should be redeveloped because "it is close to the financial district . . . and contains slopes on which apartments with fine views can be erected." "In view of the characteristically low incomes of colored and foreign-born families," it added, "only a relatively small proportion of them may be expected to be in a position to occupy quarters in the new development."[45]

160

As the 1950s wore on and the newly established Redevelopment Agency did little, downtown leaders of Bay Area Council stature decided to push for faster action. In late 1955, industrialist James Zellerbach enlisted Charles Blyth, head of an investment banking firm and major holder of Hewlett-Packard stock, to form the Blyth-Zellerbach Committee "to serve as a catalyst for the entire renewal effort." They recruited nine other corporate leaders who, according to Zellerbach, "can provide money when it is needed." "The magnates of downtown decided," one observer noted, "to assume some of the civic responsibility which the politicians seemed bent on abdicating."[46] These gentlemen, most of whom also served on the BAC executive committee, contributed $50,000 to the City Planning Commission so that it, not Zeckendorf, could do the initial planning for the Golden Gateway, leading to more federal funds in 1958.[47]

Members of the B-Z Committee, like those in the Vault, were interested in seeing that urban renewal had sufficient bureaucratic power to redevelop the right parts of San Francisco. This led the B-Z Committee to hire Aaron Levine, head of a civic committee dedicated to the advocacy of renewal in Philadelphia, to advise them on political strategy. His report, "The Urban Renewal of San Francisco," was a model of political clarity.

Noting that San Francisco had "bold plans but no results," Levine's report criticized the organization of current redevelopment efforts and proposed what he called "a complete teamwork approach of political leadership, renewal agency initiative, planning department skill, and citizen participation." He criticized the San Francisco Redevelopment Agency's use of work orders as an "organizational relationship which is unsound and time consuming." The SFRA's staff was too small, and not sufficiently qualified; the planning department budget, too, was "exceedingly small," the lowest per capita for forty major California cities. He proposed to strengthen the SFRA and launch a three-part business political offensive to provide backing for it.

"The first citizen interest," he argued, "must occur at the level of top business leadership of the community." Top managers must realize "their decisions concerning private investment can

161

be supported and even protected by careful public expenditure.''
Elsewhere, ''amazing progress'' occurred when ''businessmen
became interested.'' The B-Z Committee, Levine argued, should
provide this leadership and add to its membership ''several men
who will be representing the top executive level of the City's
business community during the next 10–15 years.''[48]

In addition to this high-level group, Levine also urged the
B-Z Committee to create a city-wide citizen's group to support
the redevelopment budget, lobby for necessary bond issues, and
work for legislative changes. ''In other cities,'' Levine noted,
''the business community has recognized the importance of main-
taining an independent citizen organization to assist the planning
program.'' He criticized the San Francisco Planning and Housing
Association as ''completely inadequate.'' He also pointed out the
need to organize support within the project areas, for ''otherwise
there is apathy and usually opposition and resentment to most
planning proposals.''[49] The Blyth-Zellerbach Committee must have
agreed with these recommendations. After 1960, with the departure of SFRA's Reilly and Christopher's reelection with their
support, the Blyth-Zellerbach Committee followed them precisely.

3. FORMATION OF THE PROGROWTH COALITION AND THE IMPLEMENTATION OF THE CORPORATE AGENDA FOR URBAN RENEWAL

Late 1959 brought together a confluence of forces in Boston
and in San Francisco: a mobilized business community, a growth-
oriented mayor willing to enlist that business support, the establishment of new and more powerful development agencies, the
appointment of strong development administrators, and, after November 1960, a Democratic president and Congress that were
willing to dramatically increase federal spending on urban renewal.

After years of preparatory work, progrowth political coalitions
were pulled into alignment in the two cities. Urban renewal reached
its apogee in the careers of Edward Logue at the Boston Rede-

velopment Authority and M. Justin Herman at the San Francisco Redevelopment Agency. Their strength was, in turn, possible because of John Collins' and George Christopher's electoral success.

Matching Plans with Political Power

BOSTON

Until the final votes were counted, it seemed likely that Senator John E. Powers, not John Collins, would be elected mayor of Boston. Powers had lost the 1955 race to Mayor Hynes by only a few precentage points. He had a strong labor record, had defeated Governor Furcolo's 1957 sales tax proposal, and had gained endorsements from most Democratic officeholders, businessmen accustomed to making campaign contributions, and even a number of important Republicans.

Powers considerably outdistanced Collins in financing his campaign. Powers raised a quarter of a million dollars at a single testimonial banquet, attended "mostly by contractors doing business with the city and large property owners who wanted assurance that tax laws would not be changed to their disadvantage."[50] His Eminence Archbishop Cushing sat at the head table and received a $34,000 contribution out of campaign funds for his efforts.

Collins' political history was much more modest. As a member of the Massachusetts House, he had opposed an unemployment insurance benefit sought by organized labor. Elected to the state Senate in 1950 and 1952, he cooperated with Powers' leadership. In 1954, he lost a race to become state attorney general, and in 1955 he made a comeback as a Boston city councillor, serving until 1957 when Governor Furcolo appointed him to the sinecure position as Suffolk County registrar of probate.

When Collins announced his candidacy for mayor in 1959, he had only an amateur campaign organization, none of the backing of major political figures that Powers had, and no prestigious "brain trust." With the slogan "Stop power politics: elect a hands-free mayor," Collins attacked Powers as a tool of special interests

163

against the common man. In a five-man primary, Powers came in with 34 percent of the vote, Collins 22 percent, and a relatively conservative Italian city councillor received 20 percent.

Two events occurred to swing the runoff vote in Collins' favor. First, opinion polls showed that many of those who did not vote for Powers believed him to be "a little crooked." A well-timed IRS raid on an East Boston bookie, who happened to have "Powers for Mayor" signs all over his bar, received wide TV coverage, gelling public opinion against Powers. Equally important, Collins appeared before Ralph Lowell, Charles Coolidge, and the other members of the Vault. Collins' pitch, according to one report, was straightforward: "What we need is a New Boston. Rebuild the Downtown area. Make urban renewal work; don't bungle it like John Hynes did with the West End. Bring prosperity back to Boston with the politicians and the business community working together."[51] Collins received the Vault members' support, who provided last-minute financial assistance and access to middle-class opinion leaders.

Antipathy toward Powers, the East Boston raid, and Collins' appeal as the "clean," reformist, nonprofessional alternative combined to give him a margin of 114,074 votes against Powers' 90,035. Powers had won in the relatively low-income heartlands of Boston Irish politics, but Collins took the middle-income Irish wards and the Italian wards. In a nonpartisan race between two Democrats, Republicans had voted heavily for Collins.[52]

In his first months in office, Collins delivered on his promises to the members of the Vault: he cut $13 million from the city's budget, reduced the number of city employees by 300, and launched a legislative program on Beacon Hill which included a key measure which made possible a special tax arrangement for the Prudential Center development. He also reorganized the BRA and hired Edward J. Logue away from the famous New Haven renewal program for a salary of $30,000, more than any other public official in the state had been paid. After a decade of rising taxes, inflated assessment rolls, and the threat of bankruptcy, Collins announced a reduction in the Boston tax rate from $101.20 to $100.70. Though symbolic, this action spoke directly to the con-

164

cerns which business leaders had raised for half a decade at the BC Citizen Seminars.

Boston politics is particularly hostile toward "outsiders," yet on the Vault's advice Collins shoved aside BRA board members who had been meddling with administrative matters, demoted a sitting administrator so that he could bring in a highly paid outsider, and created a special tax treatment for a new, outsider-financed office building construction.

Logue drove a hard bargain with Collins over moving to Boston. According to a contemporary observer,

> Logue decided at once that the Redevelopment Authority was the biggest stumbling block to a coordinated renewal program, that its staff was considered incompetent by renewal experts everywhere, and that neither federal officials nor private developers could work well with it. He also felt that Authority members . . . interfered too much in administration.[53]

He therefore insisted that he have full executive powers as development administrator, including the power to hire staff, and that BRA board members would not interfere in his work. Though the BRA Board initially resisted these demands, Collins strongly sided with Logue. Collins also secured the abolition of the Boston City Planning Board and the assignment of its functions to the BRA.

Logue took control of the BRA's program in the fall of 1960. The breadth of his aspirations may be measured in three different documents: the September 22, 1960, "90 Million Dollar Development Plan," which set forth the administration's initial goals, the more mature "1965/1975 General Plan for the City of Boston," and specific project plans, such as the 1965 "South End Urban Renewal Plan." Logue managed to put one-quarter of the city's land area and half of its population into some form of federally assisted renewal, probably a record for expanding the jurisdiction of a redevelopment agency.

Following on the completed New York Streets and West End projects, Logue set four major downtown commercial projects into motion: Prudential Center ($202 million to be invested), Gov-

165

ernment Center ($217.1 million to be invested, net loss of 989 low-rent dwelling units), the Waterfront ($131.4 million to be invested, net gain of 2,310 mostly luxury dwelling units), and the Central Business District 8 ($314.6 million to be invested, 450 luxury units). He also established major residential renewal projects for Washington Park in the black Roxbury neighborhood ($64.8 million to be invested, 2,570 units actually cleared, 1,550 to be constructed), the South End ($232.1 million to be invested, 5,250 low-rent units to be cleared, 4,100 mostly market rate units to be constructed), and Charlestown ($115.4 million to be invested, 925 low-rent units to be cleared, and 1,400 market rate units to be constructed).

These projects emphasized central business district and non-profit institutional expansion. They targeted neighborhoods close to the CBD for partial clearance and major upgrading in population status. Only middle-class areas on the city's periphery escaped his plans. At the end of the Collins administration in 1967, when Logue departed from the BRA, these projects had demolished 9,718 low-rent units while constructing only 3,504 new units, of which only 982 were federally subsidized. Some twenty-two thousand low-income individuals were thus displaced. Logue had secured federal financial commitments of over $200 million, raising Boston from seventeenth to fourth place in per capita renewal grants. About 3,223 acres of city land were involved with active renewal projects financed locally in large part with $30 million in capital improvements the city would probably have undertaken anyway.[54] He also built the BRA from a staff of seventeen and a budget of $250,000 into a 700-strong parallel government with an annual cash flow of $25 million by the time he left in 1967.

Logue stressed that BRA action should "provide the incentive to public and private enterprises both to develop and to maintain land at its highest and best use."[55] True to these words, Logue's CBD-oriented renewal projects generated approximately one-half billion dollars in office building investment within renewal boundaries by 1967. Truly, as historian Stephen Thernstrom has noted, "Here was a potent force for change: a brilliant and aggressive executive like Logue and a massive injection of outside funds, to be devoted to the building of 'the New Boston' along lines especially appealing to downtown businessmen, bankers, realtors, and newspaper editors.''[56]

SAN FRANCISCO

A similar series of events occurred in San Francisco. In 1959, with strong support from the San Francisco business community, George Christopher won reelection over Russell Wolden, the second generation city assessor. Wolden, a Democrat, came from a family with a long political history and, because of the assessor's power over commercial tax bills, a broad base of small business support. A preelection opinion poll for Christopher showed that he was behind in the race, and also that Wolden was benefiting from a popular antipathy toward Christopher's close ties with downtown.

Christopher, in turn, sought to capitalize on hints that Wolden would loosen up on law enforcement vice activities. In the end, he triumphed by 145,009 votes to 92,252. (Wolden was subsequently indicted for running his own San Francisco version of Boston's abatement racket.) Having won a second and final term, Christopher immediately set out to get the Golden Gateway and other renewal projects going as his top priority.[57]

In 1958, Christopher took the first step in this direction by appointing Everett Griffin, a "wealthy and able chemical engineer" and candidate of the B-Z Committee, to head the SFRA Board. With the retirement of SFRA Executive Director Riordan in 1959, Christopher finally got control over the Agency. After a nationwide search, Griffin and Christopher appointed M. Justin Herman to the job. A fifty-eight-year-old federal civil servant, Herman had headed the San Francisco regional office of the HHFA between 1951 and 1959. In that capacity, he oversaw urban renewal in the western states, and had been a leading critic of San Francisco's delays. For most of 1959 he served as a special assistant to the HHFA's administrator in Washington, D.C.

A brilliant and aggressive official who would later be called "the last of the Robert Moses autocrats . . . a flamboyant, autocratic wheeler-dealer," Herman had much in common with Ed-

167

ward Logue.[58] He knew the federal program and the urban development business backward and forward, had close personal ties to the Washington bureaucrats whose cooperation would speed his activities, and had strong views about the importance of public control over urban design. Like Logue, he got an assurance from Christopher that he could run the SFRA without political interference. His powers included the hiring and firing of staff, the authorization to build up his own staff, and the assurance that Christopher would use his power and business community ties to back Herman against recalcitrants inside and outside of government.

The Blyth-Zellerbach Committee and its political consultant Aaron Levine had urged exactly these terms. As one HUD official later commented, "Herman could move rapidly on renewal—demolition or construction—because he was absolutely confident that he was doing what the power structure wanted insofar as the poor and minorities were concerned."[59] Christopher also appointed to the SFRA Board such pillars of the downtown establishment as BAC founder James Folger, of Folger Coffee, and U.S. Steel executive James Black, Jr.

Herman set about getting rapid results. He fired a number of the sixty pre-Herman staffers, and proceeded to build up the Agency staff to several hundred within two years. At its peak in 1972, the SFRA had 462 employees and, like the BRA, constituted a kind of parallel government exercising strong powers over physical investment patterns. (Unlike Boston, however, the SFRA never controlled the city planning function, and in the late 1960s and early 1970s, the Department of City Planning became something of a counter-voice to Herman's, much to his disgust.) Again following Levine's recommendations, San Francisco Planning and Urban Renewal Association (SPUR), which the B-Z Committee had organized to replace the SFPHA, was named the SFRA's official citizen's advisory committee. SPUR helped build a middle-class, professional constituency on behalf of renewal.

This support allowed Justin Herman, like Edward Logue, to launch a truly impressive battery of urban renewal projects. In addition to speeding up the Western Addition A-1 clearance project and the Diamond Heights new housing development projects, and, of course, the Golden Gateway, Herman expanded the SFRA's scope to include CBD-oriented projects in Chinatown (a $12.5 million Holiday Inn, constructed under the guise of including a "Chinese Cultural and Trade Center") and the Yerba Buena Convention Center ($114 million to be invested, including private hotels and office buildings, with four thousand people, mostly single, blue collar retirees, actually displaced). The Golden Gateway Center, only a concept before Herman's arrival, became his centerpiece, attracting $221.3 million in new investment to build luxury high-rise apartments, condominium townhouses, a Hyatt Regency hotel, four high-rise office towers rising from thirty-four to forty-five stories each, and the twenty-four story Alcoa office building.

Herman also proposed a dramatically expanded new residential renewal project for the Western Addition ($221.1 million to be invested, four thousand structures housing almost eight thousand individuals to be cleared), a project in the black Hunters Point area ($103 million to be invested, several hundred units of World War II "temporary" housing to be removed), and an industrial park in the China Basin area adjacent to Hunters Point ($45 million to be invested, 272 residents to be displaced).

These projects called for half a billion dollars of private investment and a third of a billion dollars of federal investment; they also involved reshaping of San Francisco's major minority neighborhoods, particularly its black community. Like Logue's projects, M. Justin Herman's urban renewal agenda dramatically expanded the central business district and undertook large-scale clearance and rehabilitation in minority neighborhoods proximate to downtown, where "blighting" social groups occupied Victorian housing stock likely to be desirable to the growing middle class that the new downtown office buildings would generate.

Renewing Strategic Neighborhoods: The South End and the Western Addition

As the first and second largest residential urban renewal programs in the mid-1960s in the United States, the South End project in Boston and the Western Addition project in San Francisco exemplify the goals urban renewal administrators sought and the new conflicts they generated. These two neighborhoods had attracted planners' attention as "blighted" neighborhoods for two decades, and both were zones of entry for in-coming minority groups. But Logue and Herman selected these neighborhoods for large-scale renewal projects because they occupied strategic locations in the geopolitical competition for central-city land. Furthermore, these two neighborhoods were located near important dominant institutions which wanted to be protected.

These projects thus amounted to experiments to see whether, in the words of the BRA's 1965 Plan, government could achieve "a reversal of the present trend toward increasing proportions of low-income groups and nonwhites in the core city." The South End and the Western Addition were chosen because they gave the greatest promise of success. To justify their actions, planners had to project an image of these neighborhoods as so pathologically disorganized as to require social surgery. Their selective perception thus excluded a discussion of the strong elements of community which existed in both neighborhoods. Renewal entrepreneurs also had to recruit support from within the two neighborhoods. The large-scale demolition and clearance projects in Boston's West End and San Francisco's Western Addition A-1 project had left a bad taste in both cities. Renewal entrepreneurs thus had to enter these neighborhoods' established leadership networks, recruit support, and to some extent even reorganize them.

Finally, renewal entrepreneurs had to promise these established neighborhood leadership networks that renewal would provide adequate relocation assistance, build low-rent housing, and stress rehabilitation, not demolition. The basic aims of urban renewal precluded fulfillment of these promises, but renewal entrepreneurs had to make them anyway to get their projects moving.

Neighborhood Designation

From the outset, planners had pointed out the underlying strategic value of the South End and the Western Addition. Both neighborhoods had originally been constructed in the latter part of the nineteenth century for the upper middle class. Both thus combined convenient location with a housing stock initially built to high standards.

The South End was built on land built up around Boston's neck in the 1850s, approximately when the Back Bay area was filled in. The picture which architectural historian Walter Muir Whitehall painted of its origins holds true today. It is

a region of symmetrical blocks of high-shouldered, comfortable red brick or brownstone houses, low fronted and high stooped, with mansard roofs, ranged along spacious avenues, intersected by cross streets that occasionally widened into tree-shaded squares and parks whose central gardens were enclosed by neat cast iron fences.[60]

After the depression of 1873, the neighborhood began a downward slide as successive waves of immigrants displaced the Yankee elite, which departed for more fashionable outlying areas. The five-story brownstones were subdivided into tenement flats and rooming houses, and

the South End became what it has been for almost a century: a community of working people, ethnically, racially, and religiously integrated. After the Irish came the Jews and Syrians, the Greeks and Italians, the Chinese and the Portuguese, the West Indians, the American blacks, and most recently, American Indians and Puerto Ricans.[61]

By 1950, boardinghouses made up 40 percent of the housing stock and tenements most of the rest.

The South End is strategically located between three institutional foci. On the Northeast, the South End is only a few minutes' walk from Boston's central business district, and close also to the Tufts New England Medical Center. Boston City Hospital and the Boston Univeristy Medical Center form the southeastern border. To the southwest lies Massachusetts Avenue, a major demarcation line between the traditional South End and largely black Lower Roxbury. To the northwest, just over a set of depressed railroad lines, lie the headquarters of the Christian Scientist Church,

171

the massive Prudential Center complex, Copley Square with its Hancock Building and chic shopping district, and the rest of the Back Bay. Though redlined in the 1950s, it did not take a real estate genius to see that with financing and rehabilitation loan funds, the South End's "faded elegance" had tremendous market potential.

The same was true of the Western Addition. As the SFHPA's 1945 pamphlet on "Blight and Taxes" had noted, "Potentially the land is worth far more, for it is in the heart of a growing city and anyone can see its latent value."[62] Or, as a 1970 Wells Fargo report put it, "The high location value of this district, being immediately adjacent to the downtown . . . should result in a total rebuilding and renovation."[63] The area was built up after 1858, like the South End, as the city's first major middle-class expansion beyond the original downtown area. Even in 1950, well over half of its structures had been built before 1900, including "the City's finest collection of Victorian mansions that had survived the 1906 earthquake."[64]

The 1906 earthquake ended the Western Addition's social exclusiveness; under the influx of refugees from other districts which had been burned out or dynamited, the surviving Western Addition was subdivided into even smaller units, with additional structures being rapidly thrown up in back lots. The great mixture of land uses in the Western Addition also dates from this period, as displaced businesses relocated there. From the turn of the century onward, the area served as the zone of entry for low-status ethnic groups, particularly Japanese and blacks. Like the South End, the Western Addition thus held an intrinsically attractive Victorian housing stock which had been converted into rooming houses and tenement apartments.

The Western Addition also occupies a strategic location. Set upon a rise immediately to the west of San Francico's City Hall and government center, it is only a few minutes' walk or transit ride from the CBD. Summer fogs often stop just to the west of the area, giving it a relatively attractive climate. Just to the north is Pacific Heights, the city's most exclusive residential area, and also several of its more important hospitals such as Kaiser Medical

Center, Mt. Zion, and Presbyterian. On the northeast corner is a cluster of major churches, including the Catholic Cathedral, which had been rebuilt there as part of the Western Addition A-1 project. Ironically, the A-1 project, a massive clearance project which displaced four thousand households for the sake of a Japanese trade center, luxury housing, and an express boulevard, itself became a justification for a much larger project in the area surrounding it.[65]

Planners' Perceptions and Neighborhood Realities

Both neighborhoods offered much evidence for planners who wished to stigmatize them. These were "bad" areas of Boston and San Francisco, with declining populations, ill-maintained housing, and declining property values. It was easy to take the step from physical disinvestment to social decay. As areas where concentrated numbers of the minority poor lived, social planners could generate statistics on the disproportionate amount of crime, disease, alcoholism, welfare dependency, and iniquitous activities going on in each of these two neighborhoods.

In the South End, social reformers had railed against the "vice dens" which characterized the neighborhood and filled it with riffraff since the turn of the century. One part of the neighborhood near the Dover Street MBTA stop had become a skid row. By the 1950s, the South End probably had more liquor licenses than any other part of Boston.

A neighborhood profile undertaken by Action for Boston Community Development (ABCD), a community action program begun by the Ford Foundation Gray Areas program under Logue's urging in 1961, noted that the income gap between the South End and the rest of Boston was wide and getting wider, that it had a disproportionately large AFDC case load, that 37.5 percent of its males between sixteen and sixty-five years of age were not in the labor force, that 78 percent of the households lacked an automobile, and that it had 28.9 percent of Boston's tuberculosis cases.[66]

This picture of social decay, in turn, justified the physical in-

173

tervention that BRA planners wanted to undertake. In San Francisco, SFRA planners made the same argument. The 1945 and 1947 studies undertaken by the City Planning Commission directly equated the Western Addition's physical and social decay. The official 1964 renewal plan summed up delinquency, tuberculosis, and venereal disease figures "which do not measure up to City averages," and turned directly to the physical means which would "eliminate blight and blighting influences."[67]

Planners ignored the strong elements of community life in both neighborhoods to arrive at their pictures of social decay. Both neighborhoods had intense ethnic community life, centered on churches, social clubs, and proximity to the street. Boston's Catholic Cathedral is located in the South End, and carries on numerous neighborhood programs. The Syrian, Greek, black, and Puerto Rican communities had their own churches, and the South End is filled with ethnic restaurants, taverns, specialty stores, and social clubs. In the Western Addition, community life centered both around the Japantown commercial center, with its several churches, and along Fillmore Street, once home to San Francisco's best blues clubs and barbecue joints. The Western Addition has four black churches whose congregations are over a century old. Both fit Herbert Gans' and Jane Jacobs' definition of urban villages, but this perception did not find its way into the planners' analyses.

"Planning with People" as Political Intervention

Because the West End and Western Addition A-1 projects had displaced eight thousand and four thousand people, Boston and San Francisco elected officials had turned against the massive clearance approach to urban renewal. As a practical political matter, Edward Logue and M. Justin Herman each had to take a more subtle approach—stressing rehabilitation rather than complete clearance—and had to build a neighborhood constituency for agency plans. In practice, this meant that the agencies concentrated on rehabilitating properties attractive to the middle class and drew those citizens who shared the agencies' interest in upgrading prop-

174

erty values into the agency planning process. Mayor Collins called this "planning *with* people rather than planning for people."[68]

In the South End, Logue set up an elaborate process in which the BRA consulted with a "South End Urban Renewal Committee" and a network of neighborhood homeowners' associations. These groups represented only a small minority of the area, perhaps 5 percent, but they constituted the main neighborhood leadership of the time.

Through the hundreds of meetings which BRA staffers undertook in fashioning the plan's details, the BRA, in effect, organized the community in behalf of its own bureaucratic interests. As one observer concluded, "The BRA was able to find within the South End a group of elite homeowners and tenants (who could afford a moderate or high rent) who aspired to make the South End a respectable middle-class neighborhood, a goal also held by the BRA."[69]

In the Western Addition, the SFRA did not undertake the same kind of extensive consultation process, but was careful to recruit support from black ministers and from Japantown merchants. Herman promised SFRA assistance in building new sanctuaries for a number of important black organizations; he also granted nonprofit housing development rights to four leading Baptist churches, the A. M. E. Church, and Jones Methodist, the black community's most prestigious congregation. Herman won support from the conservative Japantown merchants by giving them their own commercial rehabilitation program in an area across the street from the monumental Japanese Cultural and Trade Center.

Promises Meant to be Broken

Earlier clearance projects inevitably made relocation and rehousing of displacees a central issue in renewal planning. In a 1960 speech to the San Francisco Council for Civic Unity, Herman himself observed that without adequate new housing construction for the poor, urban renewal critics would be justified in thinking that "a program intended to rehouse properly the slum dwellers

175

has been converted into a land-grab for the rich and a heartless push-out for the poor and nonwhites.''

Renewal planners and administrators faced a difficult bind: on the one hand, all the political and economic incentives pointed toward supplanting a ''blighting'' population and its ''blighting'' land uses with a higher-status population. On the other hand, they could not acknowledge to those about to be displaced, or perhaps even to themselves, that they were engaging in highly regressive social engineering. Renewal entrepreneurs resolved this bind largely by denying it. Official agency plans systematically underestimated the likely displacement and overestimated housing alternatives for those displaced. BRA and SFRA staff members thus made many promises which by their nature were bound to be broken.

In the South End, for example, Dick Green, the BRA staffer in charge of formulating the 1965 South End Urban Renewal Plan, told the Boston City Council hearing on the project that ''anybody who wishes to stay in the South End, we believe we have adequate facilities for them.''[70]

Relying on a League of Women Voters study of the South End Plan, City Councillor W. J. Foley warned that ''there is no intention of making anything but a shameful token effort in the South End for that substantial majority of those displaced who are poor. . . . [The Plan may rehabilitate the area] but only at the expense and through the misery and suffering and pain of between 10 and 15 thousand poor people. It is as simple as that.''[71] Yet the Plan was adopted.

Similarly, the black residents of the Western Addition feared the implications of such documents as Mel Scott's 1947 study, which projected that few displacees could return. In the 1948 public hearing on the proposed project, the representative of the black Ministerial Alliance said, ''We are tremendously concerned . . . as to whether or not the displaced persons from this particular area will, when they are once displaced—will they have the same opportunities to return?'' A realtor commented on the planners' belief that ''they will find comparable housing for [displacees]. . . . It isn't true; it isn't here!'' A small landlord asked, ''I would like to know where the tenants that have been in [my] properties for 15 and 20 years—where they are going, and whether they can come back. And I know full well that they can't come back when a redevelopment takes place, with the cost of building today." Dr. Carleton Goodlett, speaking for the NAACP, related how when he had asked for guarantees against black displacement at the legislature, he had been told "this is not the time" to raise such issues. When he had approached the local committee framing the project, he had again been told "this is not the time." Goodlett would not compromise with those who would defer discussion of the issue: "Experience has taught minority peoples," he concluded, "that if we don't start out right we might not end up right."[72]

To sooth these voices, the chairman of the supervisors' urban renewal committee assured the audience that "before any redevelopment can take place there must be an affirmative finding by the Board of Supervisors that there is housing available for everyone who is displaced at comparable rent." Dan Del Carlo, head of the building trades, member of the mayor's renewal committee, and lobbyist for state renewal legislation, promised that displaced people "will be taken care of; minority groups will be taken care of; that the low income groups will be taken care of."[73]

Later, on the eve of the adoption of the Western Addition A-2 renewal plan in 1964, the United San Francisco Freedom Movement issued a "Critique of the Redevelopment and Relocation Plans Proposed by the San Francisco Redevelopment Agency for Western Addition Area II," which detailed the mismatch between projected displacees' housing needs and the actual resources available. The report attacked the SFRA for demolishing the most concentrated black areas and for substantially reducing the city's low-rent housing stock. In response, the Western Addition A-2 plan blandly promised that "if they so desire, some 1,225 families and some 1,560 single individuals can remain or be rehoused in Area S-2" or would be "assisted in finding housing which is . . . within their financial means, in reasonably convenient locations, and otherwise suitable to their needs."[74] Justin Herman repeatedly promised that the Agency would provide adequate relocation. As in the South End, this promise would prove to be a weak reed.

177

Clearing Blight: The Neighborhood Urban Renewal Plans

The official renewal plans for the South End and Western Addition A-2 projects called for demolishing the most dilapidated structures, typically located in the poorest parts of the neighborhoods where minority concentrations were highest. The plans required rehabilitation of almost all of the remaining structures (only a small fraction had been found to satisfy local housing codes prior to renewal). Both estimated that only the buildings to be demolished would generate displacement, thereby ignoring the possible impact of private rehabilitation efforts. Finally, neither plan proposed to build anywhere near the number of low-rent units that would be demolished.

The South End Urban Renewal Plan (SEURP), adopted in late 1965, makes clear its basic objective of upgrading the area's physical composition rather than upgrading the quality of housing opportunities open to its current residents. Its principal objectives were to "improve the quality . . . of existing dwellings," to "remove the concentrations of deteriorated and deteriorating buildings which depress the physical condition and character of the area [and] impair the flow of investment," and to "protect and expand the city's tax base . . . [and] protect private investment," as well as to "provide appropriate sites for the necessary expansion of . . . medical, institutional, and industrial facilities."[75]

Of the 606 acres of land covered by the SEURP, 186 acres (30%) were to be acquired and demolished by the BRA. Forty-three percent of this land was to be used for new residential purposes, while 25 percent would be turned over for institutional expansion and commercial uses; the remainder went to streets and public facilities. Of the approximately 22,000 dwelling units in the neighborhood (about 20,000 occupied), 5,215 units in 1,300 townhouse structures were to be acquired and demolished. BRA projected that demolition would displace about 7,500 individuals (1,730 largely black and Puerto Rican families and 1,820 single, largely elderly, white lodging-house boarders), more than two-thirds of whom qualified for public housing.

178

The Plan included construction of 3,300 units of subsidized housing, including 2,500 moderate income Section 221(d)(3) units, 300 units of public housing for families, and 500 public housing units for seniors. Mayor Collins also got the city's mortgage lenders to end their redlining of the South End and promised not to raise property tax assessments on rehabilitated properties. Together with federal rehabilitation loan funds, the SEURP thus paved the way for massive amounts of new private investment in the South End housing stock.[76]

San Francisco's Western Addition A-2 renewal plan contemplated an even more massive impact on its 276 acre project area. The Plan sought "discovery and exploitation of the City's best economic potentials," building new housing to serve "middle income families now attracted to suburban areas," "strengthening the City's tax base," and "the elimination of slums" by drastically reducing the low-rent housing stock.[77]

The Plan indicates that the SFRA would acquire and clear 103 acres of the site, including two-thirds of the land previously in residential use. Of the 6,900 housing units in the project area, the SFRA planned to demolish all but 2,408, building an additional 3,752 new units. Of these new units, only 200 would be public housing, 800 private senior citizen housing, 1,400 subsidized moderate rent housing, and 1,352 units would be new, market-rate housing.

The Agency estimated that approximately eighteen hundred families and twenty-five hundred individuals would be displaced by demolition, or approximately eight thousand people. These figures did not include displacement from private rehabilitation. Most of those displaced could afford only public housing. Further, demolition was to be concentrated in the predominantly black Fillmore area in the center of the project area, while rehabilitation would take place on its white, relatively better-off periphery. It was, as a Freedom House analysis pointed out, "not a *war on poverty* but rather a *war on the poor*."[78]

179

Consequences of the Neighborhood Revolt against Renewal

By successfully using federal urban programs as a method for shaping support from urban constituencies, national Democratic political entrepreneurs provoked conservative countermovements within national politics. As local Democratic entrepreneurs and their allies, each motivated by their own reasons, implemented these programs in cities like Boston and San Francisco, they also provoked a second, even more troublesome reaction.

By assaulting low-income neighborhoods like the South End and the Western Addition, urban renewal and similar programs stimulated what Daniel Bell called a "community revolution."[1] New organizations and new neighborhood leaders challenged the right of the BRA and SFRA to demolish their communities, challenged the older neighborhood leaders who had cooperated with these agencies, and sought to confront and deter the broader progrowth coalitions which had made their practices possible. As sentiments like these spread within the large, old central cities like Boston and San Francisco, they called the stability of progrowth administrations into question.

The local and national political systems responded to this challenge in a variety of ways. In part, they blunted and resisted the thrust by neighborhood activists to gain control over urban development programs affecting their neighborhoods. In part, however, local and national Democrats also modified renewal practices to contain this thrust and, through the Great Society, developed new programs to absorb and benefit from it. In the end, the community revolution significantly altered both the urban political terrain and the practice of federal urban development programming.

180

Federal urban programs had a second impact on urban politics in cities like Boston and San Francisco as well. They hastened the market forces which the early backers of urban renewal had hoped to stimulate. During the 1960s, Boston, San Francisco, and similar cities experienced an unprecedented boom in downtown office building construction, the growth of government centers, and the expansion of hospitals and other service institutions. Investment in these institutions, in turn, reshaped the labor markets in these cities and, ultimately, the demographic composition of their resident population. The successful implementation of federal urban programs thus created not one but two kinds of new actors in urban politics.

Alongside the community organizations which arose in low-income minority neighborhoods, a new stratum of educated middle-class professionals became a force in urban politics. Those of this stratum who have chosen to live in central cities have tended to come from the baby-boom generation. Their values and household formation and location choices have differed from those of their suburban parents. Many chose to become "urban pioneers," living in racially mixed but interesting and improving neighborhoods like the South End. As traditional blue collar constituencies have become less numerous and less important in urban politics, this new stratum has become more important. It has developed communal interests which are distinct from and sometimes opposed to those of the other residents of the working class neighborhoods which they have entered. But it has also taken up the banner of community activism, contributing political resources which low-income residents generally lack. The successes of pro-growth politics thus unexpectedly generated a powerful counter-movement from within the heart of the New Deal Democratic coalition itself.

1. The Impact of Renewal and the Rise of Neighborhood Activism

After years of planning, the South End and Western Addition urban renewal projects entered their execution phase in 1966. The

181

BRA and SFRA moved rapidly to acquire the properties they wished to demolish. The agencies also demanded that all properties not acquired be brought up to code, and provided financing for private rehabilitation efforts. Because many of the absentee owners who held buildings in these neighborhoods had been looking for ways to get their money out, it was easy for new investors to buy up South End and Western Addition properties.

During the early project execution years, the shells of South End row houses could be purchased for as little as $5,000 while sound structures went for around $20,000. Western Addition structures were going for about $5,000 per unit. Tenants in such units paid less than $75 a month in rent.[2] Considering location, underlying quality of the housing stock, market potential, and new sources of financing, these neighborhoods offered more potential for return on low initial investments than any other in Boston or San Francisco. The first wave of new, young, professional immigrants and real estate investors were not slow to act on these realities.

The combination of urban renewal and private investment devastated prevailing residential patterns in the two neighborhoods. Many likened it to wartime bombing. One South Ender told a 1968 public hearing that the neighborhood "was beginning to look like a bombed-out European city," while a Western Addition activist drew an angry analogy with Vietnam. The story of Vernon Thornton, who lived in the Western Addition neighborhood, perhaps best illustrates the impact of renewal acquisition on both project areas.

After World War II, the Western Addition had a thriving black commercial life. Its main commercial artery, Fillmore Street, featured every manner of convenience, including nightclubs like the Café Society, Esther's Breakfast Club, Jimbo's Bop City, and the Both/And. Vernon Thornton owned a popular bowling alley on Fillmore. As renewal began execution, according to Thornton, the SFRA held off purchasing his thriving business, even though it was located in the area to be demolished for a new shopping-center-style commercial development. Instead, the SFRA demolished much of the surrounding housing, displacing Thornton's clientele and driving him out of business. Only then did the Agency take his property, offering him a fraction of what it had once been worth.

The SFRA demonstrated a coldly calculated business sense in driving down commercial property values. This approach reduced acquisition costs and made business owners amenable to whatever the Agency was likely to offer. But it also deprived small businessmen of a lifetime's work and destroyed the commercial center which gave the Fillmore its identity. By 1969, the Fillmore was indeed like a barren field. Much the same took place in various parts of the South End.

Many owners also abandoned maintenance efforts on their properties. As a result, many more units were ultimately demolished than the agencies had anticipated. In the parts of the South End and the Western Addition close to Boston's Prudential Center or San Francisco's Mt. Zion Hospital, real estate investors rapidly acquired the Victorian housing stock and reconverted it to single family or rental apartment use. New owners often required old owners to evict their tenants without benefit of BRA and SFRA relocation services or payments. Tenants, often elderly, intimidated by renewal officialdom, unfamiliar with bureaucratic maneuvering, poor and unorganized, simply caved in before these pressures.[3]

As the largest and most identifiable source of this perceived attack on the low-rent housing stock, the BRA and SFRA became the focal points for community conflict over the direction of neighborhood development. The years between 1966 and 1968 showed that neighborhood fears about relocation had been justified. By January 1968, the BRA had relocated only five hundred families, most to housing outside the South End. Contrary to BRA promises, only twenty-five had been rehoused in rehabilitated units within the South End. The first wave of relocation had exhausted the South End's low-rent relocation resources, and further displacees would clearly be forced out of the area. Further, construction had begun on only a fraction of the promised subsidized housing.[4]

Since the SFRA sought to clear even more of the Western

183

Addition, the impact was even greater on that neighborhood. As of May 1968, only 700 households of 1,800 which actively needed relocation had been rehoused, 200 of them temporarily. Of these 700, 338 had relocated to standard private housing, generally at considerably higher rents, 115 were in public housing, and the remainder had self-relocated into substandard units or were temporarily located in units yet to be torn down within the project area. Almost 15 percent of the households had been forced from the city altogether, and 60 percent were forced out of the Western Addition, despite the fact that an overwhelming percentage of displacees wanted to remain in private housing within the neighborhood.[5] This relocation record was technically legal only because the SFRA could offer relocatees places in public housing projects which it knew they were likely to turn down.

This growing disruption of the community fabric produced a new kind of militant community activism aimed at halting and redefining the renewal process.[6] The BRA and SFRA had carefully enlisted support from established neighborhood organizations and institutions which shared the agencies' interest in upgrading property values and performing "physical surgery" on neighborhood social problems. As the renewal agencies began to demolish low-rent housing, however, dissident voices emerged.

In the South End, activist white ministers influenced by Saul Alinsky, black social workers employed at United South End Settlements (USES), poverty program employees, Puerto Rican community organizers, and ideologically motivated white young professionals joined together in opposition to the BRA. These individuals worked at jobs which gave them wide contact networks among ordinary South End residents. Mel King, for example, was a black social worker for USES; for years he had organized summer recreation programs for kids. A highly skilled and articulate individual, he had run unsuccessfully for the Boston School Board. Father William Dwyer, a Spanish-speaking Episcopal minister, whose church served as a community center, got church grant money to hire organizers to mobilize the Puerto Rican tenants in the area surrounding his church. Ted Parrish, another black social worker at USES, organized tenants of a major South End slum lord in order to get control of and rehabilitate his units. With help from middle-class professional allies, such as those working for Urban Planning Aid, an advocacy planning group organized by MIT and Harvard advocate planners, these individuals and the following they galvanized became a powerful voice against the BRA.

These leaders organized three particularly important groups: the South End Tenants' Council (Parrish played the key role), the Emergency Tenants' Council (later Inquilinos Boricuas en Acción, or IBA, organized by Dwyer, Carmelo Iglesias, and others), and the Community Assembly for a United South End (CAUSE, an umbrella antirenewal group). The first two sought to develop community-owned, nonprofit, subsidized housing projects, while the third, CAUSE, sought to halt demolition and relocation, to build more subsidized housing, and to control the BRA's actions in the South End.

Dismayed by BRA activities and the failure of established organizations to counter them, these leaders and their organizations began door-to-door organizing campaigns. In the case of SETC and ETC, these campaigns revolved around protests against poor maintenance or trash-filled lots and demonstrations in favor of low-rent housing development. Parallel to these efforts, CAUSE held a series of community-wide meetings to push the Boston City Council into halting further demolition by the BRA.

In late 1967 and 1968, these three organizations sponsored a series of increasingly militant demonstrations. In the first six months of 1968, for example, CAUSE launched a sustained attack on the BRA, armed with Urban Planning Aid and Urban Field Service reports on the inadequacy of the BRA's relocation and rehabilitation efforts. In January, it drew eight hundred black and Puerto Rican tenants to the first of two city council urban renewal committee hearings on CAUSE demands. After the BRA director Hale Champion said he could not halt demolition, six hundred tenants turned out at a second hearing in March. These tumultuous events produced anguished statements about how the BRA was destroying the South End, as well as more dispassionate statements from advocacy planners documenting the same point.

On April 1, CAUSE gave Mayor White a one-week deadline to respond to its demands.[7] Receiving no response, CAUSE members first occupied the BRA South End site office and jostled and jeered the mayor when he appeared to tell them they would be arrested. Although Mel King tried to stave off mass arrests by convincing the occupants to leave at 5:00 P.M., twenty-three were arrested when they blocked a paddy wagon containing King and two other CAUSE leaders, Martin Gopen and David Smith.

Two days later, CAUSE members seized a parking lot leased to a Boston fire commissioner. The lot had housed one hundred poor families before the BRA cleared it. Two hundred CAUSE sympathizers established a "Tent City" to highlight the need for a crash subsidized housing construction program. A few weeks later, dissident USES employees active in CAUSE also took over the USES central office to dramatize their opposition to its BRA relocation services contract. Concurrent with these activities, SETC conducted a series of demonstrations designed to embarrass a major South End slumlord and force him to turn over his properties for subsidized, neighborhood-sponsored rehabilitation. The Emergency Tenants' Council did the same in Parcel 19, and opened negotiations with the BRA about being named sole developer for the parcel. The mood was one of excitement and confrontation, with direct action finally forcing "the system" to notice real community needs.

Similar events took place in the Western Addition. In 1963, the Congress of Racial Equality and its white allies had established Freedom House in the Western Addition to agitate against the urban renewal plan. Though their efforts failed when Freedom House fell apart in the face of Justin Herman's and Mayor Shelley's strong support for the A-2 project, it did manage to organize a tenants' union and homeowners' association whose members later became active against renewal. (Liberal Democrat Shelley succeeded Christopher in 1964 but continued to back renewal.)

The Black Students' Union at San Francisco State and other civil rights groups also provided new leadership against the SFRA's activities. In 1965 and 1966, activists from these groups organized the Community Action Program in the Western Addition, though

186

Mayor Shelley ultimately forced them out. The election of Mayor Joseph Alioto (former SFRA chairman) in 1967 and President Richard Nixon in 1968 ensured that the CAP would not be used as a vantage point for organizing.

As in the South End, a group of activist white ministers provided the impetus for some of the most important Western Addition organizing. Three of them had attended a conference led by Saul Alinsky in 1966, and with the help of a white former Freedom House activist decided to pull together an Alinsky-style neighborhood-wide "people's organization." During 1967, they gathered people the Freedom House had organized and began a door-to-door campaign, sometimes attracting as many as fifty people, mostly blacks, to their weekly meetings. Blacks soon claimed leadership of the group, which became known as the Western Addition Community Organization, or WACO, and began to focus its attention on displacement and housing construction.

WACO activists included Hannibal Williams, a charismatic one-time bouncer who was attending San Francisco State on his way to becoming an ordained minister, Ken and Eva Brown of the Homeowners' Association, Tenants' Union activist Mary Rogers, and other residents without affiliation to the neighborhood's older, more established institutions. An activist minister obtained a church grant to pay for organizing, and by spring, WACO had enlisted support from twenty-six black organizations.

On April 12, 1967, WACO announced to the press that it was launching an all-out attack on the SFRA. WACO's spirit was forcefully articulated by Williams, who became chairman of the organization. At an abortive "peace-making" session with Mayor Shelley, Williams said,

We've been misrepresented by a lot of people who don't speak for us. I'm a humble man, but one thing I'm sure of, somewhere in federal law there must be something about self-determination. It's our right and we're here to get it. We're not begging or asking for anything. It's our right, and we want it.[8]

This launched a series of actions throughout 1967 and into 1968 which included picketing the SFRA site office, large-scale com-

187

munity meetings attended by more than three hundred people, and seizing the stage at various public hearings. Here, too, passion in service to a just cause ran high. In several instances, WACO members sat in front of bulldozers at demolition sites in order to halt displacement and increase the number of subsidized units.[9] Unlike its counterparts in the South End, WACO also enlisted the services of public interest lawyers to sue the SFRA to halt displacement. In late 1968, a federal judge restrained HUD from disbursing further funds for the project until the SFRA came up with an acceptable relocation program.

These events polarized both the South End and the Western Addition and the larger arena of city politics. In the neighborhoods, new leadership networks challenged those of established leaders, who were attacked for "selling out." This heightened level of tension was repeated at the city-wide level as well, as the general environment of political confrontation created divisions within elite organizations and City Hall itself. Many of the younger, more liberal professionals working in the BRA, SFRA, and city government and politics felt that the protesters had a point.

The dilemma which neighborhood protest posed for the United South End Settlements illustrated the polarization of the neighborhoods. Founded to serve the poor, USES had accepted a large contract from the BRA to provide relocation services. USES felt this was part of "the bridging role USES had traditionally played between 'downtown' and the community." But, in the words of USES' director, "The failure of urban renewal . . . has created deep political division in this community" and made it "difficult, if not impossible, for this agency to perform its basic services for the people of this community."[10] Though it took a sit-in by eleven dissident employees, USES did finally terminate its relationship with the BRA. This painful conflict was echoed in many ways.

Conflicts like those in the South End also polarized Boston City politics. On the strength of his renewal performance, Ed Logue had run for mayor in 1967. Though supported by members of Vault, developers, and planners, he ran a poor fourth behind Kevin White and Louise Day Hicks. Vault members then supported

White in the runoff. Though a backer of "the New Boston," White also drew support from neighborhood groups which opposed the BRA. Strong support in areas like the South End gave White a narrow victory over Hicks. White "seized on the alienation of people from government and vowed to respond to the needs of the neighborhoods." His administration, at least at the outset, combined wily Boston polls and "able administrators, progressives, drawn from all parts of the U.S."[11]

Once in office in 1968, White set up a Little City Hall program to keep better touch with neighborhood political currents. Some members of the White administration identified with the demands being made by community groups from places like the South End. In sharp contrast to the Collins administration, the White administration responded to, and benefited from, the rising tide of neighborhood activism. These efforts led working class Irish supporters of Louise Day Hicks to resent "Mayor Black."

The late 1960s also polarized Western Addition and San Francisco politics. Many traditional Western Addition institutions depended on resources from the white community. Black churches, for example, often took money from white politicians who wanted to influence black parishoners at the ballot box. The rising WACO leadership challenged the right of traditional leaders to speak for the community and criticized their complicity with the SFRA. Even WACO became a forum for confrontation, as younger, more radical groups like the Black Panthers challenged the older civil rights activists like Williams.

Neighborhood activism in the black Western Addition and the Latino Mission district (where the Mission Coalition was being organized in the same period) contributed to growing city-wide opposition to "growth at any cost" politics in San Francisco. Jack Shelley, a Democratic U.S. congressman and former trade unionist, had become mayor at George Christopher's retirement in 1963. Liberal Democrats, unions, and minority groups had backed Shelley, but he also had downtown ties. He was considered so inept, however, that many of these supporters deserted him in 1967. (He did veto a 1967 Board of Supervisors resolution asking for

189

a halt to displacement in the Western Addition and opposed neighborhood control over the poverty program.)

In the 1967 race, Joseph Alioto combined all the elements of progrowth politics in a successful campaign against a Republican and a liberal Democrat. Downtown corporations contributed heavily to this former SFRA chairman, and the building trades also gave him strong support. Alioto gained minority neighborhoods' backing by indicating he would give good appointments to black trade unionists from the Laborers' Union and the International Longshoremen. Upon election, Alioto strongly backed M. Justin Herman.

During Alioto's two terms, he effectively thwarted the rising tide of neighborhood activism. "At heart," his planning director noted, "the Mayor was a laissez-faire development man. His advocacy of most big development proposals allowed for no mistake as to where his sympathies were."[12] Community organizations, middle-class neighborhood preservationists, and liberal activists increasingly opposed Alioto. Finally, in 1975, they united with sufficient force to elect George Moscone mayor and to reform the city charter so that supervisors would be elected by district. Mayor Moscone's subsequent assassination stemmed in part, however, from the continuing high level of underlying hostility within the city. Moscone's murderer came from a conservative, Catholic civil-service background which had a low opinion of the mayor's ties with the gay community, blacks, and liberal activists.

2. THE LOCAL POLITICAL SYSTEM RESPONDS TO NEIGHBORHOOD ACTIVISM

However unpleasant the growing conflict within neighborhood and city politics during the late 1960s and 1970s, it made change possible. Neighborhood activism created a new "political space" which allowed, and sometimes forced, urban politicians and administrators to interact with new contenders for power. These new interactions ended the days in which corporate officials and redevelopment agency administrators could quietly formulate and execute large-scale development plans on their own. The new contenders failed, however, to change the overall trajectory of neighborhood and city development.

Urban Renewal Project Administration

Initially, Boston and San Francisco renewal administrators resisted the demands of the South End and Western Addition organizations. Mayor Kevin White of Boston and his new BRA director, Hale Champion, showed a greater desire to conciliate CAUSE, ETC, and SETC, than did Alioto and Herman toward the Western Addition. White had seen old-style BRA insensitivity defeated in 1966 and 1967 electoral contests; in San Francisco, the old order did not fully change until after Herman's untimely death in 1971 and George Moscone's subsequent election in 1975. Nevertheless, neither White nor Champion wanted to turn control of renewal over to community groups.

Neighborhood confrontation with City Hall slowly and painfully evolved into collaboration between 1968 and 1975 in both cities. Neighborhood organizations gave up their oppositional stance in order to get influence in City Hall and access to Great Society-era federal program benefits, including those offered by renewal. Both found common cause against the Nixon administration, especially after the 1973 housing program freeze. City officials backed away from their initial resistance and ultimately learned that they could turn these new, hostile voices into political support. They could, in short, be tamed.

Though Champion at first refused to halt demolition and displacement in the South End, in January 1968, he did increase the planned nonprofit, moderate rental housing which would be leased by the Boston Housing Authority from 10 percent to 30 percent. He also sought to get the long-stalled construction of these units moving, promising to begin on 1,286 such units during the summer of 1968. After continued sit-ins, the BRA announced in May that it would temporarily halt demolition in the South End and would increase the number of subsidized units to be built by nonprofit sponsors under the moderate-rent 221(d)(3) program.

191

The last act of the Great Society in 1968 was to increase dramatically funding for this program, renamed Section 236.

Because of the city council hearings on the South End, and HUD's LPA letter 458 of June 1968, which mandated "maximum resident participation" in project area committees, Mayor White also conceded that some sort of neighborhood advisory committee would be set up. CAUSE pressed for strong community control over renewal.[13] The city council finally passed a compromise version in May 1969, giving a new advisory body the right to review any South End matter being sent to the BRA Board for decision, but no veto over it. Nor did it mandate tenant representation.

CAUSE opposed the city scheme and set out to hold its own election for a project area committee. The CAUSE polling drew 3,141 voters, while the official city election drew 2,416 three weeks later. The city's South End Project Area Committee (SEPAC) had twenty-five white property owners, including thirteen who had helped to fashion the original urban renewal plan, as well as eight blacks and two Puerto Ricans. In contrast, the People's Urban Renewal Committee had twenty-four blacks, four Puerto Ricans, and fourteen whites, the majority of whom were tenants. This group conducted sporadic activities for a year, but ultimately collapsed in the face of SEPAC's two staff members, a $35,000 city budget, and official status. In subsequent SEPAC elections, a number of those who had been active in CAUSE and PURC ran for SEPAC office, and by 1973 had won control of that body.

During the fall of 1969 and into 1970, the BRA also designated SETC, ETC, and a number of other community organizations as developers of nonprofit housing projects. Through these designations, the BRA revised the 1965 South End Renewal Program, thereby increasing the number of subsidized low- and moderate-rent housing units to be constructed from the initial 3,100 to 3,910.[14] Six hundred twenty-five of these units were developed on Parcel 19 by Inquilinos Boricuas en Acción, successor to ETC. In commenting on his negotiations, the BRA director said, "I think we had too much arguing with neighborhood groups. When we all sat down together, we found we had the same objectives."[15] The black South End Tenants' Council, operating as the Tenant Development Corporation, rehabilitated 285 units in the fifty-six buildings it successfully acquired from the slumlord it had challenged.

In the end, however, these victories proved to be limited. With the Nixon administration's freeze on subsidized housing in 1973 and the advent of the Community Development Block Grant Program in 1974, it became clear that funds would not be available to complete the original 1965 Plan, much less the additional units that community groups wanted. HUD also ruled against building further subsidized housing in so-called impacted areas like the South End. Although Boston spent 20 percent of its $30 million in 1976 CDBG funds on urban renewal activities, $2 million of it in the South End, the block grant program spread money rather than concentrating it in renewal project areas. With the advent of a more vocal and radical majority on SEPAC in 1973, the mayor had even less incentive to favor the area. By the mid-1970s, the South End urban renewal program had effectively come to an end, and SEPAC expired with it.

Though the SFRA and its executive director, Justin Herman, resisted community demands more firmly, the Western Addition experienced similar results. Herman stoutly opposed WACO, calling it "a passing flurry of proletarianism." He told a gathering of renewal officials that "there must come a time in any community's life when the interests of the total community must dominate those of the neighborhoods. At such times, in my judgment, a [neighborhood] veto is not in the interest of having a desirable community."[16] At another point, he said, "No little popular group is going to put together a multi-million dollar project. They aren't going to stop one either."[17] In the SFRA *Annual Reports* of these years, Herman accused WACO of trying to "turn back the clock," attacking "the right of a city to survive by renewing and replacing its worn out parts," and being a "dissident minority voice" which should not be "mistaken for a majority."[18]

Despite these attitudes, WACO made progress on two fronts. Because of the federal participation requirement, the SFRA set

193

up a Western Addition Project Area Committee (WAPAC). WACO was able to name most of the members of WAPAC's initial board (it was not elected, as was SEPAC's first board). For a time, Hannibal Williams served as chairman of both groups. WAPAC's initial budget was set at $88,000, and like SEPAC, the organization was charged with reviewing SFRA activities in the Western Addition. WAPAC soon became the focal point for conflict within the Western Addition, however, and his opponents forced Williams to resign, accusing him of self-aggrandizement and selling out to the Agency. Tension within WAPAC increased to the point that several years later one of its staff members was murdered and its offices burned down by an arsonist.

WACO achieved greater leverage through its suit against HUD and the SFRA. On December 16, 1968, Federal Judge William Sweigert granted WACO a restraining order, stating that "there had been no compliance by the local agency with some of the provisions on temporary relocation as required by the federal government" (*WACO* v. *Romney*, 294 F. Supp. 433, N. D. Cal. 1968). Herman, however, called the suit "foolish and without foundation" and attacked WACO's Neighborhood Legal Assistance (SFNLAF) attorney as "a clever, well-financed, able, ambulance-chasing lawyer who has no respect for poor people, is wrong and intellectually dishonest."[19]

Nevertheless, the suit allowed WACO and its SFNLAF attorneys to monitor further relocation practices and prevent involuntary displacement. It also led Herman to increase subsidized housing construction from the mere 569 which had been constructed through 1970 to a total of 1,868 for 1971. Despite the internal turmoil affecting WACO and WAPAC, and despite Herman's resolute opposition, the pace of subsidized housing construction increased, displacement was monitored, and the number of community-based housing development sponsors increased.[20]

In 1975, a broad coalition of labor unions, neighborhood and minority groups, and middle-class liberal activists elected George Moscone mayor. Moscone named new members to the SFRA Board, including Reverend Hannibal Williams and two other liberals. (Moscone later replaced Williams with a less abrasive black minister.) Williams and his board allies ''set the agency on its ear.'' They chose Wilbur Hamilton, a black former ILWU trade unionist who had become Western Addition A-2 project director, to head the agency. With the completion of its downtown projects in the early 1970s, the SFRA's main activity became subsidized housing construction by community sponsors in the remaining project areas, particularly the Western Addition.

As in Boston, the housing freeze and the CDBG Program cut into the SFRA's monopoly over HUD funds and reduced its ability to deliver on its new mission. As HUD itself acknowledged in 1971, ''Funds for the remaining 1,913 Section 236 units needed to complete the plan are not presently available nor likely to be in the foreseeable future.''[21] By 1979, 2,525 units had been constructed; displacement ran well ahead of this construction.

Neighborhood Leadership Networks

Interaction between community organizations and city officials had five effects on South End and Western Addition leadership networks:

1. Traditional networks persisted and were reinforced.
2. New networks became institutionalized and increasingly turned to service delivery, especially community-based housing development.
3. New white, middle-class, home-owning professionals also formed their own leadership networks.
4. Individuals from the new leadership networks experienced upward mobility and became integrated into local government and dominant local institutions.
5. Government reached into the neighborhoods and designated its own ''leaders.''

In the short run, the last trend received great attention as neighborhood leaders accused others of ''selling out'' to outside institutions. Many were labeled ''poverty pimps.'' But as community mobilization subsided, so did the money that outside institutions would spend on creating co-opted leadership. In the longer term, such leaders have not sustained legitimate followings.

The upward mobility which the new leadership experienced has also received considerable attention. In the South End, Mel King became a state representative; others went on to employment at the Boston University Medical Center and the MIT Department of Urban Studies and Planning. Another became a judge, while SETC's founder went on to become part of a black development effort in North Carolina. In the Western Addition, key activists found employment with the SFRA, the Housing Authority, a community design center, and with an urban management consulting firm. These were predictable outcomes. While the departure of some leaders has reduced neighborhood resources, it has also given these neighborhoods contacts in dominant institutions which command greater resources.

The institutionalization of the new leadership networks and their shift from protest to service delivery has had the greatest long-term impact. In the South End, SETC and IBA became major housing developers and augmented their construction activities with job training and placement, individual and group counseling, art and theater projects, and child care. Even the South End institutions which provided traditional leadership came to rely increasingly on administering government programs. After the United South End Settlements built a new central facility, it became heavily reliant on government reimbursement for providing social services.

Major Western Addition organizations followed the same trajectory. WACO, which had lost much of its reason for existence after WAPAC was founded and its lawsuit was resolved in 1971, turned to providing surplus food to needy area residents. WAPAC became progressively more involved with securing SFRA jobs. (Its staff members formed the Fillmore Economic Development Corporation to undertake a small rehabilitation project.) Hannibal Williams, WACO and WAPAC's charismatic early leader, became the minister of the New Liberation Presbyterian Church in the neighborhood. It, too, runs government-funded summer youth programs.

196

In short, in these neighborhoods, as elsewhere, the activism of the 1960s has evolved into a new layer of government, the neighborhood-level, nonprofit, alternative social service providers. These groups have become major claimants on the public budget, receiving funding from the Community Services Administration, DOL's CETA Program, HEW's Title XX, the state, as well as an important part of the HUD-funded construction activity.

This transformation inevitably altered the relationships between neighborhood leaders and their followings. Leaders have come to view neighborhood needs in programmatic rather than political terms. They want more funding for service programs like CETA or care of the elderly. This orientation differs strongly from the universalistic, political outlook which had characterized earlier demands for "community control." It has increased their dependence on City Hall, as well. The neighborhood competition for scarce budgetary resources also decreases the chance for political unity among them.

When political leaders become program administrators, their constituents also become clients. Neighborhood housing sponsors have "creamed" their applicant pool for the best tenants, who are not usually the most needy. In the most extreme cases, these tendencies have produced what might be called "programmatic tribalism," with fragmented clans, each with its own patrons and clients, maneuvering against the next.

No matter how much such outcomes weaken neighborhood political independence, though, neighborhood leaders had little choice but to go in this direction if they wished to survive. By developing a program orientation, neighborhood leaders have become more influential in city-wide decision-making, have increased their resource base, and, to some degree at least, they have preserved the values and visions with which they emerged on the political scene in the mid-1960s.

Middle-class "new immigrants" to the South End and Western Addition have also produced leadership networks. In the South End, they formed the Committee for a Balanced South End, a group which opposes further construction of subsidized housing. The "Balance Committee," as it has become known, sued three

SEPAC- and BRA-approved projects in 1973 and 1974. Though two of these cases (brought on environmental review grounds) were dismissed, in the third the developer agreed in an out-of-court settlement to make 25 percent of the units available at market rates. The Balance Committee has lobbied effectively against additional Section 8 units and helped convince Mayor White to terminate SEPAC's funding in 1977. As the South End project is closed out, the Balance Committee has also argued strongly for using the key sites remaining in BRA possession for private market development rather than subsidized projects.[22]

In the Western Addition, the white influx into the Victorian housing stock which remains standing around the core of the project area has come from multiple-income, white, gay households. According to one study of the San Francisco gay community, the Western Addition "has emerged as a [gay] concentration area in the mid-1970s. The area—representing one of the highest concentrations of gay households—has undergone a significant transformation."[23] While politically liberal, the gay culture is highly organized and concerned with issues like assault and crime which inevitably pit it against black residents in the Fillmore. Gay numbers and political influence are clearly on the rise in San Francisco, while black numbers are declining, a fact blacks resent.[24]

Even for blacks, however, the gentrification of the South End and the Western Addition have not been completely negative. Many white newcomers are committed to the same values which minority leaders sought to advance. They possess strong political resources and often want to preserve a multiracial, multiclass balance within the neighborhoods. These new groups hold the potential for cooperation as well as conflict.

Neighborhood Development Patterns

Neighborhood activists largely failed in their quest to control the trajectory of neighborhood development. Many community-sponsored housing projects faced severe financial difficulty in 1973–1975 and were saved only by Section 8 leasing as public housing units. (The post-1968 expansion in federal housing subsidies thus failed to produce a proportionate growth in new units.) Many of those projects which survived the fiscal crunch (about 15 percent did not) became islands of permanence in a surrounding sea of private market change.

In the South End, abandonment and private market rehabilitation removed far more low-rent units from the housing stock than the BRA demolished. According to a 1975 comprehensive housing review undertaken by SEPAC, "Comparing the 1965 plan with the 1974 demolition list, the number of units lost through demolition and conversion in the South End exceeded what had been projected by the plan by 125 percent."[25] The number of licensed lodging houses, which had accounted for about half the neighborhood's units before renewal, fell precipitously. Between 1960 and 1979, the total number of occupied units in the South End project area census tracts dropped from 14,012 to a low of 7,277 in the early 1970s, recovering to 9,395 by 1980.[26] (See Table 3, which presents figures calculated on a slightly different geographic basis than the actual project area.) SEPAC estimated that of the ten thousand South End units lost by 1974, the BRA had removed about thirty-five hundred, unplanned demolition about three thousand, and private conversion about three thousand. Against these precipitous declines in the low-rent housing stock, the increase in subsidized units built under BRA auspices from 3,100 to 3,910 seems modest indeed.

Although the net South End population has declined from roughly twenty-seven thousand in 1960 to twenty-one thousand in 1980, the gross out-migration probably amounted to twenty-five thousand people (offset by nineteen thousand newcomers). Single elderly whites, black families, and blue collar ethnics have contributed most to this exodus. Their place has been taken by younger, childless, multiincome households, with substantially higher education and rates of professional employment (see Table 3).[27] While Boston's white population plummeted, the South End's shrank only a little. By 1979, a typical rehabilitated South End row house cost well in excess of $125,000.

The same has happened in the Western Addition. As Table 4

199

TABLE 3 Neighborhood and City Development Trends
in the South End and Boston

| | 1940 | | 1950 | |
	SE	Boston	SE	Boston
Total population	41 320	770 816	44 323	801 444
White population	35 105	745 466	32 699	785 700
Black population	6 052	23 679	11 198	40 057
Spanish speaking	—	—	—	—
Foreign born	11 338	180 864	7 987	144 092
Total employed	16 503	337 817	18 871	311 816
Professional and				
technical	1 356	23 871	1 551	32 461
Operatives	2 791	50 538	4 187	61 170
Median income ($)	—	—	1 457	2 643
(households)				
Occupied units	10 285	197 393	10 840	218 103
Owner occupied	1 239	41 236	1 091	54 266
Median rent ($)	18.51	36.67	28.25	35.40

SOURCE: U.S. Department of Commerce, Bureau of the Census, 1940–
1980 *Censuses of Population.*

a Category changes from foreign born to foreign born or child of foreign
born in 1960 and then back to foreign born in 1980.

b White decline overstated by change in classification of Hispanics.

1940–1960 Census Tracts for South End: 11-14, J2, L1-L6.

1970–1980 Census Tracts for South End: 0704-0712.

These census tracts do not correspond exactly with urban renewal project
area boundaries.

shows, the SFRA demolished several thousand units, reducing
the total number of housing units from 12,334 in 1960 to a net
of 10,306 in 1970 (even after the construction of more than a
thousand units). In the process, the SFRA displaced 3,155 families
and 3,984 single persons, 60 percent of whom self-relocated with-

| | 1960 | | 1970 | | 1980 |
SE	Boston	SE	Boston	SE	Boston
27 439	697 197	18 820	641 071	20 949	562 994
16 984	628 704	9 106	524 709	8 871	393 937[b]
8 550	63 165	6 919	104 707	7 331	126 229
430	1 033	1 529	17 984	2 911	36 068
10 670[a]	317 064[a]	6 001[a]	237 089[a]	4 219	87 056
12 335	288 246	7 851	266 505	10 120	256 047
777	33 476	987	44 894	1 292	51 977
2 665	52 175	1 211	27 895	830	17 320
2 247	4 438	3 450	5 921	14 069	16 062
14 012	224 432	7 277	217 622	9 395	218 457
1 283	61 165	841	59 230	936	59 504
41.80	60.00	83.11	98.00	191.00	203.00

out public assistance. Private reconversion of lodging houses and other multifamily structures accounts for several thousand of this loss. Though twice as much subsidized housing was actually constructed as the 1,300 units initially projected, resulting units could at best house no more than a quarter of those displaced, leaving the neighborhood with less than half the units it had in 1950, before renewal began.

The process of change has been traumatic. As one gay real estate speculator in the Western Addition commented, "Before 1977, you could pick up anything, kick out the blacks and put in gays, unload it in three months, and make $30,000. What do you think 'good tenants' means in the multiple listing books? It means the dirty work has been done."[28] By some estimates, less than 25 percent of the 3,177 units which urban renewal left standing in the Western Addition project area are still occupied by blacks.

TABLE 4 Neighborhood and Cith Development Trends
in the Western Addition and San Francisco

	1940		1950	
	WA	SF	WA	SF
Total population	37 849	634 536	43 612	775 357
White population	28 419	602 701	23 364	693 888
Black population	2 144	4 846	14 888	43 502
Japanese	5 087	—	5 383	—
Foreign born	9 913	130 271	5 406	120 393
Total employed	16 177	271 306	19 212	330 616
Professional and				
technical	902	20 999	1 312	35 915
Operatives	1 920	39 534	2 977	44 186
Median income ($)	—	—	2 105	3 009
Occupied units	16 104	206 011	16 369	257 734
Owner occupied	895	64 398	1 486	94 594
Median rent ($)	21.17	30.13	34.82	40.27

SOURCE: U.S. Department of Commerce, Bureau of the Census, 1940–
1980 *Censuses of Population.*

ᵃ Category changes from foreign born to foreign born or child of foreign
born in 1960 and then back to foreign born in 1980.
ᵇ White decline overstated by change in classification of Hispanics.
  1940–1960 Census Tracts for Western Addition: J1-J2, J6-J13.
  1970–1980 Census Tracts for Western Addition: 0151-0152, 0155,
1058-0161.
  These census tracts do not correspond exactly with urban renewal project
area boundaries.

The remaining black community has been crowded into large,
grim public housing projects and the subsidized housing. As in
the South End, where much of the new subsidized housing is
clustered at the end of the neighborhood closest to Boston's traditional black ghetto, urban renewal has increased racial segre-

1960		1970		1980	
WA	SF	WA	SF	WA	SF
28 019	740 316	22 210	715 674	21 460	678 974
9 474	604 403	8 671	511 186	7 915	360 841[b]
14 631	74 383	10 926	96 078	10 266	86 190
3 914	—	2 613	—	1 310	—
7 916[a]	321 802[a]	5 004[a]	317 045[a]	3 445	192 212
12 307	331 156	9 853	318 311	9 444	342 484
1 061	40 446	1 691	55 878	1 650	65 592
1 252	38 161	566	23 247	288	15 487
3 178	4 757	5 315	6 765	11 734	15 867
12 334	291 975	10 306	295 174	11 078	298 274
1 017	102 182	926	97 036	1 339	100 719
57.29	68.00	112.71	128.00	—	285.00

gation and interracial hostility in San Francisco. A meeting called by liberal activists and WAPAC members to discuss the "gay invasion" only narrowly averted violence between the groups.

A recent study has shown that while 46 percent of the housing turnovers in one part of the Western Addition went to blacks in 1976, that figure fell to 19 percent by 1979. In this subarea, adult male households without children climbed from 19 to 52 percent of the in-mover population.[29] Another study in the same subarea showed that rents and housing costs "outpaced the overall rate of inflation for housing in the city or in the U.S. as a whole." Values from two- and three-unit structures increased 319 percent between 1970 and 1979, and they now sell for more than $175,000.[30] As Table 4 shows, in the project area census tracts, the number of blacks declined 6 percent between 1970 and 1980, and their incomes lagged. In the larger area of the Western Addition as a whole black population declined 18 percent. Since 1960, their

203

numbers have been reduced by half, while the number of residents of Japanese ancestry was reduced by two-thirds.

City-wide Development Patterns

Neighborhood efforts have been even less successful in influencing city-wide development patterns. Since the early 1960s, the Boston and San Francisco CBDs have experienced a sustained boom in office building construction, reflecting their dramatic expansion in headquarters and high-level service employment. Boston and San Francisco have the fourth- and fifth-largest amounts of CBD office space of all large U.S. cities, and among the highest construction rates in the late 1970s.[31] The growth of these new functions, in physical and employment terms, has generated a new social stratum within Boston and San Francisco: the middle-class professional, typically highly educated, well paid, and increasingly drawn from the baby-boom age cohorts.

A series of reports from the Boston Redevelopment Authority outlines these trends for Boston. As of 1976, Boston had 44 million square feet of office space in 378 buildings, 40 percent of which was built after 1960. Some 10 million square feet of space was built between 1970 and 1976 alone.[32] About one-third of this space had been constructed in such urban renewal projects as Prudential Center and Government Center. Additional commercial projects, particularly Park Plaza and South Station, are expected to generate hundreds of millions of dollars in additional investment.

Of the $1.45 billion in private, nonresidential physical investment which Boston estimated in 1975 would be put in place between 1975 and 1980, one-third would go to commercial urban renewal projects and another one-sixth to new office building construction. Significantly, medical facility expansion accounted for $413 million, or 28 percent of the planned investment, while educational institutional expansion accounted for another $179 million, or 12 percent. The City of Boston anticipated spending $332 million on public facilities and urban renewal, and $244 million on street repair. The state highway department, the port-airport authority, and the transit system would spend an additional $1.44 billion. Residential construction was expected to add $880 million to this amount, for a grand total of predicted infrastructural investment between 1975 and 1980 of $4.4 billion.[33] Most of these plans were carried through.

These physical investments have had a strong impact on Boston's demographic makeup. According to the BRA, "In the past decade, the City of Boston economy has experienced an extraordinary process of transformation, upgrading, and growth . . . accompanied by an upgrading of the income and educational level of the population. . . ."[34] A new class of people were being attracted to Boston, creating "a new age structure and neighborhood pattern."[35] Table 3 shows, for example, that white collar professional and technical workers grew from 33,476 in 1960 to 51,977 in 1980, while blue collar operatives shrank from 52,175 to 17,320. Real median income also rose by a third.

The same patterns are apparent in San Francisco. San Francisco is a headquarters and business service node second only to New York and Chicago. By January 1, 1974, according to a major study of San Francisco's high-rise development, the city contained 50 million square feet of office space, of which 23 million had been constructed since 1959. Approximately 2.8 million square feet, or 12 percent of this new space, was built in the Golden Gate urban renewal project, while the Yerba Buena Center urban renewal project located across Market Street from the financial district may generate 5 million more square feet.[36] The acreage occupied by hospitals also quadrupled from 46 to 166 acres between 1964 and 1970.

Since 1974, the pace of construction picked up: between 1974 and 1980, another 11.3 million square feet of prime high-rise office space was completed, and 8.6 million more was being constructed or actively proposed through 1982.[37] As in Boston, this physical investment and expansion has been accompanied by rapid growth in CBD employment and the entry of a new social stratum into the San Francisco housing market.

A slightly higher proportion of San Francisco's office-building employees lived within the city, according to the 1974 survey, than in Boston (40 percent as opposed to 31 percent). Those who lived within the city tended to hold clerical jobs, but significant proportions of higher level employees also lived within the city. Other sources such as the University of California Medical Center also attract young professionals to San Francisco. Signs of middle-class invasion and succession are unmistakably present throughout the crescent of intrinsically attractive and convenient, although poorly maintained, Victorian housing stock which stretches from the Western Addition south through the Castro and Noe Valley and eastward into the Mission District.[38] Table 4 gives city-wide trends for San Francisco. Of all the major central cities, San Francisco is the only one in which the absolute number of blacks was reduced between 1970 and 1980; their number declined 10.1 percent. As in Boston, the number of professionals climbed by more than half while the number of operatives was cut by more than two-thirds.

City-wide Political Competition

Though neighborhood groups could not control neighborhoods or city-wide development trends, they *did* influence city-wide political competition. Demographic change has weakened some traditional components of progrowth coalitions while political mobilization during the 1960s made excluded but growing constituencies more important. As a result, since the 1970s "neighborhood oriented" mayors have often replaced old-fashioned, progrowth political leaders like Collins or Alioto.

Boston and San Francisco demonstrate this trend in contrasting ways. In Boston, Mayor White has used neighborhood-oriented programs and control over the allocation of program benefits to neighborhoods to build a strong, if currently embattled, political organization. Its allegiance and political capacity cannot be transferred to other offices and candidates, but it has enabled White to overcome repeated challenges and consolidate his hold on city government. The vote-producing abilities of groups like the South End's IBA helped give White staying power, especially in the latter 1970s.

San Francisco's political system by contrast is much more fragmented, with neighborhood activists occupying various points of influence. George Moscone's 1975 mayoral victory engendered their rise to influence. A passionate liberal, Moscone was backed by minority groups, community organizations, the liberal wing of the labor movement (particularly the public employees), the gay community, and liberal activists. Moscone narrowly beat a law-and-order conservative supported by the white property-owning middle class, the business community, and the building trades. Moscone was subsequently assassinated, along with gay Supervisor Harvey Milk, by a white, conservative, working class, ex-policeman who was evidently incensed by what he considered to be the perverted forces which Moscone had led to power. Moscone's coalition went on to elect his moderate emergency successor, Dianne Feinstein, over a conservative opponent.

Mayors White and Moscone continued to back major development projects (such as Park Plaza in Boston and Yerba Buena Center in San Francisco), and neither neglected ties to business and development interests. Both, however, built a strong neighborhood orientation into their programming. Mayor White established a Little City Hall program, which, together with a City Hall staff, gave him an analytic capacity on neighborhood-related policy issues. A head of the East Boston Little City Hall, for example, helped to take on the Logan Airport noise problem and later organized opposition to the Inner Belt, which White also strongly opposed.

As the White administration has aged, it has become more conservative and less responsive to neighborhood issues. In part, competition from Louise Day Hicks and other busing opponents pushed him to the Right. With the advent of the Community Development Block Grant Program, he shifted resources from black Roxbury and the South End to white ethnic neighborhoods, and from subsidized housing to rehabilitation grants and loans to homeowners and neighborhood commercial districts. Nevertheless, Boston spent some $500 million on neighborhood capital improvements between 1968 and 1975, six times more than in the previous seven years.[39]

207

San Francisco did not develop administrative mechanisms like Boston's Little City Hall program. It is politically far more decentralized, however. For five years, district supervisors kept in close touch with various neighborhoods, and were far more accessible to, and even beholden to, neighborhood organizations than were their at-large predecessors. Though conservatives won a reversion to the at-large system in 1980, supervisors originally elected on the district basis still dominate the board. Mayoral appointments to San Francisco's many boards and commissions have broadened considerably from Mayor Alioto's days, when they were dominated primarily by his big business and big labor supporters. Moscone appointed neighborhood preservationists to the Planning Commission and renewal opponent Hannibal Williams to the Redevelopment Agency Board. The San Francisco community development budget, like Boston's, was also shifted toward neighborhood improvements. In contrast to Boston's, a substantial fraction of the city's CDBG funds have been spent on community-based social service providers.

In sum, while the rise of neighborhood activism in Boston and San Francisco has neither controlled key development decisions nor banished traditional progrowth politics, it has definitely influenced how political leaders compete for power. This, in turn, has influenced the kinds of programs enacted and the way they are administered. Public intervention now focuses on distributing a variety of program benefits to neighborhood constituencies. In both cities, mayors have used CDBG funds to rehabilitate owner-occupied properties and neighborhood business districts, thereby reinforcing their political support. Yet in both cities, a strong undercurrent of conflict over the issues which initially prompted the "community revolution" can still be felt.

3. THE NATIONAL POLITICAL SYSTEM RESPONDS TO NEIGHBORHOOD ACTIVISM

The South End and the Western Addition experiences illustrate how Great Society programs pushed local Democratic electoral coalitions to include new elements, thereby expanding the Democrats' national electoral base. Local officials used the Community Action Program, Model Cities, the 1968 Housing Act programs, and such devices as the HUD requirement of project area committees to absorb the mobilization of those who had been aggrieved by past policies. It was a conflict-laden process, but it worked. Cities like Boston and San Francisco provide national Democratic candidates a major source of votes as a result.

Beginning in 1969, the Nixon administration attacked the complex relationships which Democrats had woven between federal urban development programs, neighborhood constituencies, and Democratic elected officials. Ironically, just as neighborhoods had won some influence over these programs, the Nixon administration began its onslaught against them, including urban renewal itself. The neighborhood cases show the local impact of the moves Nixon took after his 1972 landslide reelection. Nixon moved forcefully to undermine the program base around which neighborhoods and Democratic City Halls had made their peace.

From 1973 to 1975, economic recession and Nixon's New Federalism pushed subsidized housing projects toward bankruptcy, halted the construction of additional projects, terminated urban renewal, and made it impossible for local agencies and officials to deliver on their promises. The Nixon administration's response threw City Halls and neighborhood activists alike sharply on the defensive.

In the South End and the Western Addition, these policies left prime development parcels up for grabs. Four major South End parcels owned by the BRA still face "close out" decisions. The famous Tent City parcel is one; situated just across the railroad tracks from Copley Square and the rapidly developing Back Bay, it is a site which South End organizations like IBA, Tenant Development Corporation, members of the now-defunct SEPAC, and former CAUSE activists want to see developed for several hundred units of subsidized housing. The Balance Committee had deployed all its forces against this notion, preferring market-rate luxury housing at much lower densities instead.

Seven empty, sandy blocks in the Western Addition's center have also lain bare for almot a decade since the neighborhood's

209

Fillmore Street commercial strip, containing Vernon Thornton's bowling alley, was bulldozed. Like Tent City, it also symbolizes unfulfilled promises. Designated as a "black cultural and commercial center," the land remains empty because no black developer has sufficient financial resources to mount an economically feasible project. A commercial development on the necessary scale would have to reach beyond the dwindling black market area, and, if successful, would surely accelerate gentrification and displacement. The land thus remains vacant. To neighborhood residents who remember what existed before, Tent City and Fillmore Street serve as painful reminders of what was lost and what urban renewal promised but never delivered.

4. Conclusion: The Demise of Progrowth Politics

This analysis suggests four conclusions. First, though the neighborhood activism during the 1960s and 1970s did not halt the postindustrial transformation of U.S. cities, it did undermine the local progrowth coalitions, built under Democratic auspices, which had set that transformation in motion. Neighborhood activism ended large-scale clearance projects, drastically revised traditional planning practices by creating citizen review and participation procedures, and created a new policy emphasis on preservation and rehabilitation. In the process, neighborhood activism led to the demise of urban renewal agencies as powerful engines of physical change. It sensitized public opinion to the defects of the "growth at any cost" mentality and the planners' assumption that physical development can solve social problems. As Marshall Berman has observed, "Neighborhood people did not even have the vocabulary to defend their neighborhoods because, until the Sixties, that vocabulary simply did not exist."[40] Today, it does.

Second, the rise of neighborhood activism laid the foundation for a new set of alliance patterns in urban politics and, potentially, in national politics. The response by national and local Democratic political entrepreneurs, while it demobilized neighborhood activism, also created a new set of neighborhood-based service delivery organizations which constitute a substantial political resource.

210

These organizations have become a strong presence in cities across the country, funded at the rate of perhaps $40 billion a year. They have built up reciprocal political ties with a new generation of urban political entrepreneurs, largely Democrats. Although this new level of government, or para-government, has taken numerous shocks from conservatives, it remains a powerful tool for national Democratic political entrepreneurs capable of galvanizing it.

Third, the South End and Western Addition experiences suggest that neighborhood mobilization also created new conflicts and problems for national Democratic political entrepreneurs. Democrats failed to deliver "a decent home and suitable living environment" for most of the low-income residents of neighborhoods like the South End and the Western Addition. Instead, many were forced out of these neighborhoods without adequate relocation assistance, and some were even forced out of their cities. In San Francisco, for example, the black population declined between 1970 and 1980, suggesting a quite large displacement impact. This continuing internal conflict is a major obstacle to the renewal of a Democratic majority.

In place of improving the quality of neighborhood life for those displaced, Democratic liberals instead enacted a variety of community-based social programs. These programs converted political leaders into processors of clients, increased competition among neighborhood-based service delivery organizations, and reduced their accountability to neighborhood residents.[41] Owing to their status as quasi-government bodies and their dependence on City Hall, these organizations have not always developed the kind of independent political clout needed to advocate their constituents' interests.

The impact of urban renewal has deepened conflict among social classes on a neighborhood and city-wide basis. In areas like the South End and the Western Addition, the conflicts between middle-class groups like the "Balanced Committee" and low-income constituencies have become endemic. While the potential for cooperation among these constituencies is real, the barriers are perhaps greater. Certainly, bridging the gap between them constitutes

211

the major challenge facing local and national Democratic entrepreneurs seeking to rebuild urban liberalism. Neither the current mayors of Boston or San Francisco nor, as we shall see, the Carter administration succeeded in bringing these constituencies together behind a common program of neighborhood development.

To the extent that neighborhood mobilization in places like the South End and the Western Addition successfully influenced city politics and urban development programs, it did stimulate the national conservative countermovement and the displacement of private investment away from the older central cities. Chapter three showed how the Nixon administration reacted against the Great Society and its political absorption of neighborhood mobilization. The South End and Western Addition cases show clearly how this conservative response made it even more difficult for liberal Democrats to deliver on their promises and circumscribed and undermined the victories won by neighborhood activism. These conservative national policy responses also interacted with and reinforced a private sector flight from the older central cities which, especially during the 1973–1975 national recession, imposed conditions of severe economic and fiscal distress on the older central cities. Neighborhoods like the South End and the Western Addition felt this distress most acutely, as they are again in the current period of conservative dominance.

Contrasting Paths Toward the Postindustrial City: The Northeast Versus the Southwest

During the 1970s, the U.S. system of cities crossed a watershed. New York City led other old, industrial metropolitan areas like Chicago, Cleveland, Pittsburgh, and Buffalo into a population and employment decline. After ten decades of consistent expansion, the largest metropolitan areas contracted for the first time. Though many of their central cities had lost population during the 1960s, suburban growth compensated for this decline. As Table 5 shows, however, not only did all ten of the largest northeastern central cities suffer heavy population losses during the 1970s, but eight out of the ten metropolitan areas also lost population.

The new cities of the Southwest present a sharp contrast to northeastern decline. Table 5 shows that they have grown explosively since World War II and continued to do so during the 1970s. Like the northeastern cities at the end of the nineteenth century, these new cities have doubled and tripled their SMSA population since 1940. Their central cities have grown quickly as well, though mostly by annexing growing suburbs. Phoenix, for example, was little more than a dusty desert crossroad trading center for a marginal agricultural region in 1940. It housed only 65,000 residents. By 1980, its metropolitan area population had swollen twenty-fivefold to 1.5 million people with migrants to the city accounting for more than 75 percent of this increase. In 1976, although California contributed 12 percent of these arrivals, 36 percent came from the Northeast-North Central industrial belt; most were upwardly mobile, well-educated, childless couples.[1] A rapid expansion of employment in the Southwest made this

213

TABLE 5 Northeast and Southwest Urban Population Changes

City	Central-City Population 1960	1970	1980	1970–1980 CC change	1970–1980 SMSA change
New York	7,782	7,895	7,071	− 10.4%	− 8.6%
Chicago	3,550	3,369	3,005	− 10.8	1.8
Philadelphia	2,003	1,949	1,688	− 13.4	− 2.2
Detroit	1,670	1,514	1,203	− 20.5	− 1.9
Baltimore	939	906	787	− 13.1	5.0
Cleveland	876	751	574	− 23.6	− 8.0
Milwaukee	741	717	636	− 11.3	− 0.5
Boston	697	641	563	− 12.2	− 4.7
Pittsburgh	667	604	423	− 18.5	− 5.7
Buffalo	533	463	358	− 22.7	− 7.9
10-city average	1,946	1,831	1,631	—	—
Los Angeles	2,479	2,812	2,967	5.5%	6.2%
Dallas/Ft. Worth	1,036	1,237	1,289	4.1	25.1
Houston	938	1,234	1,594	29.2	45.3
San Diego	573	697	876	25.5	37.1
San Antonio	588	708	785	20.1	20.7
Phoenix	439	587	765	30.9	55.3
Denver	494	515	491	− 4.5	30.7
San José	204	483	637	38.4	21.6
El Paso	277	322	425	32.0	33.6
Tucson	213	263	331	25.7	51.1
Albuquerque	201	244	332	35.7	36.4
11-city average	677	828	957	—	—

SOURCE: 1980 *Census of Population*, "SMSA's and SCSA's: 1980," PC80-S1-5.

interregional migration possible. On average, southwestern SMSA employment grew more than three times faster than in the northeastern metropolitan areas. The faltering of the northeastern cities compared to rapid southwestern urban growth suggests an important rupture in the previously largely stable size-rank patterns among U.S. cities.

This rupture has produced widespread comment among academic analysts and journalists. Much has been heard of "the end of the metropolitan era" (Alonso's phrase), "the death of the cities" (William Baer in *The Public Interest*), and "New York: Future without a Future" (*Society* magazine).[2] Economists have typically explained this shift arguing that northeastern cities simply cannot compete against their southwestern rivals because of high labor costs, land prices, tax loads, aging capital plants, or high energy costs. According to this analysis, northeastern cities have become obsolete and unproductive compared to the newer, lower cost, and more profitable locations in the Southwest. They therefore deserve their fate, or, at any rate, cannot escape it.[3]

To be sure, economic forces have influenced the differing fates of the northeastern and southwestern cities during the 1970s. The decline of old manufacturing industries, the rise of new ones which have made different location choices, and the increasing importance of administrative and service activities have all heavily influenced the distribution of growth across metropolitan areas. Objective economic factors have undoubtedly affected the way rising economic sectors have made their locational choices. Increasingly, however, political factors have even more strongly influenced these choices. A purely economic analysis cannot explain the timing or magnitude of the contrast in urban growth rates between the Northeast and the Southwest. Two political factors have played key roles in channeling economic activity: the conservative thrust in federal urban development policy which has emerged over the long run since World War II and the short-run impact of urban conflict and co-optation in northeastern cities—and the absence of this challenge to progrowth politics in the Southwest.

The cases of Boston and San Francisco show how Democratic

215

federal urban programs facilitated the gradual assembly of progrowth coalitions which, in turn, removed the barriers impeding CBD office building construction and the expansion of service institutions. Similarly, the conservative thrust in federal urban development policy accelerated the growth of southwestern cities and fostered a far more conservative progrowth politics much less reliant on public intervention. Where the transformation of older cities like Boston and San Francisco heightened conflict over growth and required an expanded public sector to contain that conflict, no such challenge arose in the cities of the Southwest. Southwestern cities thus benefited twice from political trends.

A comparison of the ten largest northeastern cities and the eleven largest southwestern cities shows that purely economic differences in factor costs for individual firms are neither large enough nor trending properly to account for these outcomes. For many of the competitive cost disadvantages that analysts focusing on purely economic factors have attributed to northeastern cities, southwestern cities have countervailing economic disadvantages that they have failed to notice. Further, while the differences in such economic factors as labor costs and real incomes have been declining between the two groups of cities, the disparity in their growth rates has increased.[4] If anything, this would suggest a negative correlation between the two.

Economic factors are clearly not irrelevant. As the beginning of this study argued, three major structural changes have been taking place within postindustrial economies: the emergence of corporate headquarters, business services, and social services as governance mechanisms of a world-scale economy; the growth of new industries like aerospace and electronics, which have followed distinct location patterns; and the decline of the old basic industries heavily located in the older metropolitan areas.

These structural changes have their roots in the marketplace and a new international division of labor. Unlike the industrial revolution, however, they have also been powerfully shaped and hastened by government intervention and the political balance of power. The increasingly central importance of administrative and service activities, for example, has helped some older cities with

216

strong progrowth coalitions and corporate economies, like Boston and San Francisco, but not the more industrial old cities. It has helped nearly all the newer southwestern cities, where conservative progrowth political patterns reign unchallenged. Fostered by conservative swings in federal policy and hastened by conservative local political regimes, the rise of new industries has also promoted growth in all the southwestern cities, while no northeastern central city and only a few metropolitan areas have benefited. Conversely, declining old industries have adversely affected the older metropolitan areas, especially their central cities, with little impact on the new cities. Racial, labor, and political conflict hastened their departure. Political factors—national development policies and local political balances—have thus both shaped the changes in economic structure and strongly influenced how they have been played out across the system of cities.

It was suggested in Chapter one that the nation's large cities can be sorted into three types. Among the northeastern cities, old, declining industrial cities like Newark or Gary have few administrative and service activities but do have a legacy of labor, racial, and neighborhood conflict. They have experienced the greatest distress and decline. Mixed cases like Boston and San Francisco have rising administrative and service activities promoted by progrowth politics have offset manufacturing decline, but have also experienced conflict over urban development. Both these groups can be distinguished from the third. These newer cities, typified by those in the Southwest, are strong service centers, have little traditional industry but branch plants instead in the new industries, and little or no conflict or even political debate over growth issues. They have benefited most from the private sector reaction against the political climate of the older cities and its search for conservative alternatives.[5]

In contrast to the Northeast, southwestern cities have had weaker public sectors, fewer calls for political accountability, little or no protest, and a far stronger military influence. Federal spending during conservative periods has favored them. Indeed, World War II military bases and defense production facilities provided the initial growth stimulus in such cities as San Diego, Phoenix, San

217

Antonio, and the Santa Clara Valley. War Production Board grants provided the initial capital for new industries like electronics and aircraft production in these cities, and subsequent periods of expanded national defense expenditures caused these cities to prosper. Federal water projects made their expansion possible.

These forms of federal intervention helped forge conservative, private-sector-oriented local progrowth coalitions which never faced political challenge. Their prosperity has, in turn, strengthened the position of conservative national political entrepreneurs. Over time, this mutually supportive relationship has developed into a kind of geopolitical counterweight to the traditional Democratic symbiosis between national electoral success, federal urban policy, and the major central cities. During the 1970s, the political competition between them hastened the economic and political disintegration of the traditional Democratic urban strategy.

A CRITIQUE OF THE ECONOMIC ANALYSIS OF CONTRASTING URBAN GROWTH RATES IN THE NORTHEAST AND SOUTHWEST

Economics has generated a sizable but inconclusive literature on the causes of the interregional differences in urban growth rates. The recent volume edited by George Sternlieb and James Hughes may be taken as a representative example of this literature.[6] The authors of this volume argue that the fate of individual cities hangs on decisions made by their producers and consumers, who engage in simple utility calculations. Producers look at how labor, land, capital, and other input costs vary across different locations, factor in marketing costs, and choose the location which optimizes profits. Consumers weigh the amenities of different locations against these housing or commuting time costs and pick a location which optimizes their satisfaction. This approach concludes that declining cities must have had unfavorable economic conditions which made them less attractive to producers and consumers, especially over the last decade.

According to Sternlieb and Hughes, northeastern cities have suffered from "a lack of [immigrant] demand as well as deterioration in physical amenities," "production methods and approaches which are no longer competitive," "high levels of union-ization" which "reduce the flexibility of the region to service new demands," "high levels of dependency," "new areas of competition" from rural areas and the Third World, loss of a monopoly over a "critical mass of consumers such as to provide a unique demand for specialized services and goods," and high operating costs resulting from an overly complex, uncoordinated system of production.[7]

It is not easy to distill such claims into empirically verifiable propositions. Indeed, market explanations have a strongly circular quality. Nevertheless, certain basic arguments can be identified:

1. Aggregate population and employment figures provide the best indicators of "health."
2. *Manufacturing* employment and the low birth rate of new manufacturing enterprises are, in Sternlieb's words, "at the crux."
3. Economic factors such as wages, land costs, and so forth, determine where manufacturing enterprises will be born and grow.
4. Older cities have some (as yet unspecified) economic conditions which make them "not competitive" with alternative locations like the southwestern cities.

When looked at from the northeastern point of view, these notions seem plausible. They inevitably lead to the bleak conclusion that northeastern cities have entered an irreversible and general decline. But does a comparative analysis of the two groups of cities really bear out these arguments and conclusions? Because they rely exclusively on the northeastern experience, these arguments in fact fall prey to a number of conceptual and empirical difficulties.

While aggregate population and employment figures certainly reveal something important about metropolitan areas, they also conceal a great deal. Aggregate figures may hide large but opposing changes in component parts. As some firms go under, for example, the remaining ones may become more efficient and productive. Or, as certain sectors, like manufacturing, decline,

219

others, particularly administrative and high-level service activities, may take their place. This has happened in some northeastern cities, suggesting a less bleak future than an argument based solely on industrial trends might predict.

Secondly, it is fallacious to conclude that the manufacturing jobs which have been disappearing from the Northeast are reappearing in southwestern cities. Manufacturing actually accounts for *less* growth in southwestern urban employment than services, and these manufacturing jobs differ qualitatively from those the Northeast has lost. Finally, those new manufacturing establishments which have located in the Southwest in preference to the Northeast have not necessarily done so to find low-wage workers, cheaper land, or closer proximity to their markets. Indeed, many firms have had to import trained labor for plants being established in the Southwest. Investment location decisions cannot be explained by the calculus of minimizing marginal input costs.

Thirdly, the analogy between cities and firms obscures the forces and institutions which operate across cities and create interdependence among them. Cities have become enmeshed in a complex network of what Alan Pred called "multilocational organizations."[8] A curious reversal in nineteenth-century capitalism has taken place in which multilocational organizations benefit from the competition among entrepreneurial governments each seeking to entice economic growth by providing the most favorable political climate.[9] Because it insists that cities are independent observations, the economic model also misses the simple but basic point that the growth of cities like Phoenix may benefit at least some parts of cities like New York.

Finally, by focusing on the Northeast, this line of argument fails to give proper weight to the economic problems facing the Southwest. Just because Phoenix is growing faster than New York does not mean that it is necessarily nicer in every respect. Phoenix can be unbearably hot and dry; its future water supply is uncertain and may become every bit as difficult as the energy problems facing the Northeast. And compared even to New York, Phoenix is in many ways more impoverished.

Table 6 presents some admittedly crude tests of the economic input differences as possible determinants of the different growth rates between the two groups of cities. It covers infrastructural investment, productivity, wage rates, market size, poverty and welfare dependency, and sectoral composition of the SMSA economies.

Sternlieb and George Peterson have suggested that lack of public infrastructure investment in the Northeast helps to account for its decline. It is difficult to assess just what constitutes an "adequate" public infrastructure. The Northeast has a much bigger infrastructure than the Southwest with an undoubtedly higher replacement value. While the southwestern infrastructure is much newer and needs less maintenance, the Southwest's most important infrastructure is its massively expensive water supply system, which was financed through no-interest and low-interest federal loans. To the extent the government moves toward "true cost pricing," consumer charges for such projects as the Central Arizona Project will mount greatly.

Table 6 indicates that while private construction for all purposes has been larger in per capita and absolute terms for the Southwest, northeasterners spent far more per capita and in total for public infrastructure. (In 1970, the northeastern mean was $503 per capita, the southwestern $380.) If aggregate size and current maintenance spending on infrastructure are the relevant measures, then this measure does not support Sternlieb's argument. Some aspects of the northeastern infrastructure will probably give that region an increasing economic advantage over the Southwest. The heavy investment in public transit in the Northeast partially insulates its cities from rising transportation energy costs; as a result, northeastern cities have been on the low end of the inflation scale, while car-oriented southwestern cities have been at the top.

Wages, while lower on the average for the Southwest than the Northeast, are closing with national norms, particularly after controlling for industry and occupation. In the mid-1970s janitors and porters earned $2.30 an hour in Phoenix and Houston compared to $4.10 in Chicago. But skilled service workers, like Class A secretaries, earned $5.28 and $5.46 hourly in those cities while they got $6.10 and $5.85 in Chicago and San Francisco.[10] Table

221

TABLE 6 Crude Measures of the Sternleib Hypotheses

City	All 1976 Construction ($ millions)	1970 SMSA Public Works $/cap.	Value Added Payroll $, 1967 SMSA Manufacturing
New York	$345	$894	3.48
Chicago	381	478	3.23
Philadelphia	432	495	3.31
Detroit	474	474	2.74
Baltimore	<150	638	3.15
Cleveland	<150	512	2.92
Milwaukee	<150	562	2.97
Boston	<150	531	3.47
Pittsburgh	<150	450	2.84
Buffalo	150	528	2.93
10 city mean		(503)	(3.10)
Los Angeles	$970	$624	3.20
Dallas/FW	601	352	3.35
Houston	751	305	4.90
San Diego	444	484	2.73
San Antonio	164	252	3.19
Phoenix	200	462	3.39
Denver	<150	502	3.48
San José	275	462	4.58
El Paso	<150	401	3.19
Tucson	<150	414	2.13
Albuquerque	170	381	3.50
11 City mean		(380)	(3.42)

SOURCES: Bureau of the Census, *Value of New Construction* (April 1977), and *1967 Census of Manufacturing.* Bureau of Labor Statistics, *Bulletin 1900–63,* October 1976, 1977. *Sales and Market Management,* "Survey of Buying Power," July 1976. Boston Redevelopment Authority, "Boston and the Flight to the Sunbelt," (October 1976). Bureau of the Census, *1973 Population Estimates* Current Population Reports, Series P-25, and 1970 *Census of Population.*

City	Class A Secretary 1975 Weekly Earnings	1974 Cost of Living % Natl. Urb. Av.	1975 State Union Membership Rate
New York	$240.50	114	35.7
Chicago	218.50	105	35.8
Philadelphia	217.00	103	37.2
Detroit	227.00	101	39.8
Baltimore	192.50	99	25.1
Cleveland	223.00	101	36.4
Milwaukee	207.00	105	31.5
Boston	212.50	117	25.1
Pittsburgh	231.00	97	27.2
Buffalo	209.00	105	35.7
10 city mean	(218.00)		
Los Angeles	$233.50	99	30.8
Dallas/FW	193.50	90	14.4
Houston	214.00	90	14.4
San Diego	199.00	97	30.8
San Antonio	153.00	n.a.	14.4
Phoenix	n.a.	94	17.5
Denver	204.50	96	20.5
San José	228.50	104	30.8
El Paso	n.a.	86	14.4
Tucson	n.a.	n.a.	17.5
Albuquerque	n.a.	n.a.	14.7
11 City Mean	(204.00)		

6 gives 1975 data on the weekly earnings for these secretaries. The northeastern weekly pay averages $218, the southwestern $204. Such differences seem too small to account for the migration of firms, particularly since the northeastern labor forces are likely to be better trained. Similar figures hold for skilled manufacturing occupations.

223

TABLE 6 (*cont.*)

City	1975 Retail Sales Market Size	1972 SMSA AFDC Case Load	1969 SMSA Percent Income ≤ $3,000
New York	$46.4	1,037,808	8.7
Chicago	23.8	517,368	6.3
Philadelphia	15.9	399,699	7.0
Detroit	13.3	281,258	6.4
Baltimore	5.5	147,216	7.8
Cleveland	8.0	140,069	7.1
Milwaukee	4.7	66,741	6.0
Boston	11.3	n.a.	6.1
Pittsburgh	6.1	126,212	7.6
Buffalo	4.0	66,078	7.1
10 city mean			(8.7)
Los Angeles	$31.6	640,721	7.7
Dallas/FW	8.3	87,384	7.8
Houston	8.9	76,095	8.5
San Diego	<4.0	69,860	8.5
San Antonio	<4.0	50,546	12.8
Phoenix	4.2	29,515	8.5
Denver	<4.0	56,201	6.6
San José	<4.0	73,069	5.2
El Paso	<4.0	11,448	12.7
Tucson	<4.0	10,322	8.8
Albuquerque	<4.0	17,881	10.8
11 City mean			(8.9)

The lower southwestern average wage reflects a greater prevalence of low-skilled, labor-intensive employment and more subemployment in that region. Firms which rely on low-wage labor might well locate in these cities because of it. But most of the growing southwestern industries do not rely on such labor. The industries which have contributed most to southwestern employ-

City	1973 SMSA Employment	Percent Services	Percent Government	Percent Mfg.
New York	4,433	42	15	19
Chicago	3,111	32	13	29
Philadelphia	1,939	32	16	26
Detroit	1,750	27	13	35
Baltimore	882	31	23	19
Cleveland	894	29	13	32
Milwaukee	635	28	12	33
Boston	1,550	35	15	22
Pittsburgh	904	30	13	29
Buffalo	515	27	16	31
10 city mean		(31)	(15)	(28)
Los Angeles	3,149	33	14	26
Dallas/FW	1,108	32	13	22
Houston	948	35	12	17
San Diego	574	26	37	12
San Antonio	378	26	36	10
Phoenix	466	31	17	18
Denver	636	32	19	16
San José	449	39	15	31
El Paso	126	34	37	17
Tucson	127	50	22	08
Albuquerque	116	56	19	08
11 City mean		(36)	(22)	(17)

ment growth in fact require above-average amounts of skilled technical and professional labor, which they typically recruit, often at considerable cost, from outside the region.

The value added/wage bill figures given in Table 6 bear out this point. Wages by themselves are not so important as what they buy. While the overall value added per wage dollar is higher in the Southwest for 1967, two outlying cases, Houston (petrochemicals) and San José (military hardware), contribute most of the

225

difference. Without them, the distribution and the averages are quite similar: 3.10 for the Northeast (or 3.01 if the top two northeastern cases are excluded) compared to 3.13 for the Southwest. Productivity increases over the last decade have been two and one-half times greater in the Southwest, but the picture is mixed in both groups. A number of northeastern cities where industrial employment has declined in absolute terms have made strong productivity gains. Thus neither the productivity differences at the beginning of the marked shift toward the Southwest nor the subsequent trends satisfactorily explain why industrial decline has been so marked in all the older northeastern cities, nor growth so rapid in the Southwest.

The figures on unionization lead to a similar conclusion. Northeastern rates are higher because long-organized basic industries predominate in these cities. Interestingly, many of the dynamic industrial sectors of the Southwest—for example, mining, electric power generation, and aerospace—have been organized from the outset. The *Wall Street Journal* of February 10, 1978, even reported instances of southern cities rejecting proposed plants because of the unions they would bring along, and describes "a little-known but widespread attitude in the South; fearful of unions and competition for local labor, community leaders in many areas have quietly been spurning Northern companies eager to move operations into the Sunbelt." Though unions are weaker in the Southwest, they are not necessarily so in its growing industries. In some rapidly growing southwestern industries such as the California aerospace industry, unionization rates are actually quite high.

Table 6 also raises doubt about the claim that the Northeast has lost its grip over "a critical mass of consumers." The only southwestern market which looks truly substantial by northeastern terms is the Los Angeles SMSA. Southwestern retail markets are small and widely separated. To the extent that producers need to be close to consumers, this factor continues to favor the Northeast.

Sternleib also cites "dependency" as a blemish on the northeastern economic picture, and indeed Table 6 shows that the older cities had far larger absolute and relative AFDC case loads in the early 1970s. (Northeastern cities hover around 20 percent, while the southwestern cities average less than 10 percent.) Interestingly, however, poverty (as defined as metropolitan families with 1969 incomes lower than $3,000 per year) is somewhat more widespread in the Southwest. Rapid growth has seemed if anything to exacerbate it.[11] Even taking cost of living differences into account, many more people would seem to be eligible for public assistance in the Southwest than the Northeast. Clearly, AFDC is administered under different political philosophies in the two groups of cities. Overall, the Northeast seems to have done a better job of providing higher wage jobs and more welfare at the cost of higher unemployment rates, while the Southwest generates more poverty and subemployment, but less welfare and unemployment.

The last three columns of Table 6 undermine the economists' belief that manufacturing employment is "at the crux." In fact, southwestern cities rely much more heavily on service and government employment (typically federal) than do the northeastern cities. They have substantially less manufacturing employment. While industrial decline may help explain the northeastern lack of growth, it does not explain why southwestern cities have expanded so rapidly. Only San José among the southwestern metropolitan areas approximates the industrial work force common within the Northeast. San Diego, San Antonio, and El Paso are all military centers with high rates of government employment. Los Angeles, Dallas, Houston, and Denver are business service centers. Overall, the southwestern cities averaged 36 percent service employment compared to 31 percent for the Northeast and 17 percent manufacturing compared to 28 percent. Tables 7 and 8 present a more detailed picture of the industries common to each area.

These two tables show how the largest industrial sectors within each SMSA changed between 1960 and 1970, and how their occupational structure looked in 1970. The Northeast presents a picture of basic industry, heavily reliant on skilled blue collar labor, experiencing decline. New York SMSA lost a third of its garment industry, Baltimore, Pittsburgh, and Buffalo lost 30 percent of their steel industry, and Pittsburgh, Milwaukee, and Boston lost substantial amounts of their electrical machinery work.

227

These industries required low amounts of professional, technical, and kindred (PTK) labor. The recessions of the 1970s amplified these trends.

The Southwest presents a different picture. As in the Northeast, southwestern industries with low PTK levels did not fare well in this decade. Food products (1.3 to 5.6% PTK) lost employment in Denver, El Paso and San Antonio. San Antonio and El Paso picked up a few thousand low-skilled apparel production jobs, an area in which New York lost heavily. But the distinctive element in the southwestern picture is the extremely large employment increases within high-PTK, high-technology industries, particularly aircraft, electronics, and ordnance. These new industries average over 20 percent PTK employment. San José stands out with industries which involve one-third to one-half professional and technical employment. This type of employment more than doubled during the decade. Within the region, Los Angeles and San Diego appeared to have lost some ground to Dallas/Fort Worth in aircraft production, and Los Angeles lost ground in electronics employment to such cities as Dallas, San Diego, and San José. But the overall picture is one of new high-technology industries oriented to aerospace, defense, and computer industry applications. Houston distinguished itself in petrochemicals.

These comparisons raise grave doubts about the four basic assumptions and arguments central to the strictly economic approach to the disparity in urban growth trends between the two regions. The data suggest that aggregates are misleading: within the Northeast, there are new, rising service sectors which in some cases offset industrial decline; within the Southwest, aggregate growth masks the fact that well-educated immigrants appear to be benefiting far more than the subemployed indigenous population. Further, southwestern service employment has grown even faster than industrial employment.

An undifferentiated focus on manufacturing employment is also misleading. The industries which are declining in northeastern metropolitan areas are not reappearing in the Southwest; the industries growing in southwestern metropolitan areas are qualitatively different from those which predominate in the Northeast.

TABLE 7 Occupational Structure and Size Changes, Two Largest Manufacturing Employers, Northeastern Metropolitan Areas

SMSA	Industry	1970 Emplmt.	60-70 Δ	1970 Occupational Structure				
				PTK	M&A	Sales	Clerical	Craftsmen & Operatives
New York	apparel	173,304	-31.9	3.5	7.2	4.9	10.9	71.5
	printing/publishing	128,700	-6.1	17.8	8.8	6.6	29.3	33.9
Chicago	electrical machinery	141,720	0.2	14.6	5.0	1.4	16.0	58.8
	nonelectrical mach.	118,793	5.5	11.5	6.7	2.8	16.3	58.9
Philadelphia	electrical machinery	66,768	-1.9	21.1	6.5	1.6	16.6	49.7
	nonelectrical mach.	56,350	15.1	17.0	7.4	2.6	15.5	54.5
Detroit	motor vehicles	266,369	8.1	14.1	2.5	0.4	11.9	64.2
	nonelectrical mach.	89,813	11.9	11.7	6.0	1.7	11.3	65.5
Baltimore	electrical machinery	26,483	36.4	27.7	5.2	1.0	15.9	46.2
	primary ferrous	24,797	-29.2	5.7	1.3	0.4	10.8	65.6
Cleveland	nonelectrical mach.	48,108	14.9	12.4	6.6	2.4	14.8	50.3
	fabricated metals	35,096	19.0	7.3	6.5	2.0	15.0	64.3
Milwaukee	nonelectrical mach.	52,755	23.1	11.9	4.4	1.3	14.7	60.6
	electrical machinery	30,963	-7.1	20.4	4.2	0.9	15.7	54.1
Boston	electrical machinery	46,970	-27.2	26.7	8.5	1.5	15.5	44.6
	nonelectrical mach.	31,112	31.8	22.7	8.6	2.2	16.8	46.1
Pittsburgh	primary ferrous	94,220	-23.8	8.9	2.3	0.5	12.7	58.5
	electrical machinery	27,553	-7.4	18.8	4.7	1.3	16.2	52.3
Buffalo	primary ferrous	25,076	-21.9	4.6	1.6	0.3	9.3	65.0
	motor vehicles	23,338	0.1	5.2	1.9	0.4	5.7	75.2

SOURCE: 1960 and 1970 Censuses of Population, industry by occupation tables.
NOTE: PTK = professional, technical, and kindred workers, M&A = managerial and administrative

TABLE 8 Occupational Structure and Size Changes, Two Largest Manufacturing Employers, Southwestern Metropolitan Areas

SMSA	Industry	1970 Emplmt.	60-70 Δ	1970 Occupational Structure				
				PTK	M&A	Sales	Clerical	Craftsmen & Operatives
Los Angeles	aircraft	118,413	-22.8	26.7	5.8	0.5	18.5	45.5
	electronics	83,772	-19.0	22.5	8.2	1.9	15.9	48.6
Dallas/Ft. Worth	aircraft	58,206	75.3	26.5	3.8	0.4	16.5	48.3
	electronics	39,420	149.5	29.8	5.9	1.3	13.7	46.1
Houston	petrochemicals	24,788	108.8	21.6	6.5	3.0	11.5	49.3
	machinery	24,298	32.6	13.0	5.7	4.0	13.6	59.4
San Diego	aircraft	17,207	-4.2	24.7	3.1	0.6	17.9	51.7
	electrical machinery	9,883	232.9	28.7	7.8	2.0	13.6	46.4
San Antonio	food products	6,452	-7.7	2.7	6.3	5.0	8.9	66.1
	apparel	4,147	64.7	1.1	1.4	1.7	6.9	86.6
Phoenix	electronics	21,412	465.2	24.5	4.6	0.6	12.5	54.6
	machinery	13,341	179.5	29.4	7.4	15.1	15.3	44.2
Denver	machinery	8,850	71.9	23.2	8.7	3.3	14.5	48.1
	food & kindreds	9,746	-15.2	5.6	8.0	4.3	9.7	61.2
San José	electronics	40,542	282.3	34.7	7.8	1.0	15.8	38.3
	ordnance	19,243	- -	46.2	7.8	0.4	17.6	25.0

El Paso	apparel	8,695	175.4	2.0	1.3	0.3	7.7	84.2
	food & kindreds	1,519	−31.4	1.3	7.8	6.8	8.0	62.1
Tucson	ordnance	2,576	– –	35.3	5.2	0.2	12.9	43.0
	electrical machinery	1,271	286.3	27.2	8.4	2.4	13.7	44.9
Albuquerque	food products	1,056	−38.2	4.3	11.7	9.7	12.2	52.7
	printing/publishing	1,016	−25.1	17.2	8.9	15.5	20.8	36.3
San Francisco	food & kindreds	23,486	−37.9	7.0	8.5	3.6	15.1	57.2
	electrical machinery	22,365	23.4	23.7	7.4	2.0	17.0	47.0

SOURCE: 1960 and 1970 *Censuses of Population*, industry by occupation tables.

They are new, typically dating from World War II, and highly technical. Such differences in composition seem far more important than marginal differences in labor, land, or energy costs in determining the difference in urban growth rates.

Something more basic is happening to the system of cities. Private capital investment decisions, channeled and reinforced by federal programs and local politics, have worked against sectors of the economy historically located in Northeastern metropolitan areas. They have also favored those which have chosen to locate from the outset in the Southwest.

Even so, some northeastern cities have a stronger future than a strict economic approach would suggest. Some northeastern cities are national centers of services requiring high proportions of professional and technical labor. They contain the educational institutions which produce a disproportionate amount of this critical labor ingredient. Were it not for the tremendous conflicts generated both by the liquidation of their industrial base and the tranformation of central-city land uses, these northeastern cities might well possess growth resources superior to those of the Southwest.

These conclusions suggest the need for an alternative analysis stressing how national and local political factors have influenced the locational choices of rising sectors. This analysis will include: (1) the importance of administrative activities and the high level services, (2) the long-term form taken by a city's progrowth politics, and (3) the short-term political conflict, or lack of it, which a given city's development has generated. As the Boston and San Francisco cases suggest, these factors have worked against each other in some older cities. In others, they have worked uniformly against economic expansion. But in the southwestern cities, they have worked fairly consistently in favor of expansion.

2. POLITICO-ECONOMIC DETERMINANTS OF CONTRASTING URBAN GROWTH RATES IN THE NORTHEAST AND SOUTHWEST

The previous discussion of postwar development in Boston and San Francisco has highlighted the importance of new kinds of institutions in the urban economy and the role government has played in helping them expand. Both of these cities combine substantial numbers of *Fortune* 500 corporate headquarters, concentrations of the high-level business service support they require, and large banking communities. These two cities house some of the most important universities, research centers, and hospitals in the country. They are also major centers of government employment; both are federal regional centers.

Nodal administrative activities like these, which influence subsidiary positions in many other places, clearly play a central role in determining a given city's economic future, and will become increasingly important in the future as the world economy becomes more integrated on a global scale. Table 9 shows that some northeastern cities have a rich supply of these activities—cities like New York, Chicago, Philadelphia, Cleveland, and Boston. Others, particularly the industrial cities like Buffalo, Youngstown, Toledo, Gary, and the others which grew up between the East Coast and Chicago in the late nineteenth and early twentieth centuries, do not. Though the conflicts experienced by the former cities as postindustrial institutions expanded caused some forms of investment to flee, the latter cities have suffered worse economic decline because they lacked such institutions altogether.

In many southwestern cities, branch plants and offices predominate over locally owned firms. Nevertheless, a number of southwestern cities have emerged as strong administrative nodes in their own right. As Table 9 indicates, Los Angeles, Houston, Dallas/Ft. Worth, Phoenix, and San Diego housed three or more *Fortune* 500 firms in 1976. All of them also provide strong banking resources—less, to be sure, than giants like New York or Chicago, but still a great deal considering the relative sparseness and newness of settlement in the region. Too, cities like Houston and Denver have become home to numerous head offices for operating subsidiaries whose parent corporations may be located elsewhere. The major southwestern cities also provide strong supporting business services; Table 9 shows that Los Angeles, Houston, and Denver all have large law firms. They are increasing

233

TABLE 9 Role in the Urban Hierarchy

City	No. 1976 Fortune 500 HQ'S	Total 1975 Bank Deposits ($ billions)	Percentage of All 50+ Law Firms 1973	Percentage of All Lawyers (1972 Census)	Percentage of All 1973 Am. Institute of CPA members
New York	112	177.5	21.2	12.3	10.5
Chicago	34	39.3	13.6	4.9	5.2
Philadelphia	11	17.0	7.6	2.4	3.2
Detroit	10	15.6	2.5	2.0	2.5
Baltimore	1	4.9	2.5	1.2	1.0
Cleveland	15	9.5	4.2	1.4	1.5
Milwaukee	10	4.6	0.9	0.8	0.9
Boston	10	13.1	4.2	1.4	1.5
Pittsburgh	15	11.8	0.9	1.0	1.2
Buffalo	1	11.8	0.0	0.7	—
Los Angeles	21	32.3	5.9	4.5	5.1
Dallas/ Ft. Worth	7	10.5	0.0	1.1	1.8
Houston	10	9.7	4.2	1.3	2.3
San Diego	3	0.8	0.0	0.5	—
San Antonio	0	0.7	0.0	—	—
Phoenix	3	3.2	0.0	—	—
Denver	4	3.4	3.4	1.8	—
San José	0	—	0.0	—	—
El Paso	0	—	0.0	—	—
Tucson	0	—	0.0	—	—
Albuquerque	0	—	0.0	—	—

SOURCE: R. Cohen, "The Corporation and the City."

their share relative to New York. Table 10 shows that south-western cities are also rich in educational and health institutions. They have grown faster in these areas than in the northeastern cities, and faster than have manufacturing activities. Though other southwestern cities, such as San Antonio, El Paso, San Diego, and San José are not corporate headquarters cities,they have benefited heavily from the growing Pentagon spending.

In sum, both northeastern and southwestern cities have prospered because of the key administrative and service activities they house. On balance, northeastern cities predominate on this score: they house 219 of the biggest firms as compared to 48 for the Southwest, and have lost only a little ground over time.[12] New York supplies much of the financial and legal services for firms located everywhere else. Seven large northeastern cities contain half of all the large law firms, while southwestern cities have only one-eighth of them, in Los Angeles, Houston, and Denver. Nevertheless, these activities have played a key role in the Southwest, as they have in the Northeast. As Table 10 shows, in these SMSAs service employment grew faster (59.9 percent) and accounted for far more of the total employment gain than manufacturing, which grew 36.9 percent. Service employment also grew rapidly in northeastern SMSAs, offsetting frequent manufacturing employment declines.

The Conservative Counterpoint in Federal Policy and Southwestern Growth in the Long Term

The difference between the economic sectors which have dominated these two groups of cities, and the different political forces which have nourished them, is striking. Northeastern cities have higher rates of industrial employment than the southwestern cities. In the Northeast, this employment is concentrated in low-technology basic industries like steel and auto production; in the Southwest, it is concentrated in new, high-technology industries like electronics, aerospace, and petrochemicals.

Much of the southwestern industrial infrastructure was provided by War Production Board grants during World War II; it was sub-

235

TABLE 10 Percentage Change in 1960–1970 SMSA Service
Employment

City	Education (60% PTK)	Health/hosp. (60% PTK)	Professional Services (60% PTK)
New York	85.7	38.3	96.9
Chicago	67.1	47.1	110.1
Philadelphia	83.8	58.1	190.7
Detroit	32.4	67.5	135.6
Baltimore	102.7	68.2	215.6
Cleveland	80.0	56.7	137.3
Milwaukee	112.0	96.5	165.0
Boston	68.0	54.8	233.3
Pittsburgh	10.3	−0.6	19.8
Buffalo	88.9	52.6	127.6
10 City mean	73.1	53.9	143.2
Los Angeles	51.9	51.4	115.5
Dallas/F.W.	114.1	102.2	215.8
Houston	141.5	122.4	223.3
San Diego	123.9	107.9	229.3
San Antonio	116.9	105.8	168.4
Phoenix	112.9	74.5	119.8
Denver	111.8	88.7	155.9
San José	122.2	128.0	182.6
El Paso	86.3	80.8	182.4
Tucson	111.3	92.4	171.7
Albuquerque	109.0	66.5	133.7
11 City Mean	109.2	92.8	172.6

SOURCE: 1960 and 1970 *Censuses of Population*, industry by occupation
tables.

PTK = professional, technical and kindred workers.

City	Public Administration (15% PTK)	Finance, Administration, R.E. (10% PTK)	Change in Total Service Employment
New York	25.0	29.2	34.4
Chicago	20.2	27.5	41.3
Philadelphia	34.4	37.4	139.2
Detroit	28.0	44.2	24.3
Baltimore	78.9	40.5	63.4
Cleveland	25.0	40.1	29.1
Milwaukee	20.2	45.0	35.6
Boston	18.0	36.0	29.5
Pittsburgh	− 20.4	− 25.2	− 13.2
Buffalo	15.9	22.4	37.9
10 City Mean	24.5	29.7	42.1
Los Angeles	18.7	27.7	31.3
Dallas/F.W.	43.7	71.5	65.5
Houston	106.1	87.3	93.4
San Diego	33.6	28.2	62.9
San Antonio	27.2	57.6	49.0
Phoenix	51.9	74.5	48.2
Denver	28.5	58.3	59.0
San José	87.4	100.2	107.9
El Paso	35.1	28.3	39.2
Tucson	48.4	61.7	61.3
Albuquerque	18.2	47.8	40.4
11 City Mean	45.3	58.5	59.9

sequently expanded during the Cold War, as missiles and highly sophisticated aircraft were added to the national armory, and during the Vietnam era. Ironically, Democrats were in the White House at the beginning of all three periods, but conservatives learned well from their efforts. Southern California, the Phoenix

237

TABLE 10 (*cont.*)

City	Nonprofits (40% PTK)	Business Services (25% PTK)	Communications (15% PTK)
New York	35.6	31.5	27.0
Chicago	14.7	44.6	7.8
Philadelphia	17.9	67.2	12.7
Detroit	30.7	56.1	23.5
Baltimore	66.4	137.9	40.9
Cleveland	27.6	61.4	54.2
Milwaukee	27.4	49.8	11.5
Boston	37.0	53.6	25.4
Pittsburgh	21.6	19.1	7.5
Buffalo	34.0	46.6	−0.1
10 City mean	31.3	56.8	21.0
Los Angeles	53.7	39.5	20.7
Dallas/F.W.	32.9	146.7	38.8
Houston	69.3	210.4	88.5
San Diego	85.2	87.3	49.7
San Antonio	43.9	72.9	51.2
Phoenix	94.0	142.0	50.5
Denver	60.1	126.8	36.6
San José	112.1	206.4	134.2
El Paso	40.7	85.0	1.9
Tucson	79.3	76.1	29.0
Albuquerque	117.2	5.3	12.2
11 City Mean	71.7	108.9	46.7

and Tucson areas, and Texas receive a disproportionate amount of defense contracts. In Phoenix, for example, Motorola, Ai-Research, Goodyear Aerospace, and Sperry Flight Systems built radar guidance systems and other defense applications of electronics. Electronics employment grew from 4,603 in 1960 to 21,412 in 1970, and to 40,000 by December 1978 in metropolitan Phoenix; it constitutes 40 percent of Arizona's industrial output.[13]

City	Change in Total Manufacturing Employment	Percent Manufacturing in PTK Class	Total Change in SMSA Employment
New York	−15.5	11.1	5.4
Chicago	−5.8	10.1	5.0
Philadelphia	−1.6	11.9	14.2
Detroit	8.6	11.5	18.2
Baltimore	5.0	9.8	26.0
Cleveland	6.7	10.4	19.0
Milwaukee	5.5	10.9	21.8
Boston	−13.5	15.6	11.0
Pittsburgh	−10.5	11.7	4.7
Buffalo	−5.9	9.4	7.0
10 City mean	−2.6	11.2	13.2
Los Angeles	−3.6	14.2	8.1
Dallas/F.W.	64.1	15.9	49.1
Houston	60.3	14.9	69.5
San Diego	4.5	20.6	38.0
San Antonio	43.7	5.5*	34.4
Phoenix	101.4	18.2	55.0
Denver	24.1	17.6	39.6
San José	85.4	28.7	79.3
El Paso	30.0	5.9*	23.0
Tucson	−3.1	18.5	36.0
Albuquerque	−0.5	12.0	25.9
11 City Mean	36.9	15.6	39.5

* Employment primarily in apparel.

(Nationally, half the electronics market is provided by Defense Department contracts.)

The San José metropolitan area, which includes "silicon valley," is the center for this industry worldwide. In the 1930s and 1940s, Santa Clara Valley abounded in apricots and cherry or-

239

chards, and San José, with 100,000 residents, was called "The Garden City." Today, the Valley has 1.1 million residents and 500,000 jobs, of which 116,000 are in electronics alone; the industry is expanding employment at 8 percent per year.[14] Also, metropolitan San José has an ordnance industry about half as big as its electronics industry. FMC, for example, builds tanks, while other firms make a wide variety of weapons. San Diego is another center of defense production, while the Los Angeles area claims several of the nation's six basic weapon system production lines. Firms like Lockheed, Litton Industries, and Hughes Aircraft are synonymous with growth in these cities.[15] Except for metropolitan Boston, little of this electronics or defense contract work is undertaken in northeastern cities.

Unlike the northeastern cities, these and other southwestern cities also house numerous defense installations. San Diego is a Navy city, while Phoenix has three major air bases, the Yuma Proving Ground and Gunnery range, and Fort Huachaca, a secret army installation. San Antonio contains the largest number of military installations clustered anywhere in the United States, including Kelley Field, Lackland Air Force Base, Randolph Field, Brooke Army Medical Center, and Fort Sam Houston. El Paso is also surrounded by Air Force installations. Few of the northeastern cities benefit from defense establishments.

Energy production and mining is another growing sector in southwestern cities. In the next two decades, western coal mining is projected to double, while uranium mining will, if nuclear power generation expands along predicted lines, quadruple. Resource extraction has a long history in the Southwest; Arizona, for example, has the nation's largest copper mine and the largest strip mine, the Navajo mine, which fuels the Four Corners electric generation plant with 9 million tons of coal annually.

Like the defense industry and military bases, the growth of energy and natural resource industries in the Southwest reflects penetration of the region by corporations headquartered elsewhere. The growth of these energy activities has also encouraged outside banks to establish branches in southwestern cities. In Denver, for example, Citibank, Mellon Bank, Bank of America,

Northern Trust of Chicago, First Pennsylvania, Morgan Guaranty, Chemical Bank, and Continental Bank have all opened offices since 1970 to pursue energy and natural resource investments.[16]

Technological factors have obviously influenced some of these firms' location decisions. During World War II, flying weather and proximity to the Pacific theater were important in locating air bases. Denver's proximity to coal deposits and Houston's to oil naturally influenced the growth of energy firms in these two cities. But in a deeper sense, the growth of high-technology industry and services in southwestern cities has been a function of the political connections between the federal programs which stimulated their growth, conservative national administrations which emphasized these programs, and the local political climate which supported growth of these policy areas. In contrast to federal intervention into northeastern urban development, which operated primarily through Democratic local government, federal stimulation to southwestern urban development worked through conservative administrations, the Interior and Defense Departments, and the local private sector.

Since, the War Production Board days, the Defense Department has never faced the kind of public review to which urban renewal was subjected. However insulated Robert Moses' renewal activities may have been, they were at least carried out through local public agencies with some formal obligation to local elected officials. In the Southwest, the Defense Department, the Bureau of Land Management, the Bureau of Reclamation, and now the Department of Energy have contracted directly with local private firms without working through local government agencies. Moses' closest West Coast analog might be Frederick Terman, Stanford's famous Dean of Engineering, who nurtured ties between the federal government, Stanford University, and the emerging electronics industry in Santa Clara County. In contrast to Moses' public agencies, Stanford University, a private organization, carried out much of the development on its own lands, with little public review.[17]

Elsewhere, working directly with local contractors, federal agencies exerted their sovereignty over state and local government

241

to set up local operations not subject to local public scrutiny. Indeed, the major federally financed infrastructural developments in the northeastern cities, interstate highway construction and urban renewal, were carried out by local public agencies. In the Southwest, such key water projects as the Central Valley Project, the Central Utah Project, the Central Arizona Project, and the Hoover Dam were carried out directly by the federal government with close cooperation from the major private interests which contracted for water rights. In Phoenix, the Salt River Project was constructed without federal controls and is an independent public utility subject to little effective review.

Conservative national administrations have encouraged these agencies to concentrate their benefits on local jurisdictions where growth would enhance conservative strength in national politics. Southwestern cities benefited not only because they were technically well placed, but also because they provided fertile ground for national private sector and conservative political interests seeking to build up their margins of influence. Southwestern local political culture thus interacted with national economic and political forces to yield southwestern urban growth.

The Southwestern Form of Progrowth Politics as an Alternative to Contested Liberalism

As expanding service and high-technology industries compared alternative sites for new investments, they were attracted to cities with favorable *political* climates. This was especially true as economic differences among cities narrowed after 1970 and political differences widened. More than on any other dimension, the southwestern metropolitan areas can be distinguished from those of the Northeast by the small size of their governments, their private sector orientation, the lack of local political conflict, and by the relatively great social stratification which underlies their conservative political cultures.

Business commentators are well aware of this distinction. A *Fortune* article on why "Business Loves the Sunbelt (and Vice Versa)," observed that

Northerners are missing a key point about the Sunbelt's boom [by focusing on cheap labor and low taxes]. It's booming in great part because it is pro-business—and Northern cities by and large aren't. Much of the region is a repository of traditional American values—patriotism, self-reliance, respect for authority—and both racial disorders and street crime are relatively rare. . . . It is also true that many Sunbelt states solicit new business with zeal and skill. . . . The most effective form of aggressive behavior . . . is the joining together of politicians and businessmen to shape state laws that favor business.[18]

As a group the southwestern cities tax and spend less, have fewer employees, and encourage growth rather than attempting to regulate it. They are typically headed by nonpartisan city managers, who, in turn, have backing from the local business community. In contrast to their northeastern counterparts, the political coalitions dominant in southwestern urban politics typically do not include labor or minorities; in many instances, they are not even Democratic. Most southwestern cities have voted Republican in presidential elections. These coalitions have rarely been challenged, nor has the growth process been as politicized as in northeastern cities. Tables 11 and 12 compare the two groups of cities along these political dimensions.

As the previous chapters have shown, national Democratic urban programs favored the major northeastern central cities, Democratic mayors, and minority groups. This combination produced large, highly politicized local public sectors. Large urban renewal expenditures triggered large political reactions, which subsequently required large compensatory programs, such as Model Cities, to abate conflict.

In southwestern cities, urban politics, federal programs, and economic development interacted in a different way. Because development took place on a clean slate, the massive clearance and redistribution of central-city land did not need to take place. The urban workers of the Southwest have not particularly gained from growth, but a hierarchical social order has hampered any political expression against this fact. Indeed, potential opposition

243

TABLE 11 Government and Racial Characteristics

City	Form of Gov't.	1977 Bond Rating	Non-ed. City Workers/ 1000	1970 CC Gov't. Exp./Cap	CC Pct. Black	CC Pct. Spanish	1950-1970 Land Area Increase via Annexation	CC Assessed Valuation Subject to Tax, 1975	Size of Vote for Lead Party 1968 Presidential Election
New York	M	BA	31.9	$894	21.1%	10.3%	0%	$39.4B	D53%
Chicago	M	AA	14.3	478	32.7	7.4	8	24.2	D47
Philadelphia	M	A	19.8	495	33.6	1.4	0	5.8	D50
Detroit	M	BAA	19.2	474	43.7	1.8	0	5.8	D58
Baltimore	M	A	26.3	638	49.7	0.9	0	3.2	D47
Cleveland	M	A	18.6	512	38.3	1.9	0	1.5	D52
Milwaukee	M	AAA	13.1	562	14.6	2.2	0	2.0	D48
Boston	M	A	27.8	531	16.4	2.8	0	1.8	D53
Pittsburgh	M	A1	11.8	450	20.2	0.1	0	5.8	D52
Buffalo	M	BAA	16.7	528	20.4	0.8	0	1.0	D54
10 City Average	M	—	20.0	556	—	—	1	$9.0B	D51.4%

City								
Los Angeles	M	AAA	15.5	624	17.9	18.4	3%	$8.5	R48%
Dallas/Ft. Worth	CM	AAA	15.8	352	24.9	4.4	128	5.0	R49
Houston	M	AAA	8.7	305	25.7	12.1	250	5.8	R42
San Diego	CM	AA	12.0	484	7.6	12.7	241	5.1	R56
San Antonio	CM	AA	12.4	252	7.6	52.2	281	1.2	R51
Phoenix	CM	AA	9.7	462	4.8	14.0	16,000	2.7	R59
Denver	M	AA	17.3	502	9.2	16.8	40	1.9	R50
San José	CM	AA	7.9	462	2.4	21.9	8,000	1.6	D48
El Paso	CM	A1	9.7	401	2.3	58.1	4,050	0.5	D48
Tucson	CM	A1	11.7	414	3.5	23.9	308	1.2	R51
Albuquerque	CM	A1	13.2	381	2.3	34.9	112	0.9	D55
11 City Average	CM	—	12.3	422	—	—	2,674	$3.1B	R48%

SOURCES: Barbara Grouby, "Profiles of Individual Cities," and Richard Forstall, "Changes in Land Area for Larger Cities, 1950–1970," in *The Municipal Yearbook 1972* (Washington, D.C.: ICMA, 1976). Bureau of the Census, *1970 Census of Population and Local Government Employment in Selected Metropolitan Areas and Large Counties: 1972 and 1974. Dun and Bradstreet Business Economics*, April 12, 1977.

TABLE 12 Political Conflict and Compensatory Spending

City	Extent of Neighborhood Organization[a]	Neighborhood Organizational Militance[a]	Extent of Organizational Coalitions[a]	Community Action Program Expenditures 1965–1969[a]
Philadelphia	high	med	med	$44.8
Detroit	med	high	high	44.6
Baltimore	med	high	high	58.8
Cleveland	high	high	high	59.3
Boston	high	high	high	107.0
Pittsburgh	med	med	med	98.2
Buffalo	high	high	high	26.0
Seven N.E. City Average	high –	high –	high –	$62.7
Los Angeles	high	med	med	$78.9
Ft. Worth	low	low	med	18.8
Houston	low	low	med	106.7
Phoenix	low	low	low	27.3
Denver	high	high	high	69.0
San José	high	med	med	35.0
Tucson	low	med	med	22.9
Seven S.W. City Average	med –	low +	med	$51.2

SOURCES:

[a] Barss, Reitzel and Associates, *Community Action and Urban Change* (Cambridge: Barss, Reitzel, 1969)

[b] Department of Housing and Urban Development, *Urban Renewal Directory*, 1970

[c] Department of Commerce, Bureau of the Census, *1970 Census of Population*

has largely been excluded from political participation. What little public oversight there was over rapid land development could typically be overcome through corruption. In many southwestern cities, self-appointed "Citizens' Committees" drawn from the local business elite have dominated nonpartisan, at-large city elec-

City	Urban Renewal Program Expenditures 1949-1969[b]	Model Cities Program Expenditures 1966-1969[a]	Spilerman Riot Intensity Index[a]	Gini Index of Metropolitan Income Inequality 1970[c]
Philadelphia	$274	$25.5	28	.338
Detroit	77	20.2	1049	.326
Baltimore	90	10.8	858	.337
Cleveland	49	8.0	29	.335
Boston	133	15.6	33	.347
Pittsburgh	111	6.3	150	.329
Buffalo	23	5.6	32	.318
Seven N.E. City Average	$108	$13.1	311	.333
Los Angeles	$40	$8.9	19	.361
Ft. Worth	2	0.0	00	.331
Houston	0	13.6	53	.350
Phoenix	0	0.0	26	.356
Denver	29	11.6	08	.350
San José	9	0.2	00	.316
Tucson	6	3.3	06	.369
Seven S.W. City Average	$12	$5.4	16	.348

tions. Such arrangements led one analyst of southwestern urban politics to conclude that "the business community has a virtual monopoly in deliberation on solutions to civic problems."[19]

Table 11 shows the large differences in government composition and spending patterns between the two groups of cities. Northeastern cities average 20.0 noneducation public employees per thousand population, while the southwestern cities average only 13.1. New York ranks first and Massachusetts fifth in terms of per capita state and local tax collections, while New Mexico is thirty-third, Arizona nineteenth, Colorado twenty-fourth, Utah forty-third, and Texas forty-first. As Table 12 indicates, seven of the northeastern cities received and spent an average of $108 million on urban renewal between 1949 and 1969, while seven southwestern cities of comparable population size spent only an average of $12 million. OEO spent an average of $5.12 million in the southwestern cities, but $6.27 million in the northeastern cities. The Model Cities differential is even greater: $5.4 million in the Southwest as against $13.1 in the Northeast. Tables 11 and 12 clearly show that the public sector was smaller, less of a tax burden, and less oriented toward social programs in the Southwest.[20]

Strongly different patterns of political influence have led to these spending outcomes. While all the northeastern cities have mayoral government, all but two of the southwestern cities have city manager government, with nonpartisan city councillors elected at-large. The latter type of government has been shown to be associated with a lack of responsiveness to working class voters, limited political participation, and an orientation toward policy outputs favorable to business.

In Phoenix, Dallas, Albuquerque, Fort Worth, and San Antonio, business elites have organized slate-designating and fund-raising bodies which typically win local elections.[21] The Phoenix Charter Government organization, for example, has lost only two city council races in over twenty years.[22] Blacks and Chicanos are underrepresented among local officials far more heavily than in the Northeast. Finally, as Table 11 shows, while all northeastern cities favored Democrat Humphrey over Republican Nixon and Independent Wallace, all but three southwestern cities gave majorities or pluralities to Nixon in the close 1968 contest. Only one city, Albuquerque, gave the Democrats an outright majority.

Table 12 shows that northeastern cities experienced much more neighborhood mobilization and racial conflict during the 1960s than their southwestern counterparts. The data on the former are drawn from a one hundred city survey of the Community Action Program's impact. In each city, a randomly selected poverty area was examined to determine the number of groups active, their goals and strategies, and the level of militance. The seven northeastern cities nearly always had extensive and militant organizations, working to a large extent in coalition. In the Southwest, on the other hand, except for Denver and to a lesser extent Los Angeles and San José (which experienced Chicano activism during this period), the level of activity was modest to nonexistent.[23] The overall averages were distinctly lower than in the Northeast. Data on the intensity of riot activity draw the difference even more sharply: northeastern cities experienced wrenching and violent challenges to prevalent authority patterns, while the Southwest experienced either no such conflict or only modest conflicts.

Table 12 also shows that the 1970 gini coeffecient of income inequality for northeastern metropolitan areas is substantially less than in the Southwest. The range of variance across all cities lies between .300 and .380, so the difference between the two averages, .333 and .348, is clearly significant. The gap between rich and poor in southwestern cities has been perpetuated by economic as well as political discrimination, particularly against Chicanos and Indians, but also against blacks. It does not appear to have diminished over time.

A pamphlet issued by Tucson's Development Authority for Tucson's Economy illustrates government attitudes toward the plight of subemployed minority workers:

> There are a substantial number of workers actively seeking employment in Tucson. And, Tucson's heritage and proximity to Mexico generate an above average Mexican-American work force. This fact, when coupled with a large underemployed group, and the unemployed American Indian, results in a large number of trainable unskilled workers who qualify for training courses and OJT assistance. Employers who have established plants in Tucson say that our Mexican-Americans are easy to train, will follow instructions, are more loyal, and equal or exceed the productivity of workers in other parts of the country.[24]

Underemployment, exclusion from high-wage occupational categories, employer and union discrimination, lack of bilingual education, and similar problems continue to plague the Southwest's minority populations, even while business booms for middle-class, white migrants to the area, boosting average per capita earnings.

In sum, nodal administrative and service activities have shaped growth patterns in some northeastern and all southwestern cities. Progrowth political coalitions, linked with federal intervention, played a key role in the emergence of these economic activities in both groups of cities. The nature of these coalitions, the forms of development they fostered, their national political patrons, and the political reception they encountered differed sharply, however, between the two regions. These differences prevailed over the whole postwar period but became particularly pronounced after the late 1960s.

From the Depression onward, the major corporations diffused industrial activity away from the northeastern central cities and sought political support for transforming them into administrative and service centers. The resulting public policies, backed by national and local Democratic political entrepreneurs, triggered strong political protests.

Southwestern progrowth coalitions took a far more conservative form. Built upon a prior conservative political order, lacking a politically strong blue-collar presence, local progrowth coalitions did not need to include labor, minorities, Democratic elected officials, or the other partners to the northeastern progrowth coalitions. Their federal sponsors were committed to conservative business constituencies. Federal investment in water projects, military production, and military installations flowed through local private contractors with little or no public accountability.

The conservative political cultures which such developments reinforced in turn attracted additional investment, especially since the 1960s. Individual desires for more attractive places to live, and the need of some firms for cheaper labor helped this process along, but hardly caused it. As northeastern urban conflict during the 1960s increased the political comparative advantage that the Southwest enjoyed in private sector eyes, a sharper change in growth rates occurred between the two regions.

These interactions between private sector decision-makers and local and national politics more clearly explain why northeastern

250

metropolitan areas faltered and southwestern cities grew rapidly since the late 1960s. Simple marginal economic differences are neither large enough, nor consistently favorable enough to one region, to account for such an important shift. Nor is their timing such as to explain why the shift would occur in the mid-1970s, rather than earlier or later. Attention to political conditions, and particularly to the outburst of northeastern urban protest and conflict between 1964 and 1972, does account for this timing. (Interestingly, Los Angeles, the southwestern city with the greatest protest during this period, resembles the northeastern cities more than any of the others in the group.)

Even when overt conflict abated in the older cities, their governments were permeated by costly neighborhood influences wanting to control the development process. No such constraint exists, for example, in Houston, which even lacks zoning. The resulting intercity competition enforced a market discipline over the liberalism of the older cities.

CONCLUSION: THE IMPACT OF INTERCITY COMPETITION

This analysis of the role political factors play in intercity competition suggests some counter-intuitive conclusions about the future of urban growth. First, if many northeastern cities can reach a new political equilibrium, they may actually face a brighter economic future. These cities contain the most important national centers of administrative and high-level service activity. Their services will prosper from growth in the world economy, including the growth of branch offices located in southwestern cities and elsewhere. Multilocational organizations headquartered in New York, Boston, or San Francisco benefit from growth in places like Phoenix or Denver. Despite the fact that their share of service employment might fall, the absolute amount can still rise. More importantly, such service centers can retain the most specialized and influential concentrations of service activity.

Retaining the monopoly over decision-making provided by such concentrations of specialized service activities, however, depends upon the striking of a new political equilibrium. For most such

251

cities, this has meant a severe retrenchment from the high points of urban liberalism. Starting with Proposition 13 and continuing through the Reagan administration, local Democratic mayors like Koch of New York, Mayor White, and Mayor Feinstein have been undertaking this retrenchment, much to the dismay of community organizations and their advocates among reform-minded professionals. Liberal forces have not been strong enough to counter this trend either in local or national politics.

In the short run, private sector decision-makers have thus found competition among cities provides good leverage on the shape and composition of the public sector. With help from conservative national political entrepreneurs, they have weakened the urban liberalism of the northeastern cities while strengthening the conservatism of the Southwest.

In the long run, however, these same trends may well be creating the conditions for future conflict within southwestern urban politics. This conflict has been slow to develop for a variety of reasons. Since public agencies are not bulldozing innercity minority neighborhoods, they have not provoked the kind of direct reaction which occurred in the Northeast. Middle-class constituencies which have moved to the Southwest in search of employment opportunities and improved living conditions have been slow to register the costs of unplanned growth and underdeveloped public services. Such costs tend to emerge only some time after growth has happened. Finally, the Chicano, black, and Indian communities which could provide neighborhood mobilization have been successfully excluded from political participation in many cities. The process of mobilization among Chicanos is only now reaching the stage that black organizations achieved elsewhere. As southwestern metropolitan areas mature, these constituencies may well become mobilized against the private sector dominance of local politics and urban development patterns.

Signs of this sort of political activism have already appeared in some southwestern cities. In the Southwest, Chicanos have pressed for greater benefits from the growth process. In San Antonio, Chicano activists have had a major impact on city politics. Albuquerque and Houston have elected relatively liberal mayors, at least compared to their predecessors, through coalitions of minority group members, middle-class professionals, labor, and other traditional sources of urban Democratic support. While such stirrings have not yet had a major impact on southwestern urban political culture, they indicate that the potential for a Democratic challenge within the conservative heartland does exist.

The competition among local jurisdictions to offer the best political climate for new investment has produced a "Gresham's Law" effect. Public-service-poor jurisdictions have tended to drive out public-service-rich jurisdictions. This dynamic has restricted the ability of either type of jurisdiction to deal with pressing urban problems, be they of growth or decline. Though this "market discipline" may have reduced the burden of government on the private sector, it has also increased the overall amount of urban distress. Despite the fact that it has forced big-city Democrats and their neighborhood organization constituents to retrench, the intercity competition has thus also increased the possibility that new cities as well as old will mobilize on behalf of a national Democratic majority.

Rebuilding Progrowth Politics?

1. INTRODUCTION

Over the five decades since the New Deal, the web of federal urban development programs and the intricate national-local political coalitions woven largely by Democratic political entrepreneurs succeeded in reshaping American cities and establishing the Democrats as the normal majoriy party. With federal program tools, local progrowth political coalitions like those fashioned in Boston and San Francisco transformed old industrial cities into modern administrative centers populated by corporate headquarters, advanced corporate service firms, hospitals, universities, and other service institutions. The same programs hastened the displacement of industrial investment to the suburbs and newly developing regions of the country. These successes dissolved the urban conflicts of the industrial city and helped build the modern Democratic party, much as Franklin Roosevelt and his New Deal entrepreneurs had hoped.

It is hardly surprising that changes of this magnitude also generated new kinds of urban conflict which the founders of the New Deal could not anticipate. Seeing Democratic successes, Republican national political entrepreneurs and the conservative coalition in Congress sought to blunt the political efficacy of Democratic programs while substituting alternatives designed to reinforce their own constituencies. Suspended between this conservative opposition and the divisions of interest among their urban supporters and within their party, Democrats could preserve only programs which reinforced market trends.

As these programs began to have a major impact on central-city neighborhoods during the 1960s, they triggered a second

254

source of opposition to the progrowth coalition which big-city Democrats and their federal sponsors had organized. Inner city neighborhoods erupted in protest and were joined by young white professionals, the "urban pioneers," in opposing the demolition and clearance practices of urban renewal agencies. The New Deal coalition found itself opposed from within as well as without. Even the Great Society's ambitious attempt to bring the newly mobilized dissident elements back into the fold did not reconcile such deep differences.

Finally, after the 1960s, decision-makers within dominant private sector institutions accelerated a trend already in evidence as they shifted industrial investment from the contested older cities toward new cities with conservative, supportive political climates. Their decisions were facilitated by, and in turn reinforced, the periods of conservative ascendancy in national politics. Especially during the mid-1970s, the politicized, older, Democratic central cities found themselves in considerable distress, as did the Democratic coalition itself.

These three political challenges—from conservative national political opponents, from within the Democratic coalition, and from private sector investment shifts—coincided with long-term changes in the political terrain caused by the success of the Democrats' programs. Postwar urban development not only dissolved the accumulated conflicts of the nineteenth-century industrial city, it dissolved the demographic base on which the New Deal was built. It created a range of new urban and suburban constituencies with quite different policy needs than those of the 1930s. Demographic change combined with political challenge to produce political and substantive disarray within the Democratic coalition.

In the older cities, this political breakdown has led to the slowing of urban physical investment and the breakdown of the public capital plant. George Peterson has shown that state and local public capital formation peaked in 1968 (at $38 billion in 1973 dollars) and has fallen steadily since. Capital outlays have also fallen from 29 percent to less than 15 percent of state and local spending. Peterson concludes that this represents "a disinvestment in existing capital facilities—a failure to repair and replace the

255

capital stock as it wears out."[1] The Federal Highway Administration estimates that local streets and roads are wearing out 50 percent faster than they are being repaired.[2] And despite considerable federal aid for water and sewer systems and mass transit, New York City is not alone in observing, as it did in its 1979 *Capital Needs Statement*, that its "basic life support systems continue to crumble."[3] Just as the cycle of political ascendancy established by the New Deal appears to have come to an end, so has the life cycle of many of its physical investments.

The breakdown of consensus around major urban development projects has also influenced private investment. Even large projects having political support from local elected officials face a tangled and costly approval process. The Portman Hotel project in Manhattan's Times Square, for example, required negotiation with thirty separate agencies and institutions. Only the most profitable and politically well-backed projects can manage to pierce such a tangled web. It is no longer possible in New York, Boston, or San Francisco for a Robert Moses, Ed Logue, or M. Justin Herman to "get things done" with a minimum of political constraint.

The unraveling of traditional Democratic programs and coalition patterns has created a great vacuum. Although some urban political actors benefit from negotiating development projects one-by-one instead of having clear rules of the game, an even greater prize awaits those political entrepreneurs capable of establishing new rules, thereby reducing the political overhead costs on urban growth. Not only will they make possible a new round of urban investment, but they will have created the kind of new "social contract," or new New Deal, upon which to build a durable national political majority. As William Baroody, head of the American Enterprise Institute, observed of the 1980 elections, "There is in fact the potential for a major sea change in the political process, a realignment, like 1932; or, perhaps, a flash in the pan."[4]

Today, as in 1896 and 1932, national political power must rest on a base of metropolitan electoral majorities. If, as Samuel Beer has said, "the New Deal outlook offers only confused and partial answers and exercises only feeble powers of aggregation'' under current circumstances, then who will succeed in seizing this political opportunity?[5] Two obvious contenders are now at work: traditional liberals are attempting to revitalize their party, while conservatives, now in power, are attempting to consolidate their position. The verve of neighborhood organizations which arose during the conflicts of the 1960s and 1970s, now embodied in a network of community-based service organizations, suggests at least the germ of a third alternative. Which will succeed in organizing a new metropolitan political consensus, if any?

This question has no simple answer. To the extent that the foregoing analysis is correct, *any* attempt to build a new consensus around urban development policy as the basis for a national political majority faces substantial structural obstacles. Yet if no simple political prescriptions for resolving these obstacles can be given, at least the obstacles themselves can be clearly outlined.

2. CORE PROBLEMS

Regardless of political standpoint, the successful national political entrepreneur must resolve four fundamental issues:

1. The decay of accountability and political and economic coherence within the existing intergovernmental program delivery system.
2. The growing chasm between the new urban middle class, which has benefited from government intervention, and the new urban working class, which has been shunted into secondary labor market jobs and which has experienced worsening conditions over the last decade.
3. The competition between older and newer cities which has undermined local efforts at redistribution and regulation of the development process.
4. The emergence of a new political terrain within both the older and newer metropolitan areas which has undermined traditional political attachments and created new, weakly incorporated constituencies.

257

These four problems led to the demise of traditional Democratic urban liberalism. Any new political strategy which does not resolve these problems is not likely to endure. Even conservatives must ultimately find a way to avoid the potential for overt conflict and uncontrolled political mobilization which these conditions create.

The Problem of Program Accountability

Partisan competition and local political conflict have cost federal urban development programs not only their effectiveness in guiding urban investment but their political coherence—their accountability to clearly defined constituencies. Programs have multiplied in size and number and fostered a geometric increase in the intermediary organizations designated to carry out policy. The result has been ironic: neither the outsiders looking at the fragmented delivery system nor the insiders who operate it feel that it can be held accountable to any clear set of purposes or decisionmakers.

Critics have questioned the urban program delivery system's impact and adaptability to new needs. Federal urban programs have spent money—three billion dollars on public service employment and five billion dollars on public housing in 1980 alone—without altering or improving such basic central-city problems as unemployment and the lack of decent, affordable housing. Indeed, HUD's 1980 document, *The National Urban Policy Report*, found that urban jobs and housing problems have worsened over the last decade despite substantial federal spending increases.[6] The Carter administration's reorganization project found that urban development programs "have been added on top of each other, with little attention to their cumulative impact or interrelationships [and as a result have] become a confusing patchwork that is duplicative, contradictory, and far less effective than it could be."[7] Republican and Democratic entrepreneurs alike have found it difficult to impose substantive and political rationality on this web of programs, intergovernmental relationships, third party providers, and client

258

groups. Their conflicting political interests have both been built into federal programming, to the detriment of all concerned.

Hugh Heclo has described this change in terms of a breakdown in the classic "iron triangle" between program administrators, congressional program advocates, and local recipients which once characterized federal urban development programs. "As proliferating groups have claimed a stake and clamored for a place in the policy process," Heclo noted, "they have helped to diffuse the focus of political and administrative leadership." The resulting "issue networks" now "overlay the once stable political reference points with new forces that complicate calculations, decrease predictability, and impose considerable strains on those charged with government leadership."[8]

If the intergovernmental program delivery system seems well insulated from political accountability to the White House, the cabinet, and Congress, it appears no more responsive to local elected officials or program beneficiaries. Development decisions in Boston and San Francisco face a multitude of pressures. Complex, case-by-case negotiations have replaced the simpler deal-making which promoted investment so dramatically during the 1960s. Boston's effort to build the Copley Place complex adjacent to the South End, for example, required negotiation with HUD for an urban development action grant (UDAG), with the Turnpike Authority for air rights, and with South End community groups which have protested that it will further accelerate displacement. In San Francisco, the construction of a new convention center on the Yerba Buena site has similarly faced several decades of lawsuits, citizen reviews, complex negotiations with many parties, and costly replanning.

Although federal officials often charge that local officials and the community-based organizations which carry out federal programs have subverted national priorities, they typically claim, in turn, that the federal government imposes clumsy rules on localities and is ill-informed about and unresponsive to their real needs. As Boston's Mayor Kevin White recently told a San Francisco audience, increasing reliance on federal aid had caused "an erosion of power" against which city governments "must insist on greater sovereignty," while New York Mayor Koch has attacked the federal "mandate millstone."[9]

The cross-checking conflict among actors in the urban development decision-making arena will not be easy to rationalize. Those brokers who can wend their way through this maze for a sufficiently well-backed project command great fees and are in great demand, and will resist the return to any more orderly, "as of right" procedure. The social cost of such complex procedures is nevertheless high; reducing it will redound greatly to the political entrepreneurs capable of establishing a new "social contract" for growth. Reforming federal urban programs lies at the heart of the matter. As Samuel Beer rightly observes, "the more fundamental question is how a polity can impose upon public expenditures any rationale, any coherent view of government action, any scale of priorities reflecting an overall view of national needs."[10] But this requires solving fundamental political problems.

The Problem of Distributive Shares

National political entrepreneurs hoping to rebuild progrowth politics must also face a fundamental political problem: though rhetorically predicated on improving the quality of life for central-city neighborhood residents, fifty years of federal urban policy have worsened conditions for many of them. As had been hoped, federal legislation has dramatically improved the overall quality of the urban housing stock and has stimulated the expansion of new institutions within urban economies. Contrary to the Democratic promise, however, these benefits did not "trickle down" to the urban poor. Indeed, some areas in which the urban poor gained during the 1950s as whites fled have now "trickled up" to the new urban middle class.

In the mid-1960s, Scott Greer observed that "at a cost of more than three billion dollars the Urban Renewal Administration has succeeded in materially reducing the supply of low-cost housing in American cities."[11] Though passage of the 1968 Housing Act helped increase subsidized housing production from fifty thousand units a year to five times that amount by the late 1970s, the low-cost housing supply has continued to shrink since Greer wrote. As the South End and Western Addition cases indicate, abandonment and demolition destroyed far more housing than even the renewal plans contemplated. Increased subsidized housing production in recent years has come nowhere near to replacing it. In Dr. Goodett's words, what didn't start out right didn't end up right either.

Forty years of federal policy have set market forces in motion within large central cities which pit two groups against each other. The expanding dominant institutions, such as corporate offices, universities, and hospitals, have gained from government intervention, as have the growing number of baby-boom cohort professionals which they employ. Aided by development policies oriented toward "brisk, urban, and sophisticated" young professionals "who wish to engage in the highly competitive trade and service activities of the metropolitan hub," to use the words of the 1947 San Francisco Planning Commission study, this stratum has increasingly entered such fashionable nineteenth-century neighborhoods as the Western Addition and the South End, displacing their working class residents, as renewal officials intended.[12]

Almost all cities with strong advanced service sectors are experiencing this "gentrification" process. An Urban Land Institute study found that it was taking place in thirty-eight out of fifty-six large central cities, while Phillip Clay found gentrification in twenty-eight of the thirty largest central cities.[13] The National Housing Law Center recently found that gentrification was involuntarily displacing 2.5 million people annually.[14]

Despite New Deal and Great Society intentions, most central-city minority group residents have not made great economic gains. To the contrary, changes set in motion by federal urban development programs have often worked against them. Neighborhoods have been demolished, blue collar employers forced to depart, and housing torn down or upgraded beyond their means. As the South End and Western Addition experiences show, community activism, while producing real gains in subsidized housing production, did not alter long-term trends in favor of central-city

261

minority residents. Indeed, in some settings government housing programs hastened disinvestment by providing a market in which absentee owners could unload their properties.

Central-city minority groups have not fared better in the urban labor market. The dominant urban institutions aided by federal urban development programs, such as corporate headquarters, hospitals, and universities, have not compiled strong affirmative action records and have not provided upward mobility for minority neighborhood residents. Among blacks, the emergence of an educated middle class has done more to make inequality among blacks resemble inequality among whites than it has to improve blacks as a group in comparison to whites. Hispanic, Caribbean, and Asian immigrant groups have done no better. Instead, urban minorities typically find job opportunities in small, low-wage service and manufacturing firms which lack market power and strong unions.[15]

Despite liberal intervention, the large metropolitan areas thus remain segregated and unequal. No effort to mobilize metropolitan electoral majorities is likely to be sustained without finding a way to reduce this always potentially destabilizing problem. This is particularly true for Democrats, who must still strongly mobilize central-city voters to win national majorities.

The Problem of Intercity Competition

Federal intervention to speed the transformation of the urban system not only provoked conflict within cities, it deepened the competition among them. As political conflict within the older cities became increasingly meshed with national partisan competition and private investment decisions, the competition became more severe and perverse. It has imposed great costs not only on the older northeastern and midwestern cities which have experienced serious decline, but also on the "winners" of the South and Southwest which gained population and employment at the cost of poor public services, weak government management of growth, and heightened inequality.

Political entrepreneurs hoping to pyramid national majority status out of metropolitan electoral victories must find ways to abate the competition. Policies aimed solely toward the older cities would preclude political contenders from building a strong position within the rapidly growing new cities toward which the balance of power is shifting. To concentrate only on the latter, however, would cost support in the older cities which still contain the majority of urban voters.

If conservatives take the simple position that cities like Detroit have no viable economic future and are doomed to continued decline, they will not only waste valuable assets but are likely to provoke even more bitter geopolitical conflict.[16] Similarly, the traditional urban liberal stress on retaining industrial employment in the older cities rests on an equally inadequate foundation because it neither addresses the structural causes of decline nor recognizes the problems rapid growth is causing in the newer metropolitan areas.

An effective strategy must go to the heart of the issue. The competition among cities prevents local elected officials in both kinds of jurisdictions from addressing their most pressing problems. It also creates an incentive for them to subordinate the public good to private gain even though, as in the case of tax incentive programs for business investment, no net gains in national business activity come from the sacrifice.

The Changing Political Terrain

In responding to these three substantive problems, political entrepreneurs seeking to rebuild progrowth politics must predicate their efforts on the changed social basis of metropolitan politics. In 1984, just as in 1932 or 1896, the candidate hoping to forge a national majority position must win the allegiance of the majority of metropolitan voters. As a result of the New Deal's programmatic successes, however, the definition of the metropolitan electorate has changed dramatically over the last fifty years. The challenge to national political entrepreneurs is to do well in designing programs and politics for the current political terrain as Franklin D. Roosevelt and his associates did five decades ago.

263

Each of the contextual elements which shaped the New Deal response has evolved profoundly since 1932. In places of a concentrated, white, ethnic, blue collar urban electorate, metropolitan areas now hold a dispersed, increasingly white-collar, racially divided voting population. The dominant position of the older northeastern metropolitan areas has been challenged by the rise of new metropolitan areas like Phoenix and San Diego.

As metropolitan areas have become more politically diverse, the balance of power within central-city jurisdictions has also shifted. In the older central cities, the traditional mainstays of the New Deal coalition have had to share the urban political arena with new claimants for power; in the newer cities, entirely new kinds of coalitions have developed. These shifts in metropolitan political demographics, the changes in the congressional balance of power they imply, and new political alignments in urban politics will inevitably influence how contemporary political entrepreneurs fashion their programmatic strategy.

RISING AND DECLINING ELEMENTS IN THE METROPOLITAN ELECTORATE

Since the New Deal, the metropolitan electorate has undergone three changes. Within the major central cities, the postindustrial transformation has reduced the importance of ethnic, blue collar constituencies while promoting the growth of a minority service sector labor force and a new stratum of young professional households. Second, suburban areas have grown steadily outward, receiving both a new suburbanized industrial labor force and a new professional and managerial middle class. These areas, in turn, have aged and slowed their expansion. Finally, new metropolitan growth nodes like those of the Southwest have arisen, typically with the ability to annex suburban growth and with economies heavily based on service activities. These cities have attracted white middle-class migrants from other regions, but are also even more racially segmented than the older industrial cities.

Boston and San Francisco typify those older cities which have been transformed into international administrative and service centers. Though both retain a heritage of blue collar ethnic politics,

264

change has eroded its social base. In these cities, the industrial labor force declined by half between 1950 and 1980, and now contributes only about 15 percent of the central-city job base. Unionized occupations such as operatives and craftsmen have dwindled, as has union membership outside the services. Simultaneously, the professional, managerial, and clerical labor force has doubled, and now accounts for half the central-city job base in these cities. While this pattern has not been as strong in midwestern industrial cities like Detroit, it is nonetheless common to all cities.

Such occupational changes have been accompanied by major demographic changes. Between 1950 and 1980, hundreds of thousands of white households moved to the suburbs of Boston and San Francisco, including unionized workers as well as middle-class managers.[17] First blacks and then other minority immigrant groups, particularly Hispanics, constituted the major counterflow to the white exodus. Increasingly, it has been matched by young white households with several wage earners, typically childless, seeking to maximize their access to professional employment. During the 1950s, the 20–34 age group contributed only a small net gain to central cities, but as the baby-boom generation has matured, this cohort has provided a veritable flood into the central cities.[18] This group, the best educated in U.S. history, has entered the professional and managerial labor force of the dominant institutions which are expanding in central-city economies.

These new groups have interests and outlooks which differ from their blue-collar ethnic predecessors. The South End and Western Addition demonstrate the struggle minority groups have undertaken to secure central-city housing and job opportunities. The young white professionals also differ in outlook from their suburban parents. They have chosen nontraditional household patterns; females have entered the labor force to an unprecedented degree, and the choice to defer or forgo childbearing has become more nearly the norm than the exception. Seattle, a city much like Boston and San Francisco, recently found that less than a quarter of the city's households are made up of families with children.[19] If this cohort remains committed to such choices as its members move through their prime childbearing years—and the best evidence suggests that many will—then advanced service cities like Boston and San Francisco will retain this renewed middle-class professional stratum.[20]

Although there are points where the interests of minority service workers and white urban professionals coincide, they also conflict. In the two neighborhood cases, the latter have forced the former out, and this drama is being replayed in many other cities as well. The Boston and San Francisco case studies suggest that the political center of gravity has shifted in two directions at once— toward minority neighborhood organizations, and also toward the reform ethos of young white professionals. While ethnic politics remains a factor, new kinds of organizations, including community-based service delivery organizations, service employee unions, and reform political organizations have become increasingly important vehicles for political mobilization.

Postwar development trends have also reshaped the suburban electorate. Before the 1950s, the suburban vote outside the South was strongly WASP and Republican. As factory production and the unionized labor force began its outward migration, suburbs became increasingly diverse in their political outlook. Blue collar ethnic households retained their Democratic affiliation, if not always their urban liberalism. Some older, inner ring suburbs came to share problems quite similar to those of the central cities, while vigorous growth in such places as Boston's Route 128 or the Bay Area's Silicon Valley created new kinds of political conflict over development. Postwar suburban development patterns triggered an environmentalist reaction, and many suburbs also now face housing shortages, traffic congestion, falling school enrollments, and fiscal distress.[21]

Suburban social heterogeneity has produced great political variety among the many small, often nonpartisan political jurisdictions which make up the outer ring. The level of conflict is less, and voter turnout lower, than in central cities, and political opinions are somewhat less partisan and more conservative. But within these generalizations lies great variation. As one observer concluded, "The future suburban political landscape will continue to be marked by the conflicting demands of highly diverse interests.''[22] Like the demographic changes of the central cities, suburban development has produced new constituencies which neither traditional liberals nor conservatives have been able to capture completely.

The same cannot be said of the growing metropolitan areas of the South and Southwest, which have produced conservative, and, even in the South, increasingly Republican electoral majorities. Formerly Democratic southern suburbs are now solidly Republican, while rapidly growing southwestern metropolitan areas like Orange and San Diego Counties in California, Harris and Dallas Counties in Texas, and Maricopa County in Arizona have voted solidly Republican in recent elections. As Chapter six pointed out, these cities have less political participation, more income inequality, and less political conflict than in the Northeast. Only the mobilization of the growing Chicano population and, to a lesser degree, the in-migration from the North and West, is likely to offer any countertrend. In a few instances, however, such as Albuquerque, Austin, San Antonio, and Houston, relatively liberal Democrats have been elected to mayoral positions. This may presage a growing political conflict in the newer cities over the terms of development.

The metropolitan electorate in 1980 thus differs considerably from the political terrain FDR faced in 1932. The older central cities, the core of Democratic support, increasingly suggest the possibility of new kinds of liberal coalition patterns based on minority neighborhood organizations and young professionals, should they be able to overcome their political differences. However, they are losing electoral weight to the suburbs and new cities. Outside the South, the suburbs are no longer exclusively Republican and in many cases are experiencing typically urban problems. In the South and Southwest, metropolitan electorates appear solidly conservative, though not immune to challenge from blacks, Chicanos, and a comparatively small liberal young professional stratum.

This distribution of metropolitan political sentiment suggests that political entrepreneurs at either end of the political spectrum

267

must move to command the suburban middle ground as well as to attempt to create political countermovements in the other's heartland. As the swing constituencies, voters in the older cities' suburbs and in the new central cities will decide which set of political entrepreneurs will prevail.

THE CONGRESSIONAL BALANCE OF POWER

These shifts in the metropolitan electorate will also influence the balance of power between Democrats and their Republican and southern Democratic conservative coalition opponents in Congress. The reapportionment of House seats which has occurred since the 1980 census has shifted representation from traditionally Democratic northeastern industrial states to the South and Southwest. New York has lost five seats, while Pennsylvania, Ohio, and Illinois have each lost two. Florida has gained four seats, Texas three, and Southern California two. Among those states losing representation, the ten districts which suffered the heaviest population decline read like a roster of minority congressmen. Robert Garcia's South Bronx district lost 39 percent of its population, while former Representative Diggs' Detroit district lost 29 percent.[23] The gains have come in states and areas which Republicans and southern Democrats have been winning. At first glance, these shifts would seem to confirm Kevin Phillips' contention that the Democrats have been done in by demography.

Several important factors, however, work against this conclusion. First, Republican gains in the South have come at the expense of conservative southern Democrats. As a result, the House conservative coalition has lost the seniority and power enjoyed by the southern Democrats without making net gains in voting strength. During the Great Society years, southern Democrats chaired ten of the sixteen most important House committees. By 1977, only one of these chairmen came from the old Confederacy.[24] Indeed, the turnover occasioned by the modernization of southern politics has hastened the advent of northern urban liberals to ranking committee positions. It has also modestly increased liberal representation from central-city districts in places like Atlanta.

268

Outside the South, urban decline and suburban growth may have given the Democrats a more conservative outlook but have not necessarily favored the Republicans in a clear-cut way. Table 13 shows the partisan balance in House seats subsequent to the reapportionments of 1950 and 1970. It shows that urban decline has removed far more Republicans than Democrats from the House in the past, while the two parties have equally split the emerging suburban seats. The Voting Rights Act is likely to ensure that central-city minority congressmen will continue to hold their seats; their districts will be expanded into areas previously represented by whites. The competition among Republicans and Democrats will thus shift increasingly to the suburbs.

Table 13 suggests that the outcome is likely to be a toss-up.[25] Of the fifty-nine new suburban seats created outside the South between the 1940s and 1970s, Democrats have won twenty-nine while the Republicans have taken thirty. Democrats improved their position from one-third of such seats to two-fifths. As Michigan Republican pollster Robert Teeters recently put it, "There are going to be less seats in core Democratic areas and more seats in suburban growth areas, the swing areas, but I'm not sure you're going to have any more seats that are core Republican."[26]

If the Democratic center of gravity becomes, as it must, more suburban, how will that affect the congressional prospects for urban legislation? Several studies show that though suburban Democrats may be more conservative than their central-city colleagues, they follow their lead in voting for urban legislation. Mayhew's analysis of party cohesion on urban votes during the 1950s and 1960s shows that nonsouthern suburban Democrats vote with their urban colleagues nine times out of ten. Murphy and Rehfuss' 1973 study of 8 key votes found the same, as did Caraley's study of 24 key urban votes between 1945 and 1974.[27] As with suburban voting patterns, no district House "suburban caucus" is likely to emerge distinct from the traditional partisan differences.

In sum, the changes in the congressional balance of power which derive from the demographic shifts across metropolitan areas do not clearly support one party over the other. The declining

269

TABLE 13 The Impact of Congressional Redistricting from the 1950s to the 1970s

	Party Representation								
	1950s			1970s			Δ	D	R
	D	R	Total	D	R	Total			
South*									
Urban	17	3	20	24	11	35	+15	+7	+8
Suburban	3	1	4	13	8	21	+17	+10	+7
Rural	79	3	82	37	15	52	−30	−42	+12
Total	99	7	106	74	34	108			
North and West									
Urban	73	40	113	68	18	86	−27	−5	−22
Suburban	27	53	80	56	83	139	+59	+29	+30
Rural	37	99	136	57	45	102	−34	+20	−54
Total	137	192	329	169	158	327			
National Total									
Urban	90	43		92	29		−12	+2	−14
Suburban	30	54		69	91		+76	+39	+37
Rural	116	102		94	60		−64	−22	−44
TOTAL	236	199		243	192				

SOURCE: *Congressional Quarterly* following first congressional election after decennial redistricting. Compiled with the research assistance of Jeff Fraas.
* South defined as the eleven Confederate states.

strength of the southern Democrats has redounded to the Republicans' benefit, leaving the power of the conservative coalition relatively unchanged. Outside the South, urban decline and suburban growth have weakened the Democratic core but have not straightforwardly benefited Republicans. As with the electorate as a whole, the future balance of power will be determined by which set of political entrepreneurs manages to capture the swing suburban constituencies while simultaneously mobilizing their core.

THE BALANCE OF POWER IN LOCAL POLITICS

The Boston and San Francisco cases suggest that demographic change has also reshaped the social basis of urban political competition. The relatively tight links between blue collar, ethnic Democratic organizations, downtown business interests and developers, and new, professionalized public agencies fueled by federal funds and national Democratic leadership have given way. New claimants for political power, such as neighborhood-based service delivery organizations and reform organizations based in the new professional middle class, have complicated matters greatly. The strength of party politics itself has declined; mayors no longer rise up through existing organizations, they assemble their own political followings out of increasingly diverse elements. In this task, even Boston Mayor Kevin White has sought out allies among neighborhood organizations and similar newcomers to city politics.

The conflicts and social changes of the past several decades have jostled the relative standing of different actors in the urban political arena. Business and labor actors, as well as traditional ethnic and solidary associations, continue to wield influence, but in many cases their numbers—and thus their strength—have been attenuated. In San Francisco, for example, the rise of public sector unionism has weakened the crafts unions' hold over the Central Labor Council. The conflicts of the 1960s and 1970s produced new political actors, and the Great Society and its successor programs gave big-city mayors like Kevin White, George Moscone, and Dianne Feinstein both the imperative and the means to in-

271

corporate them into the dominant coalition, albeit in a secondary and dependent position.[28]

The building of any new national consensus in favor of progrowth politics must rearrange these urban building blocks. Conservative entrepreneurs like those in the Nixon administration understood the need to discipline these new actors and strike a new local political balance through program termination, fiscal austerity, and aid to friendly constituencies. Traditional liberals have attempted to increase resources flowing to all such claimants, but have not faced up to the conflicts among them and the need to rationalize urban political coalitions along postindustrial dimensions.

National political entrepreneurs thus work on a local political terrain which differs greatly from that encountered by FDR in the 1930s as they attempt to resolve the core problems which are his legacy. The history of the intervening years suggests that there are two basic traditions for approaching this set of political problems. The first has been that of urban liberalism, stressing public works, federal intervention, and attempting to provide something for everyone in the urban development process. The Carter administration may be taken as a kind of test of how well or poorly this traditional urban liberal approach now works. The second approach has been that of the conservative tradition reaching back through Nixon and Eisenhower to the triumph of the conservative coalition in the late 1930s. The Reagan administration offers a useful test of how well or poorly a vigorous application of the conservative tradition is likely to fare in solving the basic problems vexing urban development programs and the political system. The legacy of neighborhood activism across the nation's major cities deserves examination, too, as an element of a future political consensus.

3. COMPETING EFFORTS TO REBUILD PROGROWTH POLITICS

As architectural historian Vincent Scully once observed,

> Redevelopment and Vietnam were intimately connected and were indeed the two massive failures of American liberalism.

. . . They have played complementary roles in the polarization of the country and in the shift of power away from the liberal center toward more extremist positions. . . .[29]

The decay of the urban liberal consensus opened the way to challenges from new points of view. The first and most obvious effort to fill this political vacuum has come from traditional liberals themselves. With the election of the Carter administration in 1976, they had a chance to revitalize the urban program delivery system.

The Carter Administration and the Traditional Liberal Model

As it entered office in 1977, the Carter administration could hardly have asked for better circumstances in which to renew traditional liberal urban programs. Republican economic policies had triggered a severe economic downturn, which mobilized urban voters and placed big-city economic distress at the top of the national agenda.

According to one analyst, "two-to-one majorities or better in New York, Boston, Newark, Philadelphia, Cleveland, Chicago, Detroit, Minneapolis, St. Louis, Oakland, and Baltimore" provided Carter with statewide victories in "New York, Pennsylvania, Ohio, Wisconsin, and Missouri, without which he would not have had the electoral votes to win the presidency."[30] And as a black political analyst pointed out, "In thirteen states, blacks provided Carter with the winning margin of victory, and eight of them were in the South."[31] This disproportionate support from urban and minority voters undoubtedly reflected their strong reaction against the policies of Nixon and Ford.

Severe recession and Watergate also gave northern Democrats an unusually strong position in Congress. Their preponderance over Republicans and southern Democrats in the House after 1974 was greater than at any time since the New Deal; nonsouthern Democrats held 204 seats, as against 87 southern Democrats and 144 Republicans. Urban liberals needed to pick up only 14 votes from their opponents to win. This legislative power was thwarted by President Ford's veto. In the 1976 election, northern Democrats

273

lost only four seats while gaining the presidency. Congress had passed some programs, like CETA, over President Ford's veto in response to the recession. With Carter's advent, traditional urban liberals appeared to be a driving legislative and political force just as they were in 1933 and 1965.

The Carter administration advanced three different urban policies during its brief tenure. The first, and most significant, involved the initial $16 billion "economic stimulus" package of 1977, along with the enactment of the dual-formula change in the CDBG Program, the UDAG Program, and a new emphasis on "targeting" aid to "distressed cities." This package constituted a 25 percent increase in intergovernmental aid to big cities; it evokes comparisons with the Great Society and the New Deal and undid some of the damage which Nixon's "New Federalism" had inflicted on Democratic programs. This urban policy attempted to breathe new life into urban liberalism by stressing public capital investment and subsidies to private investment in the older central cities. Rather than reforming existing programs, it substantially expanded them. Politically, it rested upon the traditional participants in progrowth politics.

A few months later, the second Carter administration urban policy provided more rhetoric but less substance for the president's big-city electoral base. In March 1978, the White House issued a formal urban policy entitled "A New Partnership to Conserve America's Communities," which pulled together pet projects advocated by various departments under the covering rhetoric of "improved performance of existing programs by coordination, consolidation, simplification and reorienting resources."[32] It proposed to continue and expand the economic stimulus package programs and, like that earlier effort, stressed targeting on "distressed cities."

Taking a lead from the President's Reorganization Project at OMB, the Carter program stressed the need for greater substantive rationality and coordination in administering urban programs and set forth the administration's political ideal—a "new partnership" among various levels of government, the private sector, neighborhoods, and voluntary associations.

274

Few of the proposed programs received congressional support; indeed, Congress proved unwilling even to extend the antirecessionary measures of 1977. The 1978 urban policy document is important primarily because, together with the reorganization project's report on urban economic development, it reveals the administration's lack of thinking about the substantive political problems afflicting the program delivery system.

When the fiscal stimulus and "New Partnership" initiatives failed to have the desired economic and political impacts, the Carter administration retreated from liberalism. Responding to persistent inflation, a ground swell of tax resistance prompted by California's Proposition 13, and congressional opposition, Carter chose to apply recessionary rather than expansionary policies for 1970 and 1980. The third policy was a premonition of the coming conservative thrust. As Richard Nathan commented,

> The last two budgets [1979 and 1980] taken together mark the turning point in federal grants policy. . . . Nonwelfare grants from the federal government to the states and localities are projected to *decline* in *real* terms by 3.3% in 1979 and 6.8% in 1980. . . . Ironically, the biggest reductions come in the programs expanded in 1977 to fight the last recession just as the next recession is about to poke its head up on the economic horizon.[33]

Antirecessionary fiscal assistance, CETA, and local public works were all phased down or out in these budgets. Despite criticism from mayors, urban policy analysts, and unions that Carter had abandoned his commitment to the cities and was jeopardizing his chances for reelection, the administration persisted. During the 1980 session, Congress not only supported but exceeded the president's proposed cuts, reducing, for example, the number of CETA jobs authorized. The revival of the urban liberal tradition could not even survive the term of a Democratic president.

How well, then, did the Carter administration's first two urban policies work? The Carter initiatives can fairly be summed up as imitating the New Deal without the financial commitment or the political reform. Where the New Deal launched $4.2 billion in

275

public works between 1933 and 1936, the Carter administration initiated $6 billion in new public works projects for 1977 and 1978, or roughly one-tenth the New Deal effort. Where the WPA employed an annual average of 2.35 million workers, the Carter administration increased the number of CETA positions authorized to 750,000. The Carter package included $3.5 billion in direct financial assistance to central-city governments hurt by high unemployment as a kind of bonus revenue sharing; it also reinvigorated such 1937 Wagner Act housing and redevelopment programs by increasing Section 8 public housing outlays by $358 million and by establishing the Urban Direct Action Grant (UDAG) Program at a $675 million authorization level.[34]

Congress passed Carter's initial legislative program swiftly. Of the 59 key House and Senate votes on this legislation, the administration won fifty-one times. In the House, the 200 nonsouthern Democrats attracted on average 60 votes from southern Democrats and Republicans, giving them a clear margin of power.[35] The administration used this influence to change the CDBG formula to favor the older, northeastern cities. HUD also required spending three-fourths of this money in low-income census tracts, while the White House supported legislation requiring a 10 percent set-aside of federally funded local public works contracts for minority firms.

Taken together, these measures simply revived the federal urban programs which the Nixon-Ford years had starved and demoralized. They did not reorganize the programs, make them more accountable to the intended beneficiaries, nor successfully use them to encourage local political reform.

Despite the much-heralded work of the Urban and Regional Policy Group (URPG) and the less well known but equally ineffectual President's Reorganization Project in OMB, the Carter administration failed to tackle the accountability problem. Instead, the URPG stapled together favored "urban initiatives" suggested by individual program offices and put them behind a covering rhetoric stressing the need to "target" resources on "distressed" cities. The administration did not succeed in enacting more than a few minor URPG suggestions; indeed, it failed to preserve the

276

main elements of its 1977–1978 stimulus package. Despite the administration's search for "an integrated development approach," the White House dropped the OMB Reorganization Project's recommendation for a new Department of Development Assistance, to encompass HUD, the EDA part of Commerce, a proposed National Development Bank, and such smaller programs as CSA, SBA, and the Agriculture housing programs.[36]

By the administration's final days, the program delivery system was, if anything, more fragmented than at the beginning. HUD's new UDAG Program competed directly with the EDA Title IX loan program, various agencies sought to get their own piece of the "urban initiative" action, and HUD, Commerce, and Treasury were fighting over control of a potential development bank. From the City Hall and neighborhood perspective, though more money was available from more sources, the new round of regulations from HUD and other agencies complicated existing programs rather than making them more effective or more responsive. New regulations and program titles designed to ensure that CETA jobs went to the minority poor, for example, made the employment system more complex, restrictive, and unresponsive. While the administration failed to require physical development grant programs to hire those trained by CETA subcontractors, it succeeded in establishing four different CETA planning cycles and more than three dozen separate CETA program titles.

The "new partnership" also failed to redress the widening gap between the urban poor and the middle class. Great Society programs like the Community Action Program and Model Cities had attempted to counter the problem of distributive shares. The Nixon administration had successfully undermined these programs, although it had not terminated all of them. Despite its emphasis on neighborhoods and voluntary associations, however, the "new partnership" contained little more than a symbolic nod toward the community organizations which had battled for a place in urban politics.

By contrast with the Great Society, the $12 billion in "new partnership" proposals contained nothing for the Community Service Administration, OEO's successor organization, only $40 mil-

277

lion to ACTION to initiate an "urban volunteer corps," and a mere $15 million for a HUD program of small grants to neighborhood groups. Congress passed only the HUD program, designating a new HUD assistant secretary for neighborhoods and voluntary organizations to administer it. The small size of the program clearly indicates its purely symbolic importance.

Perhaps the administration's boldest attempt to "reorient resources" in favor of the central-city poor involved new HUD regulations for the CDBG Program requiring that 75 percent of a city's entitlement be spent in low-income "neighborhood strategy areas." While this requirement marginally increased the amount of funds flowing to relatively poor areas, it neither changed the use of these funds (largely for housing rehabilitation) nor the decision-making mechanisms which allocated them. As a recent evaluation of the CDBG Program's citizen participation procedures concluded, "The important decisions concerning CDBG are made centrally. Despite the rhetorical stress on neighborhood which surrounds CDBG, it is a neighborhood program only in the sense that most expenditures attributed to it go to residential areas."[37] Housing rehabilitation does little to improve household incomes of previous residents while potentially worsening their housing situation through displacement.

As Harvard economist John Kain has observed, the Carter program's emphasis on property improvement and investment missed a basic point:

> The true causes of urban distress, in contrast [to the URPG argument], are racial discrimination and poverty. . . . Direct anti-discrimination and anti-poverty measures should therefore be the cornerstone of a national urban policy. . . .[38]

Instead, the "new partnership" focused on subsidizing private investment in the "distressed cities" of the Northeast. The UDAG Program offers a clear view of what the Carter administration sought in the "new partnership." Enacted in 1977 as an amendment to the Housing and Community Development Act, the UDAG Program authorized $400 and later $675 million annually in discretionary grants to private developments in large, old, declining cities. UDAG provided, in other words, a new and more flexible form of urban renewal in which federal assistance could "sweeten" development deals negotiated between local government and private builders.

A 1979 study of the first 241 UDAG awards found that three-quarters of the grants had gone to large central cities predominantly located in the Northeast. (Only 28 percent of the funds went to the South or West.) The $487 million in federal grants were matched by $2.86 billion in private investment. Of this total, $1.36 billion went to industrial projects, $935 million to commercial projects, $291 million to new hotels, and $276 million to residential projects. Though this emphasis on urban-renewal-style downtown office, shopping, and hotel projects provoked a "vehement reaction of pro-neighborhood groups," subsequent grants were not significantly different.[39] A large round of UDAG grants awarded during the 1980 presidential primaries, for example, included $12.8 million for department store and office space in downtown Detroit and $6.4 million for luxury harborside housing and a downtown office and shopping complex in Baltimore.[40] At the same time as the administration pursued these subsidies to private capital investment, it failed to achieve either general welfare reform or enactment of the more limited but equally critical youth employment proposal formulated by the Vice President's Task Force on Youth Employment. Indeed, it even failed to assure that needy central-city residents got the jobs "created" or "retained" by its subsidies to private capital.

The Carter administration's stress on "targeting" urban aid to the older northeastern cities did address the third major problem plaguing the urban program delivery system. Just as the Nixon administration shifted program benefits away from traditional Democratic beneficiaries by inventing "print-out politics," the Carter years saw successful attempts to "target" (or more properly "retarget") benefits back toward Democratic constituencies.

The austerity and recession of the Nixon-Ford years had induced fiscal distress and budgetary retrenchment in those local jurisdictions which had most actively challenged urban-renewal-style progrowth politics during the 1960s and early 1970s. As a result, local elected officials became more eager to promote the kind of downtown development which the UDAG Program meant to foster. Thus, while the older cities regained some competitive parity with the newer cities of the South and West during the Carter years, they put it to traditional uses. More favorable local political attitudes and more aid helped promote the resurgence in downtown office development which occurred after 1976 in Boston, San Francisco, New York, and other older cities with corporate services concentrations. But they also promoted heightened urban tensions.

The failure of the Carter administration's programs suggests that traditional liberal Democratic approaches do not address, much less resolve, the basic pathologies afflicting the federal urban program delivery system. At heart, the traditional liberal approach rests on subsidies to the agency administrators, local elected officials, developers, and their allies who benefit directly from the development process. It thus tends to ignore the accountability of these development interests to the neighborhoods, underemployed minority groups, or the public interest as a whole, who are supposed to benefit from growth. It also ignores the framework of competition within which this investment occurs, and which undermines local attempts to regulate the distribution of its benefits. Because it ignored these key relationships, the Carter "economic stimulus" package proved to be more effective in promoting inflation than in reestablishing a political consensus on urban development policy.

The Carter administration's version of traditional liberalism also failed because it lacked a political strategy. The Carter programs offered nothing designed to mobilize such rising metropolitan electoral constituencies as central-city young professionals or the suburban, unionized labor force. Nor did Carter attempt to appeal to the minority groups living in newer cities like those in the Southwest who have not yet been mobilized as a force in urban politics. Instead, the administration shied away from anything resembling the Great Society.

It might be said that Carter failed because he was not enough of an urban liberal and did not take the risks necessary to mobilize new constituencies. While true, it must be underscored that there was little in the existing urban programs, the tradition of liberal Democrats in Congress, or the constituencies of the Democratic party itself to push him in this direction. Thus the failure of urban liberalism in the Carter years can be attributed to structural features of the tradition as well as to weak political leadership.

Rather than modernizing the local political coalitions on which national Democratic majorities must rest, the "new partnership" played to the same old crowd. As one black participant in a HUD-sponsored "equity forum" put it, "Urban redevelopment cannot be sold as a social program; it has real economic potential which can only be tapped if the business model is followed in its exploitation."[41]

By failing to use national programs to mobilize new local constituencies and by championing "distressed cities," the Carter administration's traditional liberalism also cost it the chance to influence the congressional balance of power. The Carter programs did not mobilize support either in swing suburban jurisdictions or in the central cities of rapidly growing metropolitan areas in the South and Southwest. This failure cost it the swing votes which had given the administration its initial victories.

While the Carter administration had many other problems which weakened it, ranging from the 1977 oil shock and the inflation rate to the Iranian hostages, it is also true that it entered office with extraordinarily favorable conditions for reforming national politics by reforming urban programs. In sum, then, traditional liberalism as represented by the Carter administration failed the political as well as the substantive challenges facing it.

The Reagan Administration and the Neoconservative Model

In contrast to traditional liberals, neoconservatives have developed a clear conception about what is wrong with federal urban program delivery systems and what to do about them. The neoconservative view builds upon the experience of earlier conservative swings in national politics. During these periods, conservative national political entrepreneurs have restrained federal

281

spending, shifted power from the public to the private sector, relied upon state as opposed to federal intervention, and supported alternative development programs, such as military spending or the interstate highway program, which work through the private sector and reinforce conservative constituencies. In their years out of power, neoconservatives sharpened these policy responses against the rapid rise of federal spending and government intervention after the mid-1960s. With their advent to power in the Reagan administration, they applied these traditional ideas with great force.

Neoconservatives believe, as Peter Steinfels has pointed out, that new claimants to power—young professionals working for government, universities, and nonprofit organizations, neighborhood groups, the black and Chicano movements, public interest lawyers and the like—must be excluded from government support.[42] The "new class" critics of the American political economy, according to this point of view, champion unproductive forces which, if they grow, would make matters worse rather than better. Or, as one Reagan supporter in Congress bluntly put it, "We're going to de-fund the left."

Conservative analysts argue that the private market works better without the distortions introduced by federal subsidies, that such programs as CETA waste resources which could be productively employed elsewhere, and that attempts to reverse the northeastern population and employment decline are pointless at best. William Simon, for example, called New York City a "disaster in microcosm" because its large and costly range of public services created "a politics of stealing from productive Peter to pay unproductive Paul, creating a new class of Americans which lives off our taxes and pretends that its institutionalized middle-class pork barrel is all for the sake of the 'poor.' "[43] Should conservatives find themselves in power, they should repeal most of the programs enacted by the Democrats.

The 1980 national elections set the stage for exactly such an effort. In contrast to the 1976 election, in 1980 Carter could not carry central cities by sufficiently large margins to carry key states. This failure not only cost Democrats the White House but drastically reduced the number of Democrats in Congress. Democrats lost twelve Senate seats, thirty-three House seats, four governorships, and 220 state legislative seats. For the first time since 1950, Republicans controlled the Senate by a margin of fifty-three to forty-seven. In the House, despite the declining importance of southern Democrats, the Republican gain was strong enough to give the conservative coalition *de facto* control. When President Reagan held all 192 Republicans he needed only twenty-six supporters from the Democratic side of the aisle to win House votes. Although some southern Democrats have remained faithful to party leadership on key issues, forty-one of them have banded together to form the Conservative Democratic Forum. This group provided almost all the twenty-nine defections President Reagan needed for the 217 to 211 House victory of his Omnibus Budget Reconciliation Act of 1981 (OBRA). Representative Phil Gramm, an author of the bill, was a prime organizer of the Forum and the resurgence of the conservative coalition.[44]

The OBRA contains the key aspects of his administration's approach to the federal urban program delivery system. It seeks to reduce the growth rate of federal spending, control transfer payments to individuals and grants to state and local governments, and shift resources to military spending. To finance this shift, OBRA (as well as the FY 1983 budget) cut domestic spending some $35 billion. Urban programs were hit hard. From FY 1982 through FY 1984, ORBA cut approximately $14 billion from existing grants to localities, and $11 billion in grants to individuals (food stamps, unemployment, and social security). An Urban Institute study projected a $27 billion loss of revenues to private, nonprofit service agencies from the total package of Reagan budget cuts for FY 1982–1984. Meanwhile, OBRA authorized an increase of $52 billion for military outlays over this period. The president's FY 1983 budget seeks even further cuts.

As the president's program for a "new beginning" made clear, he sought and won "severe reductions in make-work job programs, governmental programs to stimulate new energy technologies, and regional and community development subsidies, as well as a host of other misdirected subsidy and spending programs."[45] Major program cuts included drastic reductions in HUD's

283

subsidized housing program (from the Carter-era 260,000 units down to 142,000 units with a 25 percent rent increase for public housing tenants), a one-third cut in the UDAG Program, termination of Economic Development Administration loans, the termination of most CETA and youth employment programs, curtailment of mass transit capital grant funds, and a large reduction in EPA-funded urban waste water projects. CDBG spending was also held below current levels despite inflation. In short, with backing from the Republican Senate and the resurgent conservative coalition in the House, the Reagan administration repealed major portions of the Democratic urban program delivery system.

The Reagan administration has also attempted to reorganize the delivery system by combining remaining grant programs into block grants flowing primarily through state governments. This continuation of Nixon's New Federalism reduces the discretion exercised by federal agency officials thought by the White House to be vulnerable to claims from politically suspect provider groups, and places decision-making power at the level of government that is most likely to be influenced by suburban and rural, as opposed to urban, political forces. It makes them, not Washington, the target of lobbying.

Along with shifting the control of federal money to those levels of government least likely to be vulnerable to urban liberal influence, the Reagan program makes an outright effort to ''de-fund the left.'' The OBRA budget package reduced the Legal Services Corporation by a third, eliminated the CETA public service jobs program, eliminated CSA and VISTA, removed one of the few neighborhood-oriented measures of the Carter administration, HUD's neighborhood self-help fund, and also ended funding for the Consumer Co-op Bank. The Reagan urban policy thus ambitiously took up where Nixon's effort to terminate Model Cities and OEO left off. In one swift initiative, the Reagan administration has phased out the many federal programs which have provided support, however qualified and tame, for the advocacy of the interests of neighborhood groups, the poor, and central-city constituencies.[46]

In place of the traditional liberal Democratic methods of stimulating local development, the Reagan administration has chosen different tools around which to structure its local support: tax cuts and defense spending. Business tax cuts, especially accelerated depreciation and tax credits for rehabilitating commercial structures, essentially reinforce private market decision-making. In nominal terms, defense spending will rise 88 percent between 1981 and 1985. Most of this increased commitment will go for weapons systems procurement rather than more military personnel and higher military wages. At this point, the administration does not know what specific weapons systems it will acquire with these new funds. Since the new spending will likely follow established patterns, however, these funds will flow heavily to the relatively conservative and already fast-growing regions of the South and particularly the West. Federal spending increases during the Reagan administration will thus heavily favor the areas which proved most crucial in electing him and influencing votes in Congress. Conversely, his cuts will fall most heavily on the older cities of the Northeast.

New York City, for example, calculated a loss of $1.075 billion in federal aid for FY 1982, with that number rising to $1.819 billion in 1984. Of the first year amount, $359.9 million will be lost from items within the city budget, particularly in CETA, health and social services, and education programs. Another $428.7 million will be removed from construction projects, including waste water treatment, bridges and highways, and UDAG and EDA projects. Finally, off-budget independent authorities such as the Transit Authority, the Housing Authority, and the Health and Hospitals Corporation stand to lose another $169 million. Although the direct reduction in on-budget expenditures will amount to only 2.5 percent of the city's total expenditures, this contraction will still be painful given the city's long-term struggle to balance its revenues and expenses. Federal cuts mean the city will terminate important services because it cannot fund them from its own resources.[47] Boston and San Francisco, which have already experienced severe financial stresses from local tax limitations measures, will have to make similar cuts.

These steps seek to solve the problem of program accountability

285

much as the Nixon administration did—by divesting unfriendly constituencies of their access to program benefits. The continuation of the Nixon-era block grant approach also removes decision-making power from those federal agencies, like HUD and DOL, which conservatives suspect have been "captured" by such constituencies. The Reagan administration has essentially repealed the "targeting" efforts of the Carter administration. CDBG spending will no longer be restricted to poor neighborhoods, nor even to public or nonprofit purposes!

As the Nixon administration understood, however, neoconservatives cannot successfully take a purely negative approach to the intergovernmental urban program delivery system. The Reagan administration has chosen to expand military spending dramatically as its method of stimulating domestic development, while also providing energy and agribusiness concessions needed to retain southern Democratic support. However problematic the political accountability of domestic development programs like UDAG or CETA, the Defense Department and the energy industry have even weaker records of responding to popular control. Thus while the Reagan administration may rationalize the federal urban development programs (at least according to its own lights), it will worsen the overall problem by relying on an even less responsive substitute. Ultimately, this is bound to deepen conflict, as the MX siting controversy and strip-mining, land use, and water disputes already have in the West.

The Reagan administration has also taken a classically conservative but ultimately problematic approach to the problem of distributive shares. It hopes to withdraw federal support from the various neighborhood-based service organizations which have arisen, as a result of pressure on the Democratic party, to speak for the urban poor. It also has trimmed entitlement programs flowing to them. It asks urban blacks, for example, to take their chances on the doubtful premise that a future rising economic tide will lift all boats, including theirs. Like its predecessors, the Reagan administration has employed sharply recessionary economic policies to discipline liberal claimants for political power, whether labor unions or neighborhood groups. The 1980–1982 recession equalled and in some respects exceeded the 1973–1975 Nixon recession in severity, throwing such groups sharply on the defensive.

Finally, the Reagan administration has also pursued a clear approach to the problem of invidious regional competition. It sought to withdraw measures designed to slow the decline of the older cities and to enhance those which will speed the growth of the not-coincidentally Republican cities of the South and West. Despite the pledge not to use tax policy to promote "social change," new rapid depreciation schedules will promote disinvestment from the older cities and reward investment in the newer ones. The rise in defense spending will also clearly benefit such rapidly growing cities as Houston, Dallas, Phoenix, and San Diego. Energy price decontrol also has the same intercity transfer effects.[48]

The conservative strategy, as embodied in the Reagan administration, is thus essentially destructive of productive capacity in at least three senses. It has badly shaken existing social service delivery systems. While conservative theorists argue that these systems are inherently unproductive and a drag on the economy, this is not necessarily so. Indeed, as the introductory analysis showed, the expansion of such systems at the behest of government has made a major contribution to the growth of the U.S. economy. The conservative strategy thus threatens major sectors of the economy as well as the central-city poor and working class constituencies which have backed the Democrats. Second, by heightening interregional competition and disinvestment in the older cities, the conservative strategy wastes valuable productive assets (the old cities themselves) and imposes social costs. Third, by shifting government investment from social spending to defense, conservatives are relying on the one function which all economists agree is the most purely unproductive. The conservative strategy thus destroys assets of the whole society.

Indeed, even if it survives, President Reagan's national development strategy will not work in an unambiguously favorable way even in the areas which will grow rapidly. A defense and, should prices recover, an energy development boom and heightened interregional migration will create new problems and new constituencies in the areas which conservative elites now safely domi-

287

nate. Housing shortages, pollution and congestion, and difficulty in financing the expansion of public services will become increasingly acute. When combined with such new constituencies as a unionized labor force and an increasingly organized Chicano community, the continued absence of political challenge cannot be taken for granted in these areas.

If the Reagan urban policy takes a head-on approach to the three major problems afflicting the intergovernmental program delivery system given its philosophy, what can be said of its merits as a political strategy? Like Roosevelt's New Deal and Johnson's Great Society, Reagan's New Beginning has a powerful political consistency. It punishes Democratic core constituencies while rewarding areas of the country which have supported Reagan. Just as Democratic programs fostered supportive coalition relationships within the urban political arenas of the older cities, the Reagan programs will foster a far more conservative set of coalitions which, if largely outside public view, nonetheless wield considerable political power.

The political and substantive coherence of the Reagan administration's strategy does not, however, guarantee its success. Indeed, just as the congenital weakness of traditional Democratic liberalism is its inability to reconcile its need for support from dominant economic institutions with its rhetorical and political commitment to the urban working class, the Republicans also have a congenital weakness. By forcefully advancing the interests of their core political supporters, they unite their otherwise fragmented political opposition and exacerbate the general level of political conflict. Since the Republican party rests on a narrower social base than does the Democratic party, this is a potentially fatal flaw.

The Nixon-Ford recession of 1973–1975 and the New Federalist attack on Democratic urban programs contributed heavily to the mobilization of core Democratic constituencies, particularly those located in the central cities in 1976. While the Reagan administration enjoyed great political momentum in 1981, as Nixon did in 1973, its essentially conflictual approach to urban policy will surely trigger opposition. Together with the fact that the Reagan

288

administration has resorted to a severe recession to fight inflation, the confrontational nature of the New Beginning has sowed the seeds of its own political demise. The 1982 congressional elections, which abated the power of the conservative coalition, hinted at this possibility.

The Neighborhood Movement as an Incomplete Alternative

Since the traditional liberal and conservative approaches have failed to resolve the basic structural problems and conflicts affecting the urban program delivery system and the metropolitan political arena, only an alternative model can ultimately be successful as a basis for a new national political consensus. The community organizations and community-based service agencies which grew up across the country in neighborhoods like the South End and the Western Addition during the 1960s and 1970s would certainly claim to offer such a model. This diverse, self-styled "neighborhood movement" lacks a coherent ideology like that of the neoconservatives, but compensates by providing a working model of how things might be done differently.[49] The South End and Western Addition cases (and indeed the prevalence of urban community activism elsewhere) suggest that such groups have become a real part of the urban political arena. Whatever its strengths, however, the "neighborhood movement" has shortcomings which prevent it from becoming a true political and programmatic alternative.

The views of neighborhood organizations like those in the South End and the Western Addition can only be extrapolated into a national platform. Such a platform would stress ideas like citizen participation and neighborhood control over government programs, self-help and small enterprise as opposed to large public or private organizations, "restoring and supporting natural coping mechanisms and helping networks rather than supplanting them with bureaucratic institutions,"[50] and rehabilitating existing neighborhoods rather than allowing decline or creating new housing elsewhere.

289

The neighborhood movement would have to be counted as hostile to the free play of market forces, particularly where residential housing is concerned. The fight against displacement by market forces (whether disinvestment or gentrification) has been a major theme of neighborhood activism during the 1970s. Yet community organizations also oppose big government as a substitute for the marketplace because they have seen it operate so often on behalf of dominant institutions. They favor government grants for owner-occupied, cooperative, or tenant-managed housing rather than direct government provision of housing.

Stimulated by the growth of neighborhood organizations and the ideas and values they have advocated, policy analysts have recently come to pay increased attention to such concepts as "neighborhood planning," "neighborhood confidence building," and "community reinvestment." In general, such analysts favor government subsidies to the kinds of public and private investments which would stem disinvestment in neighborhoods threatened by racial transition or, conversely, they favor aid to current residents to gain an equity stake in neighborhoods facing upward transition.[51]

Expanding these concepts within federal urban development policy would require a shift in the use of CDBG and UDAG funds away from large, downtown-oriented commercial projects toward neighborhood-based projects. It would also require an increase in federal funding for the kinds of programs suggested but never enacted by President Carter's "New Partnership." These would include enlarging grants to community organizations, expanding the manpower available to them through VISTA, CETA, or some equivalent source, and administering federal grant programs, whether they be for social services, education, housing, or economic development, through "alternative" community-based providers.

Although community-based providers are now part of the urban development program delivery system and all its problems, some feel they do a better job than government agencies. As the Ford Foundation observed in an internal memorandum leading up to the establishment of the Local Initiatives Support Center:

Community organizations have conclusively proven their worth. When well managed and adequately funded, they have displayed an ability to plan and implement complex physical and economic development projects, to offer an array of needed social service programs, and to assure that all residents share in the fruits of their activities, whether in the form of better housing, jobs or services. . . . They represent a critical mass of development and programming potential more available and accountable to community people than the traditional public or private sectors. And most important in the case of urban revitalization, nonprofit community groups are prepared to take development risks in areas long since abandoned by business and industry—and often government—in hopes of stimulating renewed private investment.[52]

On this basis, Ford committed millions of its own money and convinced major corporations to match their contribution.

In Boston and San Francisco, the CDBG funding allocations clearly reflect the influence of community organizations and the political credit to be gained by supporting neighborhood-oriented projects. National evaluations show that not all local chief executives have found it in their interest to incorporate such groups into their governing coalition, and that many do so in a way that does not concede them real power. Nonetheless, a surprising number of major cities, perhaps as many as a third, have gone a considerable distance in this direction.[53] According to one study, nearly forty large cities have also experienced drives to elect councillors by district since 1970, and more than half were successful.[54]

The community organizations and community-based service agencies which have arisen in such numbers since the 1960s thus suggest a distinctive approach to the three core problems plaguing the federal urban program delivery system. They would improve accountability neither through stronger federal oversight nor by turning to market solutions, but by turning even more federal programs over to local nonprofit organizations. They would approach the problem of distributive shares by reducing federal aid

291

to programs like UDAG and EDA loans (or the military), which emphasize large-scale development projects, and by shifting that aid to programs which deliver social services, such as CETA, Title XX, and Section 8. Such aid, they might well argue, would allow working class minority neighborhood residents to hold their own with, and perhaps even join with, urban young professionals in a campaign to improve the quality of neighborhood life.

The shortcomings of community organizations as a base for an alternative approach to the construction of a national political consensus on urban development are immediately apparent, however. First, the inherently local nature of the "neighborhood movement" has prevented it from addressing the structural sources of conflict over urban development. The movement has little to say, for example, about the private sector reaction against the relatively modest penetration of development decision-making that community groups have already achieved. Nor have community activists dealt successfully with their failure to build strength in the suburbs and the growing cities of the South and Southwest that now hold the swing vote in the national electorate. Indeed, community groups have often forsaken electoral politics altogether! This lack of a national political presence inherently undermines community organization as an alternative source of political rationalization.

Even if they were so inclined, the great diversity of neighborhood organizations and service agencies would find it hard, perhaps impossible, to build such an autonomous national political presence. As the Western Addition and the South End suggest, neighborhoods contain a great welter of interests even at the block level, and neighborhood organizations do not mediate among these interests well, much less represent them in any accountable way. Indeed, because they have typically chosen the role of service delivery in place of the role of political advocacy, community organizations have converted their constituents into clients. Though they may have a more responsive and humane way of processing these clients than public welfare agencies, the relationship remains suspect nonetheless. There is thus something strongly self-serving about the call for greater devolution of public functions to community-based service agencies.

It could well be argued, in fact, that greater reliance on this method of providing services would worsen the fragmentation and lack of accountability that now characterize the intergovernmental program delivery system. It is notoriously hard for government grant administrators to hold grantees to any but the most modest standards of performance. On the other hand, the danger that public officials could condition grant-giving on political allegiance is ever present. Further reliance on community-based providers might thus heighten the potential for political manipulation from above rather than accountability from below.

The "neighborhood movement's" reliance on social services also begs a fundamental point. These social service activities attempt to clean up the social damage after it has already been done rather than address its structural sources. Where young white professionals are displacing minority service workers from a central-city housing and employment market, for example, a program of interest-free loans for increasing minority homeownership or rehabilitating cooperative housing is beside the point. The key issue is, instead, what sources of upward mobility will operate in our cities and who will get access to them. In this light, expanding community-based social services can at best be only remedial and inadequate.

Like the traditional liberal and conservative approaches to the current programmatic and political stalemate around national urban development policy, the "neighborhood movement," therefore, does not constitute a workable basis for achieving a new national consensus. The picture is not entirely negative, however. The "neighborhood movement" has qualities upon which a successful consensus can build.

First, the "neighborhood movement" provides a constituency base (greatly expanded because of the mobilizations of the 1960s and 1970s and the Great Society political response) which new types of political entrepreneurs, like the late Mayor George Moscone of San Francisco, can use and have used to build new kinds of leadership in urban politics. As the Reagan administration budget

293

reductions cut deeply into this constituency (and remove perhaps one-third of the approximately $39 billion in federal funds local nonprofit service providers received in 1980), they will strengthen prospects for such leadership.

The "neighborhood movement" has also established a political rhetoric of citizen participation, participatory planning, and community review which challenges the prevailing ideologies of progrowth politics, whether of the liberal or conservative variety. No longer can government so easily engage in regressive social engineering. Finally, community organizations and agencies provide the organizational infrastructure through which citizens at the grass roots participate in political life on a daily basis. Under the right national circumstances and with other networks which spread into the citizenry (the labor movement in particular), they could become part of a national organized political base. They could become a vehicle for political mobilization as well as a mere electoral potential. The urban political movements of the 1960s and 1970s will thus likely play a major part in a progressive resolution of the national urban policy impasse even if they are inadequate to do so on their own.

5. Toward a New Social Contract?

The preceding argument has shown how national Democratic political entrepreneurs painfully and gradually built up a durable political coalition around programs fostering urban development. This strategy worked well in both the private marketplace and the political arena. In the economy, Democratic federal programs hastened the postindustrial transformation of the troubled industrial cities. The federal budget became a tool for social change, promoting suburbanization, transforming central-city economies, and promoting new nodes of development in new cities as well as old.

In the political marketplace, the Democrats' postwar progrowth strategy succeeded in forging links between Washington, City Halls, the traditional sources of Democratic support such as the political machines and labor unions and from new sources of

294

support from large corporations, the emerging professional stratum, and even minority neighborhoods. This worked to reinforce the power of Democratic presidents and mayors alike.

These Democratic successes created new kinds of political conflict, however. In national partisan politics, the conservative coalition, championed by Republican national political entrepreneurs, fought to undercut the favorable political impact of Democratic programs and to adapt Democratic tools to their own conservative political ends. Their skills in doing so increased both the substantive and the political disarray of the "bipartisan" urban program framework.

The Democrats' failure to deliver on their promise to improve life for the central-city poor created opposition within the Democratic coalition. As it became clear that Democratic urban programs designed to improve urban life actually meant sacrificing central-city minority communities in favor of dominant institutions, cities across the country erupted in protest. The mobilization of the 1960s left Democrats painfully suspended between two choices: they could respond to urban protest by reorienting their programs toward the new urban working class, or they could ignore this protest and continue as before. To do the first risked attack from conservatives and the dominant institutions well served by earlier policies. To do the second risked loss of support from a strategically placed and growing constituency, and hence loss of majority status. Democrats sought to keep each side happy, but managed instead to displease both.

Dominant private sector institutions, seeing racial conflict, urban turmoil, increasing political challenge in the older cities, and conservative political climates in the newer cities of the South and Southwest, "voted with their feet," at least for new investments. Conservative national development policy under Republican administrations reinforced this choice. By steadily shifting investment away from the contested older cities toward the quiescent newer cities, private sector actors sought to restore their influence over national urban development policy.

The decades of success enjoyed by the Democrats thus generated three decisive conflicts—partisan opposition, internal con-

295

flict, and private disinvestment—which destroyed their normal majority status, leaving behind a political vacuum. Two major forces have attempted to fill it. Conservatives, championed by the Nixon and Reagan administrations, have sought to dismantle the Democratic framework and erect a new one which will ensure that Republicans will capture the emerging constituencies and become the normal majority party. Traditional urban liberal Democrats countered with new money for old ideas. The Carter administration testified to the failure of traditional liberal remedies for achieving a programmatic renewal equal to that of Franklin Roosevelt, or even of Lyndon Johnson. The Reagan administration may well do the same for its own tradition.

Each party faces a central dilemma. The Democrats must overcome the conflict among their constituencies. If they fail, then conservatives and the Republican party may shift the course of American political development. If so, the country may well retreat from its commitment, however hobbled, to social justice, and create instead an even less democratic and more unequal and segmented social order.

Conservatives have their own Achilles heel, however. Their strategy dismantles not only neighborhood-oriented programs but major segments of the American middle class which depend directly or indirectly on the welfare state. The more powerful the conservative political thrust, therefore, the more likely it will cause the warring factions among Democrats to bury their differences and respond to the common enemy. But this reconciliation will only be temporary and, like the Carter administration, ineffectual until Democratic entrepreneurs find a way to overcome the profound inner conflicts generated by their own past policies.

How likely is this outcome? What shape will it take? These questions still have no simple answer. At the heart of the current impasse lie a series of conflicts—between dominant institutions and urban residents over who is going to control and benefit from urban development patterns, between urban liberals and conservatives over who is going to wield national and local political power, and between the supporters of urban liberalism themselves over whether all, or only some, will benefit from their power.

296

The successful new social contract—the new "New Deal"—must find ways to resolve these deep conflicts. Though the costs of continued polarization may eventually move all parties—conservative corporations as well as activist community groups—toward some new consensus, at present it is hard to see how it will be achieved or what it will contain. Yet even if no immediate marching orders can be given, at least some general principles for erecting such a consensus can be discussed.

First and foremost, a new social contract must distribute economic opportunity more equally across urban constituencies. Urban liberalism unraveled because it promised to do so but in the end did not. The reasons for this failure had as much to do with the organization of the American state and American politics as they did with liberal intentions, which suggests that substantive equality of opportunity (if not of outcomes) must go hand in hand with renewed political reform. Left to their own devices, dominant private sector institutions have never shared opportunity with less powerful groups. On their part, progressive national political entrepreneurs must take the risk of mobilizing such constituencies in the suburbs and newer cities as well as within the old. They must also seek to control the competitive framework that private institutions have exploited to undermine redistributive politics in the past. But they must offer the private sector some *quid pro quo* if massive, debilitating conflict is to be avoided.

What could the private sector gain by cooperation? One major objective should be to provide the education, training, and support services necessary to provide greater upward mobility for minority workers in the new and old metropolitan areas. This would require the advanced service institutions to do better at affirmative employment efforts. In return, government could increase its efforts to improve their competitive advantage.

Measures which would allow the new urban middle class to join forces with the new minority, urban, service working class around a program of neighborhood renewal and quality of neighborhood life also have undeniable appeal. Such a program would have to go beyond physical upgrading of private property to include neighborhood and city-wide public goods and services. It

297

must heighten the quality of civic life. If national measures ensured that minority service workers had a more equal chance at employment and housing opportunities, it might well be possible to overcome the conflict between the "gentry" and the "underclass." In the present context, such a hope may seem naive and utopian, but the cost of failing to realize it will be an even more deeply divided and fearful existence, and not just in the large, old central cities.

To some extent, such measures must be forced on the national political economy by the weight of mobilized political action. It has already shown that it will not adopt them of its own accord. Such political action cannot be merely local; this is a great failing of the neighborhood movement. To succeed locally, both a national majority and national policy initiatives are necessary. Only national action, for example, can restrain the intercity competition which has undermined local reform efforts. And only national action can ensure the more equal distribution of economic opportunity through affirmative action standards and a commitment to full employment, with government employment as a last resort. Finally, national sponsorship proved to be crucial for local reform efforts during the New Deal and the New Frontier/Great Society, and the same is true today.

Successful political action cannot be carried out merely at the national level, however. National political influence necessarily rests on a local foundation. The most difficult systemic conflicts take place within the larger metropolitan areas and particularly within the older central cities. Whatever models of national consensus eventually emerge, they will likely be patterned after new coalitions in the urban political arena. National political entrepreneurs must think consciously, then, about how federal programming can foster new local coalitions, while local political entrepreneurs must undertake the arduous task of overcoming the widening gulf which separates them from each other. In this task, the networks among community organizations offer a good beginning, but no more.

What must such new local coalitions seek to achieve? Obviously, they must combine interests which are now often in

298

opposition. Community groups and the labor movement, for example, must find a way to take common stands, for each is likely to falter without support from the other. They, in turn, must work on negotiating a master agreement with the corporate and development interests of their cities. Such agreements should specify the minority employment and training goals and moderate-rent housing production which must accompany downtown development. Successful mobilization to win local electoral majorities would help to make such negotiations much more possible. Local political leadership, particularly within the Democratic party, can play a crucial role in this respect, though it has so far failed to do so. An important part of overcoming systemic conflict lies within the reach of local politics.

If there is a final lesson to be learned from the rise and fall of urban liberalism as a guiding force in American urban development, it is this: we are not captives of history and social structure. The political balance of power, the forms of government intervention, and the courage of political leadership have had a vast and demonstrable impact on the course of urban development. We may well fail the challenge which the demise of traditional urban liberalism has set before us. Certainly, we face many forbidding obstacles in rising to this challenge. Yet, others faced similar obstacles in the past and found ways to overcome them. With the courage to take risks and seek change, those who strive to improve our cities, and through them our politics, can do so as well.

NOTES

INTRODUCTION

1. This concept was first developed in my article "The Post-War Politics of Urban Development," *Politics and Society* 5:2 (Winter 1975). My thinking on the subject was stimulated by Robert Salisbury, "Urban Politics: The New Convergence of Power," *Journal of Politics* 26 (November 1964), pp. 775–797, and Robert Caro, *The Powerbroker* (New York: Knopf, 1974).

2. For thoughts along these lines, see Theda Skocpol, "Bringing the State Back In" (Paper presented to a Conference on "States and Social Structures," Seven Springs Conference Center, Mount Kisco, N.Y., February 25–27, 1982).

3. ACIR, "The Dynamics of Growth in Federal Functions: An Analysis of Case Study Findings," in *The Federal Role in the Federal System*, Report A-86 (Washington, D.C.: GPO, June 1981), p. 11.

4. For a seminal statement, see John Kain, "The Distribution and Movement of Jobs and Industry," in J. Q. Wilson, ed., *The Metropolitan Enigma* (Cambridge: Harvard University Press, 1968).

5. Statements of this view include David Harvey, *Social Justice and the City* (Baltimore: Johns Hopkins University Press, 1974), and David Gordon, "Capitalist Development and the History of American Cities," in L. Sawers and W. Tabb, eds., *Marxism and the Metropolis* (New York: Oxford University Press, 1978).

6. The grandfather of the view that cities are generative is, of course, Lewis Mumford. For neo-Marxist statements of this line of argument, see Ira Katznelson, *City Trenches* (New York: Pantheon, 1982), and Manuel Castells, *The City and the Grassroots* (Berkeley: University of California Press, forthcoming). My own earlier musings may be found in "Community and Accumulation," in M. Dear and A. Scott, eds., *Urbanization and Urban Planning in Capitalist Society* (London and New York: Methuen, 1981), pp. 319–338.

CHAPTER ONE

1. Allan R. Pred, *The Spatial Dynamics of U.S. Urban Industrial Cities 1800–1914* (Cambridge: MIT Press, 1966), and Maury Klein and Harvey Kantor, *Prisoners of Progress, American Industrial Cities 1850–1920* (New York: Macmillan, 1976), are excellent on this period.

2. George W. Sternlieb and James Hughes, "New Regional and Metropolitan Realities of America," *Journal of the American Institute of Planners* 43:3 (July 1977), p. 238.

3. For discussions of this ethnically segmented occupational/industrial mosaic within and across cities, see Beverly Duncan and Stanley Lieberson, *Metropolis and Region in Transition* (Beverly Hills: Sage, 1970), David Ward, *Cities and*

Immigrants (New York: Oxford University Press, 1971), and Sam Bass Warner, Jr., *The Urban Wilderness* (New York: Harper and Row, 1972), chap. 4.

4. Allan R. Pred, *City-Systems in Advanced Societies* (New York: John Wiley, 1977), esp. pp. 98–166, gives a path-breaking empirical analysis of such linkages for U.S. cities. See also Stephen Hymer, "The Multinational Corporation and the Law of Uneven Development," in J. N. Bhagwati, ed., *Economics and the World Order* (London: Macmillan and Co., 1972), pp. 113–140, and Robert Cohen, "The New International Division of Labor, Multinational Corporations, and Urban Hierarchy," in Michael Dear and Allen Scott, eds., *Urbanization and Urban Planning in Capitalist Society* (New York: Methuen, 1981), pp. 287–315.

5. Lewis Mumford, *Sticks and Stones* (New York: Boris and Liveright, 1924), p. 87.

6. Everett C. Ladd, Jr., *Where Have All the Voters Gone?* (New York: W. W. Norton, 1978), and "The Shifting Party Coalitions—from the 1930s to the 1970s," in S. M. Lipset, ed., *Party Coalitions in the 1980s* (San Francisco: Institute for Contemporary Studies, 1981), p. 147.

7. Daniel Bell, *The Coming of Post-Industrial Society* (New York: Basic Books, 1973), and J. K. Galbraith, *The New Industrial State* (Boston: Houghton Mifflin, 1971) are perhaps the best-known works on the subject, which goes back at least to J. A. Schumpeter's classic *Capitalism, Socialism, and Democracy* (New York: Harper and Brothers, 1950). My thinking has also been influenced by James O'Connor, *The Fiscal Crisis of the State* (New York: St. Martin's, 1973) and the works of Claus Offe.

8. Charles Lindblom, *Politics and Markets* (New York: Basic Books, 1977), p. 37.

9. Alfred D. Chandler, Jr., "The Beginnings of 'Big Business' in American Industry," *Business History Review* 33 (Spring 1959), p. 25.

10. John Kasarda, "The Changing Occupational Structure of the American Metropolis," in Barry Schwartz, ed., *The Changing Face of the Suburbs* (Chicago: University of Chicago Press, 1976), pp. 120–121. Kasarda calculates his figures on the basis of constant 1950 central-city boundaries, thus controlling for the influence of annexation in the Southwest. The seminal statement on these trends remains John Kain, "The Distribution and Movement of Jobs and Industry," in J. Q. Wilson, ed., *The Metropolitan Enigma* (Cambridge: Harvard University Press, 1968), pp. 1–41.

11. U.S. Department of Housing and Urban Development, 1980, *President's National Urban Policy Report* (Washington, D.C.: GPO, 1980), pp. 1–6 and pp. 3–11. See also Sternleib and Hughes, "New Regional Realities."

12. Roger Schmenner, "The Manufacturing Location Decision: Evidence from Cincinnati and New England," report to the Economic Development Administration, U.S. Department of Commerce, March 1978, "Summary of Findings," p. 2.

13. Ibid., pp. 8, 10–11. See also Roger Schmenner, "Industrial Location and

Urban Public Management,'' in A. P. Soloman, ed., *The Prospective City* (Cambridge: MIT Press, 1980), pp. 446–468.

14. UAW, *Bargaining Fact Book 1979* (Detroit: UAW, 1979), pp. 3, 15, 24. The UAW represents all but a few of the major auto production plants. Bargaining units largely coincide with plants, although a few locations have more than one unit.

15. Institute for Iron and Steel Studies, *Steel Industry in Brief: Databook USA 1977* (Greenbrook, N.J.: IISS, 1977), pp. 9–11.

16. My thanks to Nina Farana for compiling these figures. The source was *1981 Who's Who in Electronics: Data in Depth* (Twinsburgh, Ohio: Harris Publishing Company, 1981), pp. 211–272.

17. Maureen McBreen, "Regional Trends in Defense Expenditures: 1950–1976," in Committee on Appropriations, U.S. Senate, *Selected Essays on Patterns of Regional Change* (Washington, D.C.: GPO, 1977), pp. 511–543; quotation from p. 526.

18. Alfred D. Chandler, Jr., *The Visible Hand* (Cambridge: Harvard University Press, 1977), p. 6.

19. Ibid., p. 10.

20. Robert Cohen, *The Corporation and the City* (New York: Conservation of Human Resources Project, 1979), chap. 3.

21. Conservation of Human Resources Project, *The Corporate Headquarters Complex in New York City* (New York: CHRP, 1977), chap. 5.

22. See Hymer, "Multinational Corporation," and Cohen, "New International Division."

23. Pred, *City-Systems*, p. 116.

24. Cohen, *Corporation and the City*, chap. 1.

25. For New York, for example, see John Mollenkopf, "The Advanced Services and the New York City Economy" (New York: Department of City Planning, City of New York, 1981).

26. Cohen, *Corporation and the City*, chap. 9, p. 12.

27. Peter Bearse, "On the Intra-Regional Diffusion of Business Service Activity," *Regional Studies* 12 (1978), pp. 563–578.

28. ACIR, "Counter-Cyclical Aid and Economic Stabilization" (Washington, D.C.: GPO, 1978), pp. 22–23.

29. Ann Markusen, Annalee Saxenian, and Marc Weiss, "Who Benefits from Intergovernmental Transfers?" in R. W. Burchell and D. Listokin, eds., *Cities under Stress* (New Brunswick: Rutgers Center for Urban Policy Research, 1981), pp. 628–629.

30. Robert Yin, "Creeping Federalism: The Federal Impact on the Structure and Function of Local Government," in N. Glickman, ed., *Urban Impacts of Federal Policies* (Baltimore: Johns Hopkins University Press, 1980), pp. 595–618.

31. Don K. Price, *Government and Science* (New York: New York University Press, 1954), pp. 77–78.

32. Gary Shannon and Alan Dever, *Health Care Delivery: Spatial Perspectives* (New York: McGraw-Hill, 1974), pp. 60–66.

33. Mollenkopf, "Advanced Services."

34. National Resources Committee, *Our Cities: Their Role in the National Economy* (Washington, D.C.: GPO, 1937), pp. vi–vii.

35. Ibid., pp. 2–3.

36. 1980 *Census of Population*, PC80-SI-5, "Standard Metropolitan Areas and Standard Consolidated Statistical Areas: 1980."

37. Gary Miller, *The Lakewood Plan and the Politics of Municipal Incorporation* (Cambridge: MIT Press, 1982). Frank de Leeuw, Ann Schnare, and Ray Struyk, "Housing," in W. Gorham and N. Glazer, eds., *The Urban Predicament* (Washington, D.C.: Urban Institute, 1976), p. 153.

38. J. Kasarda, "Occupational Structure," p. 124; and U.S. Department of Commerce, Census Bureau, "Social and Economic Characteristics of Metropolitan and Non-Metropolitan Populations: 1977 and 1970," Special Studies P-23, No. 75 (Washington, D.C.: GPO, 1978), p. 13.

39. National Resources Committee, *Our Cities*, pp. v, 37.

40. Regina Armstrong, "National Trends in Office Construction, Employment and Headquarters Location in U.S. Metropolitan Areas," in P. W. Daniels, ed., *Spatial Patterns of Office Growth and Location* (Chichester, England: John Wiley, 1979). Data from pages 88–92. See also Armstrong's *The Office Industry: Patterns of Growth and Location* (Cambridge: MIT Press, 1972).

41. William Alonso, "The Population Factor and Urban Structure," in Soloman, ed., *Prospective City*, pp. 32–51, and Kathleen Gerson, "Hard Choices: How Women Decide about Work, Career, and Motherhood" (Ph.D. diss. Sociology Department, University of California at Berkeley, 1981).

42. See, for example, Boston Redevelopment Authority, "Boston's Highrise Office Buildings" (Boston: BRA, 1973), a survey of the residential and racial characteristics of high-rise office workers, or "Historical Housing Location of San Francisco Workers by Occupation," in San Francisco Municipal Railway, *Five-Year Plan 1981–86*, vol. 2, p. 2–2.

43. Richard Nathan and Charles Adams, "Understanding Central City Hardship," *Political Science Quarterly* 91:1 (Spring 1976), pp. 47–62.

44. "Urban Renewal, a Statistical Profile," *Journal of Housing* 9 (1970), p. 469.

45. National Resources Committee, *Our Cities*, pp. 4, 52.

46. U.S. Department of Commerce, Bureau of Economic Analysis, "National Income and Product Accounts of the United States, 1929–74, Statistical Tables" (Washington, D.C.: GPO, 1975), Table 1.1. Office of Management and Budget, *Supplemental Studies to the 1979 Budget*, "Special Analysis G" (Washington, D.C.: GPO, 1979), pp. 158–159; and Paul Taubman and Robert Rasche, "Subsidies, Tax Law, and Real Estate Investment," in Joint Economic Committee, U.S. Congress, *The Economics of Federal Subsidy Programs: Part I* (Washington, D.C.: GPO, 1972), p. 367.

47. U.S. Department of Housing and Urban Development, *Programs of HUD* (Washington, D.C.: GPO, 1978).

48. V. O. Key, Jr., *The Administration of Federal Grants to States* (Chicago: Public Administration Service, 1937), pp. 1, 4, 5.

CHAPTER TWO

1. National Resources Planning Board, *Our Cities* (Washington, D.C.: GPO, 1937), p. 51.

2. The seminal discussion of the conservative coalition is V. O. Key, Jr., *Southern Politics* (New York: Random House, 1949). See also John Manley, "The Conservative Coalition in Congress," *American Behavioral Scientist* 17 (November–December 1973), pp. 223–247.

3. This point has been stressed by Demetrios Caraley. See *City Governments and Urban Problems* (Englewood Cliffs, N.J.: Prentice-Hall, 1977), p. 152. See also Gary Orfield, *Congressional Power: Congress and Social Change* (New York: Harcourt Brace Jovanovitch, 1975).

4. Carl Degler, "American Political Parties and the Rise of the City: An Interpretation," *Journal of American History* (June 1964).

5. The phrase is that of Roscoe C. Martin, *The Cities and the Federal System* (New York: Atherton, 1965), p. 111.

6. Everett C. Ladd, Jr., with Charles D. Hadley, *Transformations of the American Party System* (New York: W. W. Norton, 1975), p. 36.

7. Ibid., p. 39.

8. Degler, "American Political Parties," p. 48.

9. Ladd and Hadley, *Transformations*, p. 37.

10. Ibid., p. 33.

11. Samuel Lubell, *The Future of American Politics* (New York: Harper and Brothers, 1952), "The Revolt of the City," p. 29.

12. Ibid.

13. Kristi Anderson, *The Creation of a Democratic Majority 1928–1936* (Chicago: University of Chicago Press, 1979).

14. Ibid., p. 117.

15. Fred Cohen, "The Theory of Corporate Power—The Origins of the National Recovery Act" (unpublished paper, History Department, Princeton University, 1972), p. 21.

16. E. Pendleton Herring, "1st Session of the 73d Congress, March 9, 1933–June 16, 1933," *American Political Science Review* 28:1 (February 1934), p. 68.

17. Nathaniel Keith, *Politics and the Housing Crisis since 1930* (New York: Universe Books, 1973), p. 34.

18. Herring, "1st Session of the 73d Congress," p. 69.

19. J. Joseph Huthmacher, *Senator Robert F. Wagner and the Rise of Urban Liberalism* (New York: Atheneum, 1968), p. 130. The internal quote is from economist Leon Keyserling, at the time Wagner's assistant.

20. James Holt, "The New Deal and the American Anti-Statist Tradition," in John Braeman, Robert Bremmer, and David Brody, eds., *The New Deal: The National Level* (Columbus: Ohio State University Press, 1975), p. 33.

21. Martin Shefter, "Parties, Bureaucracy, and Politics: Change in the U.S.," in Sage Electoral Studies Yearbook, vol. 4, *Political Parties: Development and Decay* (Beverly Hills: Sage, 1978), Lewis Maisel and Joseph Cooper, eds., pp. 211–266.

22. Ed Flynn, *You're the Boss* (New York: Viking, 1947), pp. 145–146, and Bruce Stave, *The New Deal and the Last Hurrah* (Pittsburgh: University of Pittsburgh Press, 1970).

23. James Farley, *Behind the Ballots* (New York: Harcourt, Brace, 1938), p. 363.

24. See, for example, A. W. MacMahon et al., *The Administration of Federal Work Relief* (Chicago: Social Science Research Council Committee on Public Administration, 1941), p. 281, and Donald Howard, *The WPA and Federal Relief Policy* (New York: Russell Sage Foundation, 1943), p. 301.

25. Donald Haider, *When Governments Come to Washington* (New York: Free Press, 1974), pp. 2–3, 49–50.

26. Samuel I. Rosenman, ed., *The Public Papers and Addresses of Franklin D. Roosevelt,* 13 vols. (New York: Random House, 1938–1950), vol. 5, p. 389.

27. Milton Derber, "The New Deal and Labor," in Braeman et al., *The New Deal*, pp. 129–130. See also Leon Keyserling, "The Wagner Act: Its Origin and Current Significance," *George Washington Law Review* 29:2 (December 1960), pp. 199–233, esp. pp. 202–203. Keyserling points out that Wagner prevailed over Roosevelt's lukewarm stance on labor legislation, demonstrating the importance of congressional, as well as executive, political entrepreneurs.

28. According to Howard Chudacoff, *The Evolution of American Urban Society* (Englewood Cliffs: Prentice-Hall, 1975), p. 220, 47,500 units went to blacks in northern and southern cities.

29. Howard, *WPA*, p. 288.

30. Anderson, *Creation of a Democratic Majority*, pp. 100–101.

31. Raymond Wolters, "The New Deal and the Negroes," in Braeman, Bremmer, and Brody, eds., *The New Deal*, p. 200.

32. Huthmacher, *Wagner*, p. 143. See also Keyserling, "Wagner Act."

33. J. Kerwin Williams, *Grants-in-Aid under the Public Works Administration* (New York: Columbia University Press, 1939), pp. 51–57.

34. Harold Ickes, *The Secret Diary of Harold Ickes* (New York: Simon and Schuster, 1953), vol. 1, pp. 53, 67.

35. Williams, *Grants-in-Aid*, p. 50.

36. Ibid., p. 248.

37. Federal Works Administration, *Final Report of the WPA, 1933–1939* (Washington, D.C.: GPO, 1942).

38. MacMahon et al., *Administration*, p. 280.

39. Ibid., pp. 281–282.

40. Timothy McDonnell, *The Wagner Housing Act* (Chicago: Loyola University Press, 1957), pp. 29–49; Huthmacher, *Wagner*, p. 206.

41. Elizabeth Longen, "The Present Status of Municipal Housing and Slum Clearance in the United States," *American Political Science Review* 31:5 (1937), p. 1126.

42. The U.S. Housing Act of 1937's story is told in McDonnell, *Wagner Housing Act*, in great detail. See also Huthmacher, *Wagner*, pp. 207–215, 224–230, and Keith, *Politics*, pp. 32–39.

43. McDonnell, *Wagner Housing Act*, p. 337.

44. As quoted in Keith, *Politics*, p. 24.

45. Nelson's testimony in House Select Committee on Lobbying Activities, 81st Congress, 2d Session, "Housing Lobby" (Washington, D.C.: GPO, 1950), p. 20.

46. Ibid., p. 21.

47. Gavin Wright, "The Political Economy of New Deal Spending," *Review of Economics and Statistics* 56 (February 1974), pp. 30–38, quote on p. 33. Roger Friedland and Herbert Wong, "Congressional Politics, Federal Grants, and Local Needs: Who Gets What and Why?" (Sociology Department, University of California at Santa Barbara, 1982).

48. Robert Caro, *Power Broker* (New York: Knopf, 1974); Forbes Hayes, *Community Leadership: The Regional Plan Association* (New York: Columbia University Press, 1965).

49. Richard O. Davies, *Housing Reform during the Truman Administration* (Columbia, Missouri: University of Missouri Press, 1966), pp. 25, 40.

50. Ibid., p. 41.

51. John Manley, "The Conservative Coalition in Congress," *American Behavioral Scientist* 17 (November–December 1973), p. 239.

52. Miles Colean, *Renewing Our Cities* (New York: Twentieth Century Fund, 1953), p. 4.

53. President's Conference on Home Building and Home Ownership, *Report of Committee on Blighted Areas and Slums* (Washington, D.C.: GPO, 1932); Edith Elmer Wood, *Slums and Blighted Areas in the United States*, Housing Division Bulletin No. 1 (Washington, D.C.: GPO, 1935); Mabel Walker, *Urban Blight and Slums* (Cambridge: Harvard University Press, 1938).

54. Davies, *Housing Reform*, pp. 62–64.

55. Ibid., pp. 118–120; Keith, *Politics*, pp. 104–105.

56. Quoted from the *ULI Bulletin*, May 1943, in Roger Feinstein, "Policy Development in a Federal Program: A Case Study of the National Politics of Urban Renewal" (Ph.D. diss., Columbia University, 1974), p. 36.

57. Keith, *Politics*, pp. 93–100; Davies, *Housing Reform*, pp. 106–115.

58. Davies, *Housing Reform*, p. 130.

59. Ibid., p. 127.

60. Feinstein, "Policy Development," p. 66.

61. Keith, *Politics*, p. 104.

62. Feinstein, "Policy Development," p. 108.

63. Marc Weiss, "The Origins and Legacy of Urban Renewal," in Pierre Clavel et al., *Urban and Regional Planning in an Age of Austerity* (New York: Pergamon Press, 1980).

64. This and the following paragraphs are based on Ladd and Hadley, *Transformation*, pp. 227–233.

65. Ibid., p. 138.

66. Mark Gelfand, *A Nation of Cities* (New York: Oxford University Press, 1975), p. 294.

67. James Sundquist, *Politics and Policy: The Eisenhower, Kennedy and Johnson Years* (Washington, D.C.: Brookings Institution, 1968), p. 33.

68. Keith, *Politics*, p. 138.

69. Jeane J. Kirkpatrick, "Changing Patterns of Electoral Competition," in Anthony King, ed., *The New American Political System* (Washington, D.C.: American Enterprise Institute, 1978), pp. 264–265.

70. Joe R. Feagin and Harlan Hahn, *Ghetto Revolts* (New York: Macmillan, 1973), pp. 92–93, 97.

71. Frances Piven and Richard Cloward, *Poor People's Movements* (New York: Pantheon, 1977), p. 248.

72. Sundquist, *Politics and Policy*, pp. 8–9, 392–415.

73. Demetrios Caraley, *City Governments and Urban Problems* (Englewood Cliffs: Prentice-Hall, 1977), pp. 152–153; Sundquist, *Politics and Policy*, pp. 347–348. See also David Mayhew, *Party Loyalty among Congressmen* (Cambridge: Harvard University Press, 1966), chap. 3.

74. Lawrence Friedman, "The Social and Political Context of the War on Poverty: An Overview," in Robert Haveman, ed., *A Decade of Federal Antipoverty Programs* (New York: Academic Press, 1977), p. 29. See also Daniel Moynihan, *Maximum Feasible Misunderstanding* (New York: Free Press, 1969), pp. 22–23.

75. Paul Peterson and J. David Greenstone, "Racial Change and Citizen Participation: The Mobilization of Low Income Communities through Community Action," in Haveman, *Decade*, p. 241.

76. Frances Fox Piven and Richard Cloward, *Regulating the Poor* (New York: Pantheon, 1971), pp. 249, 256.

77. Keith, *Politics*, pp. 139–150.

78. Ibid., pp. 159–168, and National Housing Policy Review, U.S. Department of Housing and Urban Development, *Housing in the Seventies* (Washington, D.C.: GPO, 1974), pp. 14–21.

79. Keith, *Politics*, p. 119.

80. Ibid., pp. 86, 96, 106, 112, 119.

81. Ibid., pp. 156–157, and "Urban Renewal: A Statistical Profile," *Journal of Housing* 9 (1970), p. 469.

82. Peterson and Greenstone, "Racial Change and Citizen Participation," p. 254.

83. Sundquist, *Politics and Policy*, p. 145.

84. Barss, Reitzel and Associates, *Community Action and Urban Institutional Change* (Cambridge: Barss, Reitzel, 1970), App. F.

85. Piven and Cloward, *Regulating the Poor*, pp. 271, 270.

86. Barss, Reitzel, *Community Action*; Bruce Jacobs, "The Political Economy of Organizational Change" (Ph.D. diss., Harvard University, 1979), chap. 3.

87. Piven and Cloward, *Regulating the Poor*, pp. 275–276; Peter Eisinger, "The Community Action Program and the Development of Black Political Leadership," in Dale R. Marshall, ed., *Urban Policy Making* (Beverly Hills: Sage, 1979), pp. 127–144.

88. Bernard Frieden and Marshall Kaplan, *The Politics of Neglect* (Cambridge: MIT Press, 1977), p. 41. The quote is from Jack Conlon, then-director of CAP.

89. Dennis Judd and Frances Kopel, "The Search for National Urban Policy from Kennedy to Carter," in Theodore Lowe and Alan Stone, eds., *Nationalizing Government* (Beverly Hills: Sage, 1979), pp. 164–166, 169.

90. Sundquist, *Politics and Policy*, pp. 392–393.

CHAPTER THREE

1. For thoughtful discussions of how conflicting legislative and administrative requirements produced the "crippled program syndrome" among Great Society programs during the Nixon years, see Steven Waldhorn, "The Role of Neighborhood Government in Postcategorical Programs," in J. D. Sneed and S. Waldhorn, eds., *Restructuring the Federal System* (New York: Crane, Russak and Company for the Stanford Research Institute, 1975), pp. 148–157, and Waldhorn, "Pathological Bureaucracies," in V. B. Ermer and J. Strange, eds., *Blacks and Bureaucracies* (New York: Thomas Y. Crowell, 1972), pp. 184–190.

2. Richard Polenberg, "The Decline of the New Deal, 1937–1940," in Braeman, Bremmer, and Brody, eds., *The New Deal*, p. 260.

3. Sam Lubbell, *The Future of American Politics* (New York: Harper and Brothers, 1952), pp. 34, 132–136.

4. Polenberg, "Decline," p. 254.

5. David Brody, "The New Deal and World War II," in Braeman et al., *New Deal*, p. 273.

6. Ibid., p. 270.

7. James T. Patterson, *Congressional Conservation and the New Deal* (Lexington: University of Kentucky Press, 1967), p. 196.

8. Ibid., pp. 203–206.

9. Ibid., pp. 263–264.

10. Ibid., p. 288.

11. Brody, "New Deal and W.W. II," p. 272.

12. Federal Works Agency, "Final Report on the WPA Program, 1935–1943" (Washington, D.C.: GPO, 1946), p. 85.

13. Brody, "New Deal and W.W. II," p. 281.

14. Phillip Funigrello, *The Challenge to Urban Federalism: Federal-City Relations during World War II* (Knoxville: University of Tennessee Press, 1978), pp. 48–56.

15. Brody, "New Deal and W.W. II," p. 272.

16. J. J. Huthmacher, *Senator Robert F. Wagner and the Rise of Urban Liberalism* (New York: Atheneum, 1968), pp. 276, 291.

17. Ibid., p. 291.

18. Fenigrello, *Challenge*, chap. 3, production figures from p. 112. See also Keith, *Politics*, pp. 40–58.

19. War Production Board, "War Construction and Facilities" (Washington, D.C.: WPB, September 1943), Table 6, p. 15.

20. Civilian Production Administration, Industrial Statistics Division, "War-Time Manufacturing Plant Expansion, Privately Financed, 1940–1945" (Washington, D.C.: CPA, 1946), p. 40. Seventy-four percent of the money came in direct grants, 26 percent in the form of accelerated depreciation over five years for private investment to be written off against high wartime profits.

21. Civilian Production Administration, Bureau of Demobilization, "The Facilities and Construction Program of the War Production Board and Predecessor Agencies, May 1940 to May 1945" (Washington, D.C.: CPA, 1945), pp. 195–196.

22. Brody, "New Deal and W.W. II," pp. 288–289.

23. Ibid., pp. 292–295.

24. Ladd and Hadley, *Transformations*, p. 228.

25. U.S. Bureau of the Census, "U.S. Census Population: 1960. Volume 1, Characteristics of the Population," part A. Number of Inhabitants.

26. Ladd and Hadley, *Transformations*, pp. 158, 164.

27. Kevin Phillips, *The Emerging Republican Majority* (New Rochelle: Arlington House, 1969), p. 69.

28. Ibid., p. 158.

29. Ibid., p. 221.

30. Ladd and Hadley, *Transformations*, pp. 159–161.

31. Keith, *Politics*, p. 109.

32. Ibid., p. 112.

33. John Manley, "Conservative Coalition," p. 236.

34. Feinstein, "Policy Development," pp. 215–216. See also Weiss, "Origins and Legacy."

35. Feinstein, "Policy Development," p. 161.

36. Colean, *Renewing Our Cities*, pp. 22–23, 63–64, 73–74.

37. Feinstein, "Policy Development," p. 162.

38. *Report of the President's Advisory Committee on Government Housing Policies and Programs* (Washington, D.C.: GPO, 1953), p. 1.

39. Ibid., p. 123.

40. Alan Altshuler with James Womack and John Pucher, *The Urban Trans-*

portation System: Politics and Policy Innovation (Cambridge: MIT Press, 1979), p. 28.

41. House Committee on Public Works, 84th Congress, 1st Session, "A Ten Year National Highway Program: A Report to the President" (Washington, D.C.: GPO, 1955), pp. xiii–xiv.

42. Keith, *Politics*, pp. 112–123.

43. Feinstein, "Policy Development," chaps. 4, 5.

44. Ibid., p. 114.

45. Keith, *Politics*, p. 119.

46. Feinstein, "Policy Development," p. 112.

47. Alan Altshuler and Robert Curry, "The Changing Environment of Urban Development: Shared Power or Shared Impotence?" *Urban Law Annual* 10:3 (1975), pp. 6–7.

48. Gary Schwartz, "Urban Freeways and the Interstate System," *Southern California Law Review* 49:406 (1976), pp. 418–419.

49. Ibid., pp. 423–426.

50. Ibid., p. 436. Internal quote from J. Burby, *The Great American Motion Sickness* (Boston: Little, Brown, 1971), p. 298.

51. Ibid., p. 445.

52. Ladd and Hadley, *Transformations*, p. 262.

53. Gary Wills, *Nixon Agonistes* (Boston: Houghton Mifflin, 1970), and Ladd and Hadley, *Transformations*, p. 262.

54. Phillips, *Emerging Republican Majority*, pp. 183, 248, 275, 449. For an analysis which clarifies Phillips' conclusion, but which unfortunately deals only with state-level data, see William Schneider, "Democrats and Republicans, Liberals and Conservatives," in S. M. Lipset, ed., *Emerging Coalitions in American Politics* (San Francisco: Institute for Contemporary Studies, 1978), pp. 183–270.

55. Phillips, *Emerging Republican*, p. 353.

56. Ibid., p. 275.

57. Manley, "Conservative Coalition," p. 240. See also A. James Reichly, *Conservatives in a Time of Change* (Washington, D.C.: Brookings Institution, 1981), pp. 79–97.

58. Floyd Hyde, memorandum to HUD Secretary Romney, February 8, 1969, cited in Bernard J. Frieden and Marshall Kaplan, *The Politics of Neglect* (Cambridge: MIT Press, 1977), p. 88.

59. Peter K. Eisinger, "The Community Action Program and the Development of Black Political Leadership," in Dale R. Marshall, ed., *Urban Policy-Making* (Beverly Hills: Sage, 1979), p. 140.

60. Richard P. Nathan, *The Plot That Failed* (New York: John Wiley, 1975), p. 49. See also Reichly, *Conservatives*, pp. 232–249.

61. Paul Dommel, *The Politics of Revenue Sharing* (Bloomington: Indiana University Press, 1974), pp. 105–128, 148–167, and Don Haider, *When Governments Come to Washington* (New York: Free Press, 1974), pp. 257–277.

62. Richard Nathan, Allen Mannel, Susannah Calkins and Associates, *Moni-*

toring Revenue Sharing (Washington: Brookings Institution, 1975); Samuel Beer, "The Adoption of General Revenue Sharing: A Case Study in Public Sector Politics," *Public Policy* 24:2 (1976), pp. 127–195.

63. Richard Nathan, "The Outlook for Federal Grants to the Cities," in Roy Bahl, ed., *The Fiscal Outlook for Cities* (Syracuse: Syracuse University Press, 1978), p. 80.

64. Nathan, *Plot*, p. 24.

65. Frieden and Kaplan, *The Politics of Neglect*, p. 19, quoting a 1965 minority report from the House Committee on Government Operations.

66. Haider, *When Governments Come*, p. 175.

67. Ibid., p. 176.

68. Frieden and Kaplan, *The Politics of Neglect*, p. 212.

69. Ibid., p. 200.

70. Ibid., p. 214.

71. Haider, *When Governments Come*, p. 272.

72. Dommell, *Politics of Revenue Sharing*, p. 174.

73. Roger Vaughn, "The Urban Impacts of Federal Policy: Volume 2, Economic Development" (Santa Monica: Rand Corporation, 1977), pp. 87–95; Advisory Commission on Intergovernmental Relations, *City Financial Emergencies: The Intergovernmental Dimension* (Washington, D.C.: GPO, 1973), pp. 31–36.

74. Dommell, *Politics of Revenue Sharing*, chap. 6.

75. Haider, *When Governments Come*, pp. 280–281.

76. Demetrios Caraley, *City Governments and Urban Problems* (Englewood Cliffs, N.J.: Prentice-Hall, 1977), pp. 153–154.

77. Taken from the Nixon speeches reproduced in Nathan, *Plot*, pp. 122–169.

78. Altshuler et al., *Urban Transportation System*, pp. 37–38.

79. Nathan, *Plot*.

80. Impact data came from Richard De Leon and Richard Le Gates, "Beyond Cybernetic Federalism" (The Urban Center, San Francisco State University, 1979), and Nathan, "Outlook for Federal Grants to Cities," p. 81.

CHAPTER FOUR

1. George Blackwood, "Boston Politics and Boston Politicians," in Murray Levin, *The Alienated Voter* (New York: Holt, Rinehart and Winston, 1960), p. 7. See also George Dorsey, *Christopher of San Francisco* (New York: Macmillan, 1962), esp. pp. 61–68, 78–80, 88–97.

2. Robert Salisbury, "Urban Politics: The New Convergence of Power," *Journal of Politics* 26 (November 1964), pp. 775–797.

3. "Mr. Moses Dissects the 'Long-Haired Planners,' " *New York Times Magazine*, June 26, 1944, p. 17.

4. Edward Banfield and Martha Derthick, eds., "A Report on the Politics of Boston" (unpublished study, Joint Center for Urban Studies, 1960), pp. vi, 114–115.

5. Franklin Phillips, "NASA, the Space Age, and the Boston Area," in *Proceedings of the 1963–1964 Series of Boston Citizen Seminars on the Fiscal, Economic and Political Problems of Boston and the Metropolitan Community* (College of Business Administration, Boston College, 1964), p. 38. Subsequently cited as *BC Citizen Seminars*.

6. California State Reconstruction and Reemployment Commission, "New Factories for California Communities," Pamphlet 11 (Sacramento: State Printing Office, July 1946), pp. 1–7.

7. "Should-Must Cities Decentralize?" *Commonwealth* (May 31, 1948).

8. Boston Redevelopment Authority, *1965/1975 General Plan for the City of Boston and the Regional Core* (Boston: BRA, March 1965), p. 92.

9. Boston City Planning Board, *General Plan for Boston, Preliminary Report, 1950* (Boston, 1950), pp. 40–45, quote from p. 42.

10. Action for Boston Community Development, Inc., "Neighborhood Profile: South End" (ABCD Planning and Evaluation Department, September 1967), pp. 1–2, citing the Boston Redevelopment Authority. Housing characteristics report on p. 21. For a turn-of-the-century view, see Robert A. Woods, ed., *The City Wilderness: A Social Survey of the South End* (Boston: Houghton Mifflin, 1898).

11. Boston City Planning Board, *1950 General Plan*, p. 25.

12. John A. Breen, Director of Administrative Services, "Address to First Citizens Seminar," *BC Citizen Seminars*, 1956–1957 series, p. 5.

13. John Mollenkopf, "The Post-War Politics of Urban Development," *Politics and Society* 5:3 (Winter 1975), p. 259.

14. San Francisco Department of City Planning, "Industrial Trends," "Commercial Trends," and "Labor-Force Trends," pp. 37–40 (San Francisco: Background Reports for the Commerce and Industry Element of the Comprehensive Plan, July 1975).

15. San Francisco City Planning Commission, "The Redevelopment of Blighted Areas: A Master Plan for San Francisco, 1945" (San Francisco, 1945), p. 2.

16. San Francisco Planning and Housing Association, "Blight and Taxes" (San Francisco, November 1947).

17. Mel Scott, "Western Addition District Redevelopment Study" (San Francisco Planning Commission, November 1947), pp. 1–12.

18. Banfield and Derthick, eds., "Report on Politics of Boston," pp. II–3–6.

19. Ibid., pp. VI–9.

20. George Blackwood, "Boston Politics," in Levin, *Alienated Voter*, p. 10.

21. Banfield and Derthick, eds., "Report on Politics of Boston," pp. II–16.

22. George Dorsey, *Christopher of San Francisco* (New York: Macmillan, 1962), p. 79.

23. Allan Temko, "San Francisco Rebuilds Again," *Harper's*, April 1960, p. 53.

24. Dorsey, *Christopher*, p. 100, quoting Christopher.

25. Temko, "San Francisco Rebuilds," p. 53.

26. Ibid., p. 55.

27. Ibid., p. 56. Dorsey, *Christopher*, pp. 124–125. See also Chester Hartman, *Yerba Buena* (San Francisco: Glide Publications, 1974), pp. 35–36, 46–47.

28. Dorsey, *Christopher*, p. 167.

29. Ibid., p. 230.

30. Ibid., p. 162.

31. Christian Herter, address to *BC Citizen Seminars*, 1954–1955 series, pp. 152–153, 164.

32. John B. Hynes, ibid., p. 8.

33. Robert Ryan, address to *BC Citizen Seminars*, 1956–1957 series, p. 63.

34. Charles Francis Adams, Jr., ibid., p. 72.

35. Richard Chapman, address to *BC Citizen Seminars*, 1959 series, pp. 7–8.

36. George Sternlieb, "Is Business Abandoning the Big City?" *Harvard Business Review*, January–February 1961, pp. 6–13.

37. Hynes, *BC Citizen Seminars*, 1954–1955 series, p. 15.

38. Cyril Herrman and Robert Ryan, *BC Citizen Seminars*, 1956–1957 series, pp. 23–24, 65–66.

39. Hennessey, *BC Citizen Seminars*, 1957–1958 series, p. 16.

40. Joseph Lund, ibid., 1959 series, p. 64.

41. Ryan, *BC Citizen Seminars*, 1956–1957 series, p. 60, Elliott, executive vice-president of John Hancock Mutual Life Insurance, ibid., p. 30.

42. John Mendeloff, "The Business Elite and the Politics of Boston with a Focus on the Issue of Urban Renewal" (senior honors thesis, Harvard College, 1969), and Charles McCollum, "The Vault: On the Business End of Politics," *Phoenix*, July 27, 1971, pp. 1, 20.

43. Stephen Zwerling, *Mass Transit and the Politics of Technology* (New York: Praeger, 1974).

44. Technical Committee of the Mayor's Administrative Transportation Planning Council, "Traffic, Transit and Thoroughfare Improvements for San Francisco" (San Francisco, March 1947), pp. 10–11. Thanks to Marc Weiss for drawing my attention to this document.

45. Scott, "Western Addition District Redevelopment Study," pp. 30, 37, 66.

46. Temko, "San Francisco Rebuilds," p. 55.

47. Hartman, *Yerba Buena*, pp. 35–36.

48. Aaron Levine, "The Urban Renewal of San Francisco," Report to Blyth-Zellerbach Committee, March 20, 1959, esp. pp. 1, 19–21. Thanks to the Bancroft Library for making this document available.

49. Ibid., pp. 22–24.

50. Banfield and Derthick, eds., "Report on Politics of Boston," pp. II–17.

51. McCollum, "The Vault."

52. Levin, *Alienated Voter*, pp. 24–25, 30–32, 78–80.

53. Banfield and Derthick, eds., "Report on Politics of Boston," pp. VI–110.

54. Project statistics from Boston Redevelopment Authority, "Seven Year Report to the City Council" (Boston, 1967), App., as reproduced in Mendeloff, "Business Elite."

55. BRA, *1965/1975 General Plan*, pp. 3, 145–146.

56. Stephen Thernstrom, *Poverty, Planning, and Politics in the New Boston* (New York: Basic Books, 1969), pp. 6–7. Interestingly, whether to avoid conflicts of interest or out of innate conservativism, a relatively low proportion of this private capital came from those directly involved in the Vault.

57. Dorsey, *Christopher*, pp. 179–198.

58. William Lilley III, "Herman Death Ends an Era," *National Journal*, September 18, 1971, p. 1939. See also Hartman, *Yerba Buena*, pp. 47–49.

59. Lilley, "Herman," p. 1939.

60. W. M. Whitehall, *Boston: A Topographical History* (Boston: Belknap Press, 1963), p. 122.

61. Boston 200 Corporation, "The South End" (Boston: Bicentennial Neighborhood History Series, 1975), pp. 2–3.

62. SFHPA, "Blight and Taxes," p. 10.

63. Wells Fargo Bank, "San Francisco Central Business District: A Growth Study" (San Francisco, 1970), p. 29.

64. Judy Waldhorn and Sally Woodbridge, *Victoria's Legacy* (San Francisco: 101 Publications, 1978), p. 30.

65. SFRA, "Report on the Redevelopment Plan for the Western Addition Approved Redevelopment Project Area A-2" (San Francisco, April 1964), p. 9. This document is the basic renewal plan for the Western Addition.

66. ABCD, "Neighborhood Profile."

67. SFRA, "Report on . . . A-2," pp. 14–19, quote from p. 19.

68. "90 Million Dollar Development Plan," *City Record*, p. 756.

69. David Stern, "Citizen Planners for Urban Renewal" (senior honors thesis, Harvard College, 1966), p. 1. See also Peter Womble, "The Neighborhood Autonomy Movement" (senior honors thesis, Harvard College, 1970), pp. 25–30, and Nancy Arnone, "Redevelopment in Boston" (Ph.D. diss., Political Science Department, MIT, 1965), pp. 71–75, 151. They suggest that Langley Keyes' discussion of the planning period in *Rehabilitation Planning Game* (Cambridge: MIT Press, 1969), pp. 35–86, overstates the range of interests and views which influenced the plan.

70. As quoted in Elizabeth Seifel, "Displacement: The Negative Environmental Impact of Urban Renewal in the South End of Boston" (MCP thesis, MIT, June 1979), p. 28.

71. City of Boston, "Proceedings of City Council," December 6, 1965, as quoted in Womble, "Neighborhood Autonomy," p. 27.

72. San Francisco Board of Supervisors, "Public Hearings on Redevelopment of the Western Addition" (transcript of meeting, June 3, 1948), pp. 22, 27, 30.

73. Ibid.

74. SFRA, "Report on . . . A-2," p. 27.

75. BRA, "SEURP," pp. 3–4.

76. Figures from App. 1, Urban Planning Aid, "Urban Renewal's Effect on

315

Low Income Housing in the South End'' (Boston, October 1967), and Seifel, "Displacement,'' pp. 31–33, and App. I.

77. SFRA, "Report on . . . A-2,'' p. 7.

78. Ibid., p. 26, and United San Francisco Freedom Movement, "A Critique of the Redevelopment and Relocation Plans Proposed by the SFRA for Western Addition Area II'' (San Francisco, May 1964), pp. 7–9. Thanks to Steven Waldhorn for providing this document.

CHAPTER FIVE

1. Daniel Bell and Virginia Held, "The Community Revolution,'' *Public Interest* 16 (Summer 1969), pp. 142–177.

2. Peter Zupcofske et al., "The Cause and Effect of Reverse Blockbusting in the South End'' (unpublished undergraduate project, Boston College Economics Department, June 1972), p. 20. Urban Planning Aid, "Urban Renewal's Effect on the South End'' (Cambridge, Mass., October 1967). United San Francisco Freedom Movement, "A Critique of the Redevelopment and Relocation Plans Proposed by the San Francisco Redevelopment Agency for Western Addition Area II'' (San Francisco, May 1964), pp. 12–18.

3. For a case study of one outside investor who renovated 56 South End buildings between 1971 and 1973, displacing many elderly and minority families, see "Goldweitz and Company, Inc,'' Harvard Business School Case 4-372-271 (Harvard Business School, 1972). The case shows that Goldweitz and his partners received a net cash flow of $156,520 annually on an initial investment of $399,380 in 32 buildings, for a 39 percent rate of return not counting appreciation (Exhibit IV). At least for one developer, the South End proved to be a spectacularly profitable "target area.'' See also Ad Hoc Committee for a South End for South Enders, "A Community Report and Call for Action against the South End Empire of Mark R. Goldweitz'' (Boston, 1973).

4. Urban Field Service, "Report on South End Urban Renewal Plan for Boston City Council'' (Cambridge, Mass., March 1968), pp. 5, 16.

5. Relocation Appeals Board, "Relocation Appeals Board Report'' (San Francisco, May 1968), Apps. A, B. Several members resigned from the board because it "was at best an irrelevant body, and at worst another instrument which provides the facade of meeting a social problem while ignoring the basic problem itself,'' p. 3.

6. For extended descriptions of this process in the two neighborhoods, see John Mollenkopf, "Community Organization and City Politics'' (Ph.D. diss., Harvard University, 1973), chaps. 4, 6. All unfootnoted quotations and assertions are documented in this source. See also Mollenkopf, "Neighborhood Political Development and the Politics of Urban Growth: Boston and San Francisco 1958–78,'' *International Journal of Urban and Regional Research* 5:1 (1981), pp. 17–38.

7. CAUSE demands included the following: relocation within the project area,

demolition phased according to the availability of replacement construction, more subsidized units, rehabilitation of properties for their current owners, and a citizen review board for the South End project.

8. *San Francisco Chronicle*, May 4, 1967, p. 2.

9. WACO demands included relocation within the project area, no displacement until new housing was constructed, more subsidized units, and a review board.

10. Ken Brown, "Why the USES-BRA Relationship in Family Relocation Should Be Terminated" (USES memorandum, May 21, 1968).

11. Alan Lupo et al., *Rites of Way* (Boston: Little, Brown, 1971), p. 21.

12. Allan B. Jacobs, *Making City Planning Work* (Chicago: ASPO, 1978), p. 148.

13. CAUSE demands at this point included adequate staff and budget, advance notice of BRA South End agenda items, the right to review and veto all plans, the right to initiate proposals, review of demolition decisions, joint determination of project employment practices, prior review of site office personnel changes, and the right to contract to provide renewal activities. "Proposed Powers for Elected Urban Renewal Committee in South End" (Boston, May 1969).

14. Elizabeth M. Seifel, "Displacement: The Negative Environmental Impact of Urban Renewal in the South End of Boston" (MCP thesis, MIT, June 1979), p. 40.

15. *Boston Globe*, December 11, 1969, p. 21, quoting then-director John Warner.

16. "Renewal Official Responds," *Journal of Housing* 4 (November 1969), p. 602.

17. Interview cited in Ann Bastian, "The Politics of Participation: A Case Study in Community Organization" (unpublished senior honors thesis, Radcliffe College, 1970), p. 83.

18. SFRA, *San Francisco Redevelopment, 1967–68* (San Francisco, 1968), p. 8, reproducing a *San Francisco Examiner* editorial of August 1, 1967.

19. "Gadfly of Redevelopers," *San Francisco Chronicle*, January 20, 1970, p. 3.

20. Herman suffered a heart attack and died in 1971 the day after Christopher Lewis, whom Hannibal Williams had described as a "thug who did more damage to the community than a hundred guys, but no one had the guts, or help, to take him on," had leapt over Herman's office desk and attempted to choke him over a hiring decision on a building site. Lewis was later murdered.

21. James Price, "Review of Relocation Actions in the Western Addition Urban Renewal Project Area" (San Francisco: HUD Area Office, April 1, 1971), p. 3.

22. Deborah Auger, "The Politics of Revitalization in Gentrifying Neighborhoods," *APA Journal* 45:4 (October 1979), pp. 515–522.

23. Karen Murphy, "Urban Transformations: The Case of the Gay Community in San Francisco" (MCP thesis, Department of City and Regional Planning, University of California at Berkeley, 1980), App. I.

24. See "Gay Migration into Black Neighborhoods," and "Black Leaders Call Housing Real Issue," *San Francisco Chronicle*, September 1, 1979, pp. 1, 4, 5.

25. SEPAC, "South End Housing Community Report" (Boston, June 1975), pp. 8–22.

26. Seifel, "Displacement," p. 38. Seifel's study is the most careful and complete concerning changes in the South End housing stock and the associated shifts in population composition. Her figures for the actual project area show a drop from 20,879 in 1960 to a low of about 10,000, rising to 14,565 in 1979.

27. Ibid., pp. 72–76.

28. "Gays Who Invested in the Black Area," *San Francisco Chronicle*, September 1, 1979, p. 4.

29. National Institute for Advanced Studies, "Market Generated Displacement: A Single City Case Study" (Washington, D.C.: draft final report on HUD Contract H-2984, T.O.2, June 13, 1980), p. 52.

30. Research Triangle, Inc., "Draft Final Report" (Research Triangle Park, N.C.: draft final report on HUD Contract H-2984, T.O.1, June 13, 1980), p. V-I.

31. Regina Armstrong, "National Trends in Office Construction, Employment, and Headquarters Location in U.S. Metropolitan Areas," in P. W. Daniels, ed., *Spatial Patterns of Office Growth and Location* (New York: John Wiley, 1979), p. 89.

32. Michael Matrullo, "The Office Industry Survey, Interim Report" (BRA Research Department, September 1977), pp. 3–6.

33. "Jobs for Boston's Future—Expanding the City's Economic Base through Capital Investment—Mayor Kevin White's Program" (BRA Research Department, November 1975), pp. 33–40.

34. Thomas O'Brien and Alexander Ganz, "A Demographic Revolution: The Impact of Office Building and Residential Tower Development in Boston" (BRA Research Department, December 1972), pp. 2–3. See also Robert Earsy and Kent Colton, "Boston's New High-Rise Office Buildings: A Study of Their Employees and Their Housing Preferences" (BRA Research Department, July 1974).

35. Mary Tomkins et al., "Boston's Population: Reversal of Two Decades of Decline" (BRA Research Department, 1973); Elizabeth Comer and Alexander Ganz, "Notes on the State Census of Population, 1975" (BRA Research Department, February 1976), p. 2.

36. San Francisco Planning and Urban Renewal Association, "Impact of Intensive High Rise Development on San Francisco: Detailed Findings" (San Francisco: SPUR, June 1975), pp. 32, 52, 62.

37. San Francisco Department of City Planning, "Major Office Buildings Constructed in Downtown San Francisco, 1945–1977" (San Francisco, 1978), Table II: Buildings under Construction or Proposed, and Gerald Adams, "Battle of the Skyscrapers," *San Francisco Sunday Examiner and Chronicle*, January 28, 1979, pp. 1, 6.

38. John Mollenkopf, "The San Francisco Housing Market in the 1980s: An

Agenda for Neighborhood Planning" (San Francisco: San Francisco Foundation, June 14, 1980). See NIAS, "Market Generated Displacement," and RTI, "Draft Final Reports" (n. 29), for a detailed analysis of the Hayes Valley.

39. Boston Office of Community Development, "Neighborhood Improvement Program for the City of Boston, 1976" (Boston, January 1976), p. 9. This view of the White years is supported by Martha Wagner Weinberg, "Boston's Kevin White: A Mayor Who Survives," *Political Science Quarterly* 96:1 (Spring 1981), pp. 87–106.

40. Marshall Berman, "Buildings Are Judgments," *Ramparts*, 13:5 (March 1975), p. 56.

41. Marilyn Gittell, *Limits to Citizen Participation* (Beverly Hills: Sage, 1980).

CHAPTER SIX

1. Arizona Republic and Phoenix Gazette, *Inside Phoenix '77* (Phoenix: Phoenix Newspapers, 1977), pp. 17–19.

2. William Alonso, "The End of the Metropolitan Era" (Harvard Center for Population Studies Discussion Paper, 1978); William Baer, "On the Death of Cities," *Public Interest* 45 (Fall 1976), pp. 3–19; "New York: The End of an Empire," special issue, *Society* 13:4 (May/June 1976).

3. See George Sternlieb and James Hughes, eds., *Post-Industrial America: Metropolitan Decline and Interregional Job Shifts* (New Brunswick: Rutgers Center for Urban Policy Research, 1975) for a statement of this view.

4. B. L. Weinstein and R. E. Firestine. *Regional Growth and Decline in the United States* (New York: Praeger, 1979).

5. For an earlier and somewhat different presentation of these views, but one from which this chapter draws heavily, see John Mollenkopf, "Paths toward the Post-Industrial Service City," in Robert W. Burchell and David Listokin, eds., *Cities under Stress* (New Brunswick: Rutgers Center for Urban Policy Research, 1980).

6. Sternlieb and Hughes, eds., *Post-Industrial America*.

7. Ibid., pp. 2–4, 40.

8. Alan Pred, *City-Systems in Advanced Societies* (New York: John Wiley, 1977), esp. pp. 98–166.

9. This insight essentially stands Charles Tiebout's approach to local public finance on its head. It was first suggested to me by Robert Goodman, who has developed it in his book *The Last Entrepreneurs* (New York: Simon and Schuster, 1980). My thinking was also stimulated by Paul Peterson, who develops his view of this dynamic in *City Limits* (Chicago: University of Chicago Press, 1981), chaps. 2–4.

10. Arizona Republic and Gazette, *Phoenix*, p. 36.

11. See Robert Firestine, "Economic Growth and Inequality, Demographic Change, and the Public Sector Response," in David Perry and Alfred Watkins, eds., *The Rise of the Sunbelt Cities* (Beverly Hills: Sage, 1977), vol. 14, Urban

Affairs Annual Reviews, pp. 197–200. See also Perry and Watkins' conclusion, pp. 293–298.

12. Roger Vaughan, "The Urban Impacts of Federal Policies: Volume 2, Economic Development" (Santa Monica: Rand Corporation, June 1977), p. 19.

13. 1960 and 1970 U.S. Census, "Arizona's Silicon Valley," *San Francisco Sunday Examiner and Chronicle*, December 29, 1979, p. 13.

14. Santa Clara County Manufacturing Group, Jobs/Housing Task Force, "Report on Estimates of Job Growth and Building Expansion of Sixty Santa Clara County Companies, 1979–1985" (Santa Clara, July 1979), p. 3; and Scott Lefaver, "Will Success Spoil Silicon Valley?" (San José: George S. Nolte and Company, 1979). My thanks to Scott Lefaver for these and other materials on problems of the County's explosive growth.

15. For a more general discussion, see Kirkpatrick Sale, *Power Shift* (New York: Vintage, 1976); and Maureen McBreen, "Regional Trends in Federal Defense Expenditures, 1950–76," in Committee on Appropriations, U.S. Senate, *Selected Essays on Patterns of Regional Change* (Washington, D.C.: GPO, October 1977), pp. 511–542. McBreen shows that these cities' prominence as defense contractors is great and increasing. California alone got 23 percent of all prime military contracts, Texas, 5.4 percent, and Arizona, 1.6 percent.

16. "What's Going on Here?" *Colorado Business* (May 1977), p. 52.

17. Biography given on the occasion of the dedication of Terman Engineering Building, *Stanford Observer* (November 1977), p. 3.

18. G. Brecker, "Why Business Loves the Sunbelt (and Vice Versa)," *Fortune*, June 1977, pp. 134–136.

19. Leonard Goodall, ed., *Urban Politics in the Southwest* (Tempe: Arizona State University Press, 1967), p. 159. This conclusion was made about San Diego, but is supported for most other cities as well.

20. Peter Lupsha and William Siembieda, "The Poverty of Public Services in the Land of Plenty," in Perry and Watkins, eds., *Rise of the Sunbelt Cities*, pp. 169–190, reach the same conclusion. This is true on a per capita as well as absolute basis.

21. Goodall, ed., *Urban Politics*.

22. *New Times* (Phoenix), July 27, 1977, p. 7.

23. Barss, Reitzel and Associates, *Community Action and Urban Change* (Cambridge: Barss, Reitzel, 1970).

24. *Arizona Daily Star* (Tucson), March 26, 1977, p. 1.

CHAPTER SEVEN

1. George Peterson, "Capital Spending and Capital Obsolescence," in Roy Bahl, ed., *The Fiscal Outlook for Cities* (Syracuse: Syracuse University Press, 1978), p. 57.

2. "Federal Plan Urged to Shape Up Roads," *New York Times*, April 1, 1978, p. 38.

3. New York City Planning Commission, "Capital Needs and Priorities for the City of New York" (New York, 1979), p. ix.

4. "Reagan Inaugural Signals Continental Tilt," *New York Times*, January 18, 1981, p. 4E.

5. Samuel H. Beer, "The Search for a New Public Philosophy," in Anthony King, ed., *The New American Political System* (Washington, D.C.: American Enterprise Institute, 1978), p. 44.

6. U.S. Department of Housing and Urban Development, *The President's National Urban Policy Report* (Washington, D.C.: GPO, 1980), pp. 4-1, 4-5, 5-2, 5-8.

7. President's Reorganization Project, Office of Management and Budget, "Work Program-Local Development Study" (Washington, D.C.: OMB, August 1977), p. 1.

8. Hugh Heclo, "Issue Networks and the Executive Establishment," in King, ed., *New American Political System*, pp. 94–95, 105.

9. "Cities Facing an 'Erosion of Power,' " *San Francisco Chronicle*, June 11, 1980, p. 2; Edward Koch, "The Mandate Millstone," statement to the midwinter meeting of the U.S. Conference of Mayors, January 24, 1980.

10. Samuel Beer, "Political Overload and Federalism," *Polity* 10 (Fall 1977), pp. 15–16.

11. Scott Greer, *Urban Renewal and American Cities* (Indianapolis: Bobbs Merrill, 1965), p. 3.

12. Mel Scott, "Western Addition Redevelopment Study" (San Francisco Planning Commission, November 1947), p. 3.

13. J. Thomas Black, "Private Market Housing Renovation in Central Cities," in Shirley Laska and Daphne Spain, eds., *Back to the City: Issues in Neighborhood Renovation* (Elmsford, N.Y.: Pergamon Press, 1980), pp. 3–13; Phillip Clay, *Neighborhood Renewal* (Lexington, Mass.: Lexington Books, 1979). See also John Mollenkopf, "The San Francisco Housing Market in the 1980s: An Agenda for Neighborhood Planning" (San Francisco Foundation, 1980).

14. Richard Le Gates and Chester Hartman, "Displacement," *Clearinghouse Review* 15:3 (July 1981), pp. 207–249.

15. A large literature on labor market segmentation and ethnic clustering in the lower rungs of the segmented labor market bear out these assertions. Basic references include David Gordon et al., eds., *Labor Market Segmentation* (Lexington: D. C. Heath, 1976), Michael Piore, *Birds of Passage* (Cambridge: At the University Press, 1979), and William J. Wilson, *The Declining Significance of Race* (Chicago: University of Chicago Press, 1980).

16. For an example of thinking along these lines, see Donald Hicks, *Panel Report on Policies and Prospects for Metropolitan and Non-Metropolitan America* (Washington, D.C.: GPO for the President's Commission on a National Agenda for the Eighties, 1980).

17. Reynolds Farley, "Components of Suburban Population Growth," in Barry

Schwartz, ed., *The Changing Face of the Suburbs* (Chicago: University of Chicago Press, 1976), p. 10, Table 2.

18. Larry Long and Paul Glick, "Family Patterns in Suburban Areas: Recent Trends," in ibid., pp. 56–57. This trend is not equally evident in all cities, but Long and Glick's figures show it to be particularly strong in Boston and San Francisco, as well as New York and Chicago.

19. City of Seattle, Office of Policy Planning, *Seattle's Growth Policies* (Seattle, May 1977), p. 8.

20. See Ralph E. Smith, "The Movement of Women into the Labor Force," in R. Smith, ed., *The Subtle Revolution* (Washington, D.C.: Urban Institute, 1979), pp. 1–30; and William Alonso, "The Population Factor and Urban Structure," in A. Soloman, ed., *The Prospective City* (Cambridge: MIT Press, 1980). For the best study of the structural forces which have contributed to these changes, and which suggests that they will be enduring, see Kathleen Gerson, "Hard Choices: How Women Decide about Work, Career, and Motherhood" (Ph.D. diss., Department of Sociology, University of California at Berkeley, 1981).

21. Ad Hoc Committee on Jobs and Housing, "Housing: A Call for Action" (Santa Clara County, 1979).

22. Thomas Murphy and John Rehfuss, *Urban Politics in the Suburban Era* (Homewood, Ill.: Dorsey Press, 1976), p. 43. See also Ann Greer and Scott Greer, "Suburban Political Behavior: A Matter of Trust," in Schwartz, *Changing Face*, pp. 203–220.

23. "Study Says Redistricting Will Hurt Northeastern Cities," *New York Times*, April 14, 1980, p. B10; "Sunbelt, West to Gain House Seats," *San Francisco Chronicle*, August 1, 1980, p. 4; "Reagan's Inaugural Signals a Continental Tilt," *New York Times*, January 1, 1981, p. 4E.

24. For an excellent review of institutional changes in Congress over the last decade, see Samuel C. Patterson, "The Semi-Sovereign Congress," in A. King, ed., *New American Political System*, pp. 125–177.

25. Calculated for me by Jeffrey Fraas from the appropriate 1952, 1962, and 1972 *Congressional Quarterly* issues.

26. "GOP is Gearing Up for Redistribution Armed with Census and Computers," *New York Times*, January 3, 1981, p. 1.

27. David Mayhew, *Party Loyalty among Congressmen* (Cambridge: Harvard University Press, 1966), p. 165; Murphy and Rehfuss, *Urban Politics*, p. 42; quote from Demetrios Caraley, *City Governments and Urban Problems* (Englewood Cliffs, N.J.: Prentice-Hall, 1977), p. 148.

28. For a brilliant argument along these lines concerning New York City, see Martin Shefter, "National-Local Interaction and the New York City Fiscal Crisis," in D. Ashford, ed., *National Resources and Urban Policy* (New York: Methuen, 1980), pp. 185–213.

29. Vincent Scully, *New York Times Book Review*, January 24, 1971, p. 8.

30. Demetrios Caraley, "Carter, Congress and the Cities," in D. R. Marshall, ed., *Urban Policy Making* (Beverly Hills: Sage Publications, 1979), p. 94, citing

unpublished research by Alfred Toizer on the impact of voting in 38 large cities on the outcome of the 1976 elections.

31. Ronald Walters, "Black Presidential Politics in 1980: Bargaining or Begging?" *The Black Scholar* 2 (March/April 1980), p. 30.

32. Office of the White House Press Secretary, "New Partnership to Conserve America's Communities" (Washington, D.C.: March 27, 1978), p. 3.

33. Richard Nathan, "Federal Grants: How Are They Working?" in Robert Burchell and David Listokin, eds., *Cities under Stress* (New Brunswick: Rutgers Center for Urban Policy Research, 1980), p. 534.

34. Advisory Commission on Intergovernmental Relations, "Countercyclical Aid and Economic Stabilization" (Washington, D.C.: GPO, 1978), Report A-69, p. 16; Robert Reischauer, "The Economy, the Federal Budget, and the Prospects for Urban Aid," in R. Bahl, ed., *The Fiscal Outlook for Cities* (Syracuse: Syracuse University Press, 1978), pp. 96–104.

35. Caraley, "Carter, Congress," pp. 81–83.

36. President's Reorganization Project, "Reorganization Study of Local Development Assistance Programs, Staff Analysis" (Washington, D.C.: Office of Management and Budget, December 1978), pp. i, ii and passim.

37. Susan Feinstein et al., "Citizen Participation in the Community Development Block Grant Report—First Year Report" (University of Pennsylvania for HUD, May 1980), p. 46.

38. John F. Kain, "Failure of Diagnosis: A Critique of Carter's National Urban Policy" (Harvard Department of City and Regional Planning, Policy Note p. 78-2, August 1978), pp. 21–22.

39. Susan Jacobs and Elizabeth Roistacher, "The Urban Impacts of HUD's Urban Development Action Grant Program, or Where's the Action in Action Grants," in N. Glickman, ed., *Urban Impacts of Federal Policies* (Baltimore: Johns Hopkins University Press, 1980), pp. 347–348, 352–353, quote at p. 357.

40. "Fifty-Four Public/Private Development Projects Started with $149.2 Million in Action Grants," HUD press release, April 11, 1980.

41. Office of Deputy Assistant Secretary Yvonne Perry, HUD, "Equity Forum Proceedings," p. 2 and passim; "Executive Summary," p. 3 (Washington, D.C.: n.d.). These discussions included minority job training and economic development experts.

42. Peter Steinfels, *The Neoconservatives* (New York: Simon and Schuster, 1979), pp. 53–64 and passim.

43. William Simon, *A Time for Truth* (New York: Berkley Publishing Corp., 1979), p. 193.

44. "New Conservative Coalition," *New York Times*, January 7, 1981, p. A15; "Conservative Democrats and GOP Form Alliance," *New York Times*, May 5, 1981, p. A1; "44 Democrats on Right Flex Muscles in the House," *Wall Street Journal*, March 25, 1981, p. 31; "Reagan's Plan Wins as Democrats Split in House on Budget," *New York Times*, June 26, 1981, p. 1.

323

45. "America's New Beginning: A Program for Economic Recovery," House Document 97-21 (Washington, D.C.: GOP, February 18, 1981), p. 21.

46. For overviews of the impact of OBRA and the tax bill, see "Review of Poverty Law 1980–1981," *Clearinghouse Review* 15:9 (January 1982), pp. 704–824; Lester Salamon with Alan Abramson, "The Federal Government and the Nonprofit Sector: Implications of the Reagan Budget Proposals" (Urban Institute, May 1981); "Effects of Tax and Benefit Reductions Enacted in 1981 for Households in Different Income Categories" (Washington, D.C.: Congressional Budget Office, February 1982); and John Palmer and Isabel Sawhill, eds., *The Reagan Experiment* (Washington, D.C.: Urban Institute, 1982).

47. Office of the Mayor, "Analysis of Federal Budget Proposals" (City of New York, March 13, 1981), pp. 1, 5–33.

48. Northeast-Midwest Institute, "The Unprotected Flank: Regional and Strategic Imbalances in Defense Spending Patterns" (Washington, D.C., 1980), and "The United American Emirates: State Revenues from Energy Non-Renewables" (Washington, D.C., April 1981).

49. For various expositions of its outlook, see *Social Policy* (September-October 1979), "Special Issue on Neighborhoods," and the National Commission on Neighborhoods, "The Case for Neighborhoods: A Progress Report" (Washington, D.C., 1978). See also Harry Boyte, *The Backyard Revolution* (Philadelphia: Temple University Press, 1980). In some cities such as San Francisco, city-wide neighborhood coalitions have compiled policy platforms.

50. The National Commission on Neighborhoods, "The Case for Neighborhoods," p. 11. See also *People, Building Neighborhoods: Final Report* (Washington, D.C.: GPO, 1979).

51. For example, Rolf Goetze, *Understanding Neighborhood Change* (Cambridge: Ballinger, 1979); Phillip Clay, *Neighborhood Renewal*; Laska and Spain, eds., *Back to the City*; Roger Ahlbrandt and James Cunningham, *A New Public Policy for Neighborhood Preservation* (New York: Praeger, 1979).

52. Division of National Affairs, "Communities and Neighborhoods: A Possible Private Sector Initiative for the 1980s" (New York: Ford Foundation, January 1979), p. 6.

53. Susan Feinstein et al., "Citizen Participation."

54. "The Comeback of Government-by-District," San Francisco *Examiner*, May 29, 1980, p. 1, citing a study by Robert Mundt, Political Science Department, University of North Carolina.

INDEX

327

LIBRARY OF CONGRESS CATALOGING IN PUBLICATION DATA

Mollenkopf, John H., 1946-
  The contested city.

  Includes index.
    1. Federal-city relations—United States.   2. Boston
(Mass.)—Politics and government.   3. San Francisco
(Calif.)—Politics and government.   I. Title.
JS344.F4M65 1983   352'.00724'0973   83-42568
ISBN 0-691-07659-6
ISBN 0-691-02220-8 (pbk.)

*John H. Mollenkopf is Associate Professor of Political Science at the
Graduate Center of the City University of New York, and Director of its
Public Policy Program.*